ROOTS OF RELATIONAL ETHICS

AAR

American Academy of Religion
Reflection and Theory in the Study of Religion

Editor
David E. Klemm

Number 09
ROOTS OF RELATIONAL ETHICS
Responsibility in Origin and Maturity
in H. Richard Niebuhr
by
R. Melvin Keiser

ROOTS OF RELATIONAL ETHICS
Responsibility in Origin and Maturity in H. Richard Niebuhr

by
R. Melvin Keiser

Scholars Press
Atlanta, Georgia

ROOTS OF RELATIONAL ETHICS
Responsibility in Origin and Maturity in H. Richard Niebuhr

by
R. Melvin Keiser

Library of Congress Cataloging in Publication Data
Keiser, R. Melvin.
  Roots of relational ethics : responsibility in origin and maturity in
H. Richard Niebuhr / by R. Melvin Keiser.
      p.   cm— (AAR reflection and theory in the study of religion;
  no. 09)
  Includes bibliographical references and index.
  ISBN 0-7885-0211-5 (alk. paper). — ISBN 0-7885-0212-3 (pbk. : alk. paper)
  1. Niebuhr, H. Richard (Helmut Richard), 1894-1962. 2. Christian
ethics—History—20th century. I. Title. II. Series.
BX4827.N47K45 1996
241'.092—dc20   95-26370
                                                 CIP

Printed in the United States of America
on acid-free paper

To Beth

Compresence in love

speaking, teaching, writing, parenting

co-working smallholders on the earth

being still and still moving

on the way

CONTENTS

PREFACE

My encounter with H. Richard Niebuhr began one afternoon in the old Earlham College library. As a sophomore with the words of my teacher, Joe E. Elmore, a student himself of both Niebuhrs, ringing in my ears, that Reinhold Niebuhr had a still more extraordinary theologian brother, I reached out to the New Book Shelf and took down the *festschrift* for H. Richard Niebuhr, *Faith and Ethics*. Opening to the flyleaf picture, I was struck by his face. Deeply etched, luminous, manifest with power, humility, and suffering, it was what I would come later to understand as the numinosity of "a wise old man." In that fortuitous moment I was transfixed by a felt sense of deep meaning and mystery in the vital mind of this embodied self. Regaled with stories of his theological acumen by my undergraduate mentor and beginning to read *Christ and Culture*, I went to Yale Divinity School to study with Niebuhr in what turned out to be the last two years of his life.

Much affected by the man as teacher and thinker, I have tried to figure out what is going on in the depths and direction of his theology and ethics of responsibility, sensing something radically different from the neo-orthodox climate in which theology was being done across the country in his final decade. Many were influenced by him in the 1940s and 1950s and went on to influential positions in the theological world. But in the 1960s Niebuhr was changing: the deep meaning of his mature thought that carried him beyond the dualistic problematic of modernity was emerging into fullness in his theo-ethics of responsibility only in the last few years of his life.

After Niebuhr's death, in an S.T.M thesis under Robert L. Calhoun at Yale Divinity School, I named this deep meaning "relationality" ("Relationality in the Theology of H. Richard Niebuhr: A Study in Niebuhr's Understanding of Man and God," 1964). Later, in a doctoral dissertation under William H. Poteat at Duke Univiersity, I named it "postcritical" ("Recovering the Personal: The Logic of Religious Discourse in the Theological Quest of H. Richard Niebuhr," 1974). My passion for Polanyi, who coined "postcritical," began at Niebuhr's direct encouragement so it was fitting to attend to Niebuhr from Polanyi with Poteat, who had also been Niebuhr's student.

With the difficulty of grasping the deeper meaning of his thought, recoverable only through inhabiting the far-flung thought-world of his past and emerging present, and my own immersion in the richness of undergraduate teaching at Guilford College opening into interdisciplinary and women's studies, the process has taken a long time. Coming to fruition first in a book on his theological method, *Recovering the Personal: Religious Language and the Post-Critical Quest of H. Richard Niebuhr* (1988), my search now reaches for articulation of his climactic theological ethics and the origins from which they come.

While I have labored to uncover the meaning of Niebuhr's relational thinking in the early 1960s, a new context of relational thought has arisen in the feminist and liberation writings of the last two decades. What Niebuhr's ethics means can best be seen, I believe, by attending from a background of postcritical and phenomenological philosophy and liberation, especially feminist, thought. I am not claiming that Niebuhr was a "feminist" or "liberation" theologian in their current meanings, but that he was working at the roots of such contemporary thinking as he sought to develop a relational point of view beyond the modern mind/body, subject/object dualism. Albeit with mortgages to his "critical" and patriarchal past, his thought has nurtured a relational perspective in myself and my students, and offers resources for the present dialogue.

My interest in the early thought of Niebuhr took me back into his days of idealistic liberalism and the effort to understand his radical conversion to "religious realism" and "divine sovereignty." The theo-ethical meaning of this conversion at the end of 1929 is, I believe, to be found most fully in his relational reflections on responsibility.

For a year of creative solitude at Hall Farm of Shipton-by-Beningbrough, outside York, England I am grateful to David and Sheila Hardisty, and for support to Guilford College. For other spaces inhabited (since we think with our bodies, as Polanyi has said and as Niebuhr, known by his students for his gestures, has shown in his teaching), I am similarly grateful: the convivium of Guilford College's dialogical community, the anonymity of Café Mairie at St. Sulpice in Paris, the witty friendliness and political concern of Steven and Deborah Hanrahan's

For Every Season Delicatessen in Meredith, New Hampshire, and the nearby earthy, wind-spirited, wave-washed presence of Laurel Island.

All thinking is collaborative--dialogical, Niebuhr would say. We write with readers and companions remembered pleasurably from the past, engaged fruitfully in the present, who for me are: my teachers with whom I have talked or worked on Niebuhr--Joe E. Elmore, Sydney E. Ahlstrom, Robert L. Calhoun, and William H. Poteat; my colleagues at Guilford College who have sustained me through interest in my writing-- John H. and Carol L. Stoneburner, Jerry Caris Godard, Jane Godard Caris, Claire Helgeson, Carter Delafield, Richie Zweigenhaft, Robert G. Williams, Joe Groves, David Barnhill; collegial friends elsewhere-- Elizabeth D. Kirk, Theodore and Annette Donovan, Christine Downing, June Yungblut, Walter Blass, Robert and Anne Welsh, Molly Mabe, Demaris Wehr, Katie Cannon, Carter Heyward, Chalmers and Pam Coe; former students turned nurturing friends in life's dialogues--Barbara T. Norton, Larry and Corinne Elworth, Robert and Syndee Kraus, Mary Louise Bringle, John Bell, Judy Whisnant, Sandy Beer, Holly Fairbairn, David Jones; current students--denizens over recent years reading Niebuhr in my "Contemporary Theology" and "Dante and the 20th Century"; those who have given access to Niebuhr materials--Lowell Zuck of Eden Theological Seminary, and the libraries of Pacific School of Religion, Vanderbilt University, Yale Divinity School, Washington University--and also permission to quote--Richard R. Niebuhr, Gene Canestrari, and Joe E. Elmore; typist, former student, Laura Lowder; proofreader, former student, David Teague; editorial friends, John H. Stoneburner and Elizabeth B. Keiser; computer consultant, Robert Kraus; financial supporters--Guilford College in bestowing a recent study leave to complete this project, Episcopal Divinity School for taking me in during the first part of that study leave as Procter Fellow, Pendle Hill for taking me in the latter part as Friend-in-Residence; and familial supporters-- David Shetter and Marjorie Hedley Keiser (my parents), Megan and Christopher Keiser (my children), Norman and Margaret Keiser (my brother and sister-in-law), and Elizabeth B. Keiser (my wife).

R. Melvin Keiser
Laurel Island, Squam Lake
New Hampshire
July 5, 1994

INTRODUCTION

Neo-Orthodoxy and Liberation in
Postcritical Perspective

Religious reflection undergoes a sea change in the 1920s and 1930s. In these decades a theological generation comes to maturity in Europe and America; seeking religious revitalization, it develops a new theology in Protestant circles which has been a luminous contribution of theological creativity unequaled except by the Reformation itself. Ordinarily this is referred to as a conversion from theological liberalism to what is variously called neo-orthodoxy, theology of crisis, dialectical theology, or Barthianism: from belief in divine immanence to transcendence (from God as spiritual ideal in cultural development to God beyond the world), from the optimistic appraisal of human nature and belief in progress (moral, cultural, spiritual) to the reaffirmation of sin and rejection of such progress, and from disregard of Reformation and biblical categories to their reappropriation.[1]

Again in the 1960s and 1970s a new theological generation of Protestants, now working much more openly with, often indistinguishably from, Catholics, emerges in Europe and America. Shifting attention to various forms of social oppression, it is critical of neo-orthodoxy, even while drawing sustenance from its theological vitality. Liberation is central, whether from racism, sexism, classism, militarism, anti-Judaism, or environmental exploitation. Neo-orthodoxy, as well as previous theologies, are criticized for not attending to these issues in doing theology and for propagating these oppressive systems.

These explicitly political theologies interpret the gospel as liberation in this life here and now by the divine at work in the world on the side of the oppressed, willing the dissolution of oppressive social systems and creating a context of human fulfillment for all. At the heart of their critique of society and theology--recognized to varying degrees by them, acknowledged especially by feminists--is the rejection of the dualism of modernity and the affirmation of our inherent relatedness to each other, nature, divinity.

In philosophy, thinkers such as Michael Polanyi, Maurice Merleau-Ponty, and Ludwig Wittgenstein have been working similarly at conceiving a new world beyond modern dichotomies. Modernity is epitomized by the "critical philosophy" of Kant and is based on the Cartesian subject/object dualism which undercuts personal (committed and constitutive) relations between self and body, and between self and other human and natural beings, by methodical doubt, by conceiving self and other as existing independently, and by treating all objects as passive, unambiguous, quantifiable, and causally determined and all subjects as agencies of conscious reason. Hence reality is of two kinds: the self as subject is deracinate mind (plucked up from the roots of bodily being in the world) and the world (including our own bodies) as objects is demented bodies (mindless matter devoid of making sense of things). Polanyi speaks of going beyond the "critical" to a "postcritical" world of "personal knowledge," which is a relational way of being in our bodies that affirms our "tacit indwelling" and unconscious creative integrating of whatever we know.[2]

From a postcritical point of view, social oppression is seen to be founded on the Greek separation of spirit and matter, reforged in the definitively modern Cartesian separation of subject and object, mind and body; these dualities are invariably hierarchical, so that one side is constructed as the superior agent and the other as the inferior recipient. The postcritical conception of new life and thought is to transcend dualism of mind and body, subject and object, dominator and dominated, by recognizing the inherent relatedness of self, world, and God. Liberation theologies are postcritical as they reach beyond systems of domination, based on dualism, to affirm that selves live in relation to each other as interactors, to the world as matrix, and to the divine as immanent in the world and human lives.

While the neo-orthodox understood themselves to have made a major break from liberalism, they nevertheless retained the same fundamental dualistic framework of modern thought. Their shift was within the subject/object split from the liberal preoccupation with the subject to a refocusing on the object: from the human as agent able to act on self, world, and God within the world to achieve moral and spiritual progress, to God as agent able to act on self and world from outside to achieve redemption of incapacitated sinful selves.[3] In Aristotelian language: liberalism saw the self as substance, existing on its own;[4] neo-orthodoxy insisted only God is substance while all selves exist in dependence upon this sole independent entity. For liberalism as for neo-orthodoxy, both self and God are defined as separate selves, atomic individuals, and the world as a system of objects.

In spite of the major differences between liberalism and neo-orthodoxy, their similar dualistic framework becomes especially evident from the postcritical perspective of liberation theologies which reject dualistic categories of human agency and divine immanence, on the one hand, or divine sovereignty and human sinfulness, on the other. What is at stake, then, amidst liberation theologies' oppositions to one form or another of social domination is the deconstruction of the modern world based on Cartesian dualism and a revisioning of self, world, and God in relational terms.

Such a new way of thinking and being is demanded by ongoing social violence, now cast within the context of nuclear and environmental crisis that threatens the survival of the human race. Although continuing oppression increases tensions that could precipitate it, we have so far avoided nuclear catastrophe. Without changing our basic way of being and thinking, we cannot avoid the environmental crisis that will make the world humanly uninhabitable. What is at issue in these explicitly political theologies is not only equality between whites and people of color, men and women, rich and poor, Christians and non-Christians, and mutuality between humans and the natural world, but a new consciousness, a new way of being.

Niebuhr's Conversion:
From Liberalism to Relationality

Although H. Richard Niebuhr is understood to be an outstanding representative of liberal theology turned neo-orthodox, in fact, his conversion from liberalism was to relational thinking that bears the seeds of a postcritical theology. His conversion replaced liberalism's dualistic separation of God, as divine individual, from self and world with the immanent interrelatedness of God, as pattern of being and value, with self and world. While he soon goes on to use the dualistic categories of Kantian thought to express the new view born of this conversion, he stretches them to their limits by historicizing subject and object in order to develop a relational view of "inner history" set in opposition to the objective causal view of "outer history." Finally, in his culminating ethics of responsibility, relational thinking breaks free of its dualistic container and expands into a comprehensive postcritical theology, actualizing, as much as he could, the relational potential of his conversion.

Born September 3, 1894, in Wright City, Missouri, Niebuhr died July 5, 1962, after a distinguished career as teacher for seven years and Dean at Eden Theological Seminary (St. Louis), president of Elmhurst College (Illinois) for three years, and professor of theology and Christian ethics at Yale Divinity School (New Haven) for thirty-one years. Along with his brother, Reinhold Niebuhr, and Paul Tillich (who came to America from Germany at the rise of Hitler in 1933), he was one of the major American figures in the golden era of Protestant theological vitality. Begun after World War I, this era featured in Germany and Switzerland such luminaries as Karl Barth, Emil Brunner, Dietrich Bonhoeffer, and Rudolf Bultmann.

Niebuhr's early liberalism is characterized by his affirmation of self and God as separable and isolable individuals, opposition of spirit to nature, and belief in the human capacity to overcome this opposition by grasping ideals and using them to permeate the world. Although optimistic in his appraisal of the self as a Cartesian consciousness able to exert the subject's power of holding ideas over the objective world, he never accepts the liberal belief in inevitable progress. While acknowledging the possibility of eventual realization of the kingdom of God on earth, he insists on the ongoing likelihood of sinful compromise.

In his conversion from idealistic liberalism he exhibits the neo-orthodox reappropriation of Reformation biblical categories. Central to him, as for all his fellow participants, is the new conviction of "God's sovereignty."[5] While this meant for his colleagues a rejection of divine immanence in favor of transcendence, for him it meant a movement *towards* God's immanence as the way to affirm divine transcendence. In the emergence of his new conviction he discovers God to be a pattern of being and value *in* the world. God is no longer a particular entity warring on the side of the human spirit against nature but is seen as the pervasive and encompassing whole and mystery that exists in intimate relation to all particulars, natural as well as spiritual.

More especially, this divine mysterious whole exists in intimate relation to the self in its being, eliciting personal commitment to it expressed in language of the first person. As he says at the end of his life, speaking of this conversion in his autobiographical essay, "Reformation: Continuing Imperative": "And now I came to understand that unless being itself . . . was trustworthy . . . I had no God at all" (*Ref* 72). Divine sovereignty means to Niebuhr reconceiving God and self in relational, and therefore experiential, terms. It means the presence of the transcendent God as pattern of being and value in the world, and the self's personal dependence upon and faith in the trustworthiness of being in its mysterious wholeness.

The transcendent nature of such an immanent God is its reaching beyond us, not as one entity is separate from others, but as a whole extends beyond the parts it encompasses. As the whole pattern of being, it forever acts upon us as parts seeking to transform our being and valuing. In the language of his culminating relational view of divine sovereignty, he says that we relate "fittingly" to all creatures as we are transformed in our relating to the divine pattern pervasive throughout the entire community of being. To speak of conscious adhering to ideals and imposing them upon recalcitrant nature inadequately expresses both the underlying relations to all of being we exist within as selves, and the need for grace, working amidst these relations, to shatter our exclusiveness and defensiveness and to open us to the entirety of being and its mysterious pattern.

While he participates in the neo-orthodox recovery of divine transcendence, he does so not in their Cartesian but his own relational terms. His conversion is not to the objective supremacy and initiative of God, and the inverse passivity of the self, but to divinity immanent in the world with which we interact, opening us to and deepening our trust in the entire matrix of being. Among his contemporaries, Tillich comes closest to Niebuhr's insight into divine relationality. Yet Tillich, while using the language of being, does not speak of a *pattern* of being *in* the world but of the *ground* of being *beneath* the world, not of the divine acting upon and interacting with selves but of the Unconditioned.

While Niebuhr at the end of his life spoke of his major theological change as coming to the "conviction" of "God's sovereignty" (*Ref* 71-72), in the early 1930s he spoke of it as a shift from "liberalism" to "religious realism" (see *Can* and *Realism*). By realism he meant that which faces the actualities of our being in the world. This includes the negativities of our existence, our sinful defensiveness, our insistence on living in an exclusive sphere of relations blocking out wider realms of being. It includes as well facing the actuality of God's presence in the world as its pattern of being and value. Tillich and Reinhold Niebuhr also spoke of their changing thought as a shift to realism. For them realism meant the honest recognition that the ideal cannot be successfully established in a non-ideal world. But for H. Richard Niebuhr it meant rejecting altogether the dichotomy between a spiritual realm of ideals beyond and the non-ideal reality of the world; his realism embraced the actual world of grace and sin understood in relational terms as divine pattern in our lives and our resistance to it and to its context, the entire community of being.

While Niebuhr understood this at the time as a move away from liberalism, he came to realize at the end of his life that he fits within a broader meaning of liberalism: a contextual meaning, that affirms the inextricable interrelation between religion and culture. Throughout his life he saw the inescapable necessity of thinking theologically and ethically in relation to a secular and scientific world, and of confronting secular history and its methods as they bear upon the Bible, the history of Christianity, and our ways of knowing. Of this he writes: "if taking our own historicity very seriously means being a liberal then I remained a liberal even in the thirties."[6] What Niebuhr objected to was idealism: the dualistic, atomistic way of thinking of late nineteenth- and early twentieth-century liberalism. It would be more accurate, then, to speak of Niebuhr's conversion as a shift within liberalism (characterized by affirmation of the interrelatedness of religion and culture) from dualistic and optimistic idealism to relational realism.

The Richness and Limits of Niebuhr's Ethics

The ethics he developed after his conversion has become one of the outstanding contributions of twentieth-century Protestantism. Always working on the foundation of his religious commitments to divine sovereignty, he is known for his classic ethical methodological investigations of historical relativism, value theory, types of relationship between religion and culture, faith, and responsibility. His interwoven theological and ethical thought culminates in his attempt to define responsibility as a third alternative to the two major traditions he distinguishes in the west: teleological or goal-striving ethics of Aristotle, Thomas Aquinas, and much of Catholicism, and deontological or law-obeying ethics of Kant and much of Protestantism.

While this final stage is represented in print by *The Responsible Self: An Essay in Christian Moral Philosophy*, that slender though rich book is but a small part of what he had eventually hoped to write. He spent many years lecturing on A Christian Ethics of Responsibility which he intended to transform into his magnum opus of theo-ethical reflections. Sudden death by heart attack a year prior to retirement prevented this completion. Fortunately, we are left with this posthumously published piece, as well as with various unpublished literary remains. Unfortunately, the fragmentary quality of these final reflections has left many questions about the meaning of responsibility in Niebuhr's mature thought. Because of this and the influence of his earlier thought, which shaped readers' consciousness through several brilliant delineations of the theo-ethical landscape, the more radical nature of the mature reflections of his final years has been overlooked.

While Niebuhr goes through several stages of thought in his lifetime, there is a continuity, I believe, running from his conversion at the end of 1929 through to his final work on responsibility. His thinking is emergent so the full theo-ethical meaning of his conversion to divine sovereignty and subsequent work in its light becomes most evident in his reflections on responsibility. My intention in this work is to show the nature of his conversion from liberalism to divine sovereignty and the culmination of these commitments in the theo-ethics of responsibility. I will work with the published and unpublished materials on responsibility so as to imagine the whole of which they are part--showing what he in fact says in the disparate pieces, educing the principles inherent in the density of his thought which he did not live to single out, locating the places of inadequacy needing major rethinking, and envisaging, where he has not, what could be aborning in his theo-social analysis.

By focusing in Part One on Niebuhr's conversion from liberalism, we shall understand better the beginnings of twentieth-century American Protestant theology and ethics, how he understood it, and his change from it to divine sovereignty. By attending in Part Two to decision-making in responsibility, we shall see how the mature articulation of his relational ethics of responsibility--its context, process, and principles of decision-making beyond dualism--is implied in his conversion to divine sovereignty as immanent divine pattern in the world. By exploring in Part Three the Christian and potentially socially transformative character of his postcritical ethics, we will discern how the impulse towards social justice can be rooted in commitment to God as being with rather than dominating over us, shaped by the symbolic form of Jesus Christ, and nurtured within the Christian church.

We will also come upon H. Richard Niebuhr's limitations. First, he nowhere provides a clear methodological statement that gives comprehensive articulation to his ethical principles. While they are embedded in his culminating reflections on responsibility, we are left with the task of elucidating and organizing them. Second is his lack of comprehensive social analysis, even though his relational perspective is an inherently social view of the self. Because of his sharp critique of capitalism's social injustice during his liberal period and his extensive work, then and later, with various social theorists, he was in an excellent position to develop "the responsible self" in its full socioeconomic and political context, showing how it is enmeshed in the oppressive systems of sexual, environmental, religious, militaristic, racial, and class domination.   While concerned about many of these aspects of contemporary life, he never develops a theo-social ethical analysis of systemic oppression.

As Beverly Wildung Harrison argues most incisively, Niebuhr fails to engage his methodological concerns of responsibility in doing an actual social analysis of the dynamics of our existence.   Fundamentally appreciative of his many contributions, she indicts this failure:

> Our judgment is that his *formal* vision of the sort of Christian ethical analysis needed is pertinent, and powerful. However, Niebuhr himself failed to realize the promise of his own best insights at this point. He did not finally "do" the sort of social-ethical analysis which he aspired to in light of his deep desire to transmute the individualism of past interpretations of Christian faith; . . . he did not develop his social phenomenology to the point where it could connect with the analysis of the actual social *praxis* of human communities and movements. He did not subject communal social action to self-critical scrutiny in a manner analogous to the way he subjected the praxis of individual agents to scrutiny. . . . What was most lacking in H. Richard Niebuhr's approach to social conflict and political process was any direct interest in the question of social and political *power* or in the *structural* character of the dynamics of power in the social world. His analysis of conflict, while useful in many respects, lacked a crucial element which deeper analysis of the *power* dimensions of social interaction would have clarified.[7]

Harrison is right there is no evidence in the social phenomenology of responsibility that Niebuhr analyzes systemically the power structures of oppression, even though he is investigating the praxis of individual agents.   What we do see in his ethics of responsibility, however, is ongoing concern for various forms of social oppression--classism, war, and racism--and rich potential for reflection on others--sexism, environmental exploitation, and the Christian imperialism of anti-Judaism.

While he never discusses anti-Judaism, he writes in *The Responsible Self* and elsewhere at the end of his life about Judaism and Christianity in a way that shows the relevance of the principles of responsibility for establishing just relations between Christians and Jews. He presents our relation to nature and develops a non-dominating view of ethics which are richly suggestive for reflecting on environmentalism and sexism, even though he does not write at all about these issues. Within responsibility ethics there is the opportunity to realize the potential, which Niebuhr never did, for dealing with these three forms of oppression.

His concern for classism goes back into his early liberal days where he wrote extensive sharp critiques of capitalism, but after the mid-1930s this interest moves from center to periphery. His writings on war similarly become a central preoccupation for a time, beginning in 1932 and running through World War II. And he speaks at length on racism, but only in his 1952 "Christian Ethics." While he carries concern for these issues into *The Responsible Self*, taking them up at various points as illustrative of different aspects of responsibility in distinguishing it from the other two ethical orientations, he nowhere begins to reconstruct their meaning and his attitude towards them in the light of responsibility. Nevertheless, there is evidence that he was dissatisfied with his handling of these social issues and saw the need to rework his treatment of them from within responsibility. How he would have rethought these we cannot know. While there is no evidence that Niebuhr would have developed them into the liberation concern for social praxis, there is a wealth of possibility in his ethics of responsibility to develop a systemic theo-social power analysis of these forms of domination.

In Chapters Seven and Eight we will explore Niebuhr's variegated treatment of these social issues, its potentialities, developments, and diminishments; discover in his ethics of responsibility a valuable resource for our own further reflections; and imagine through a particular example of socioeconomic conflict how his principles could be applied. Throughout these two chapters' investigation of social oppression, we will gather clues to explain the absence of any move in Niebuhr's thinking, even though implicit in the logic of responsibility, towards social praxis.

While limited by this lack of systemic social ethical analysis, his responsibility reflections are pregnant with valuable principles for theo-social analysis and transformation. Maieutic reflections on these relational ethics can contribute significantly to our present dialogue. Affirming in them the *immanent* presence of God acting continually in our daily lives; the *existential* involvement of self in its living; a *phenomenological* attending to the actuality of our present being in the world; a *postcritical* overcoming of mind/body and spirit/nature dualism; a *hermeneutical* stress on interpretation and the linguistic transformative possibilities of our being in the world; a potential for *transformative analysis* of systems of domination and modernity's underlying way of being; and thus affirming through all of these a *relational* ethics of a self inherently connected to, rather than dominating over, its own existence, other selves, and nature within the total community of being and sweep of time--we will find that Niebuhr's mature thought can assist contemporary theo-ethical explorations of liberation.

What is true of social action is also true of the communal nature of the Christian life as the church. While he wrote a definitive description of the nature of the church, *The Purpose of the Church and Its Ministry*, in 1956, he did not live to rethink it in the language of responsibility. Nevertheless, as with his approach to social domination, we can, in Chapter Nine, weave together threads from his last writings to envisage how what he has said would give shape to the church as the Christomorphic community of responsibility.

PART ONE

THE EMERGENCE OF RELATIONAL REALISM

And now I came to understand that unless being itself, the constitution of things, the One beyond all the many, the ground of my being and of all being, the ground of its "that-ness" and its "so-ness," was trustworthy--could be counted on by what had proceeded from it--I had no God at all.

(Ref 72)

CHAPTER ONE

LIBERALISM: A HERITAGE OF IDEALS

Young Niebuhr was committed to a theological ethics of idealistic liberalism. His earliest writings, beginning with a poem (1912) from an in-house publication of Eden Seminary,[8] through his first published essay, "An Aspect of the Idea of God in Recent Thought" (1920) in his synodical periodical, to his first book, *The Social Sources of Denominationalism* (1929), represent this perspective. But his two unpublished academic theses, "The Problem of the Individual in Richard Dehmel" (1917) and "Ernst Troeltsch's Philosophy of Religion" (1924) explore mystical philosophical idealism. He never embraces Dehmel's romantic cosmic egoism or Troeltsch's monadological idealism, even though in his conversion he will draw upon relational aspects in the latter's thought. The theo-ethical language he uses is that of ideals within the dualistic framework of Protestant liberalism rather than the monistic idiom of mystical union with divine reality.

Idealistic Liberalism

Originating in idealistic liberalism, Niebuhr's early theo-ethical reflection is characterized by nine themes. 1) The *framework* is Cartesian and Kantian "critical" *dualism* in the form of *spirit/nature opposition.* 2) *God* is conceived as an *individual subject* set over *against* the *objective* world of nature, and is 3) an *ideal* or *spiritual entity* separated from and opposed to nature. He is a "finite God" who did not create nature and therefore is not responsible for it or for the evil present in it. As creator of the spiritual part of mankind and as the power that works for the victory of spirit over nature, God is present in the world wherever the human spirit makes him present by bending nature to serve spirit.

These three points are evident in "An Aspect of the Idea of God in Recent Thought." In a sympathetic appraisal of William James's belief in a finite God, Niebuhr writes:

> God is a part and not the whole. It is not necessary to judge his goodness by referring to all the deeds of nature and life. "As God is not all things He can be an eternal (i.e. unceasing) tendency making for righteousness and need not be, as on all other theories he must be, the responsible author of evil." So God also becomes the creator not of the totality of nature, but of the spiritual life (*Aspect* 41).

In H.G. Wells's similar belief, Niebuhr makes clear that, while Wells is "deny[ing] that God is Providence or an omnipotent Creator," God is nevertheless "a personality"--"as real as a bayonet thrust." Identifying Wells's view with the Christian--except for his triumphalist assertion of "the risen Christ" which diverges from the Christian affirmation of "resignation" and "non-resistance" manifest in "the symbol of the crucified"--Niebuhr expresses in his own voice his objection, like James's and Wells's, to the Hegelian assertion of an infinite God:

> There are of course many points of contact between such an idea of [a finite] God and the Christian belief in God. For every-day Christian belief God has never been the Absolute of the Hegelians nor been present in all the accidents and futilities of life except as the spiritual nature of the victims put him there, making such things serve them for good thr[o]u[gh] love of Him. Nor has he been for the Christian "the responsible author of evil" as he must be according to Hegelian conceptions, against which the proponents of the faith in a finite God inveigh. Belief in his omnipotence has been faith in the potentiality of his power and in the victory rather than a belief in his active causation of all events (*Aspect* 43-44).

In this evident upholding of a spirit/nature dualism, Niebuhr is emphatically rejecting here the belief in divine sovereignty that he will later come to affirm centrally, although never in Hegelian language. God in this first period is not being itself but only part of reality, not the creator of all but only of the spiritual part of humanity. Nor is God present in all events but only where the spirits of men make him present by bending nature to serve spirit. As responsible only for the spiritual part of being, God is not liable for evil which occurs in nature's opposition to spirit.[9]

4) The *self* is similarly conceived as an *individual* within this *spirit/nature dualistic framework*, which underlies the subsequent five themes. In the face of the opposition of the impersonal forces of nature and the industrialized social world, Niebuhr affirms 5) the "*absolute value of personality*" (*CSP* 279), which 6) is essentially *social*. Shaped by society, the individual self expresses and realizes itself:

> The power of man to create a thing, to express his self in the work of his hands . . . is a thing of infinite value to the individual and often to the world. . . . The principle of the kingdom [is] that individual life finds its purpose and its realization in the identification of its interest with the interests of the kingdom of God. The end of life is social.

Salvation is social, as participation in the society of God's kingdom; sin is similarly social, lying not only in human nature but "within the social structure to which this human nature must make its adaptation" (*CSP* 288, 281, & 284).

7) The real *problem* is *compromise*. True in the church's unsuccessful relating to labor, industrialization, and society in general, it is as well the case within the church, evident in its denominational fragmentation. The necessity of compromise is that we live in bodies within the natural world devoid of spiritual meaning, so that the objective ideal can never be fully incorporated into the world of material objects without significant loss of its reality.

> This proneness toward compromise which characterizes the whole history of the church, [sic] is no more difficult to understand than is the similar and inevitable tendency by which each individual Christian adapts the demands of the gospel to the necessities of existence in the body and in civilized society. It has often been pointed out that no ideal can be incorporated without the loss of some of its ideal character. When liberty gains a constitution, liberty is compromised; when fraternity elects officers, fraternity yields some of the ideal qualities of brotherhood to the necessities of government. And the gospel of Christ is especially subject to this sacrifice of character in the interest of organic embodiment; for the very essence of Christianity lies in the tension which it presupposes or creates between the worlds of nature and of spirit, and in its resolution of that conflict by means of justifying faith. It demands the impossible in conduct and belief; it runs counter to the instinctive life of man and exalts the rationality of the irrational; in a world of relativity it calls for unyielding loyalty to unchangeable absolutes (SSD 3-4).

8) The *solution* to this problem is the individual's *self-sacrifice* through *love*. Acknowledging the inevitability of compromise, the self must reach outside of self and world for justification by the ideal reality of God:

> At the end, if not at the beginning, of every effort to incorporate Christianity there is, therefore, a compromise, and the Christian cannot escape the necessity of seeking the last source of righteousness outside of himself and the world in the divine aggression [which is the "inclusiveness of divine love"], in a justification that is by faith.

What God demands of us is that we strive to "penetrate"[10] the natural world with the divine ideal, moving toward spiritual victory, not through employing the forces of nature, but through the way of the cross understood as resignation and self-sacrifice. Resigning oneself before nature is possible because one has sacrificed oneself and realized one's larger self in the kingdom of God, "tho[ugh] complete self-realization be impossible until the social group include the whole of man's social environment, God and mankind" (*CSP* 281). While the self is essentially social, society consists of individuals who possess themselves in such a way that they can sacrifice their individual selves, and thereby achieve the expansion of their individuality into "better selves":

> The road to unity is the road of sacrifice which asks of churches as of individuals that they lose their lives in order that they may find the fulfilment of their better selves. But it is also the road to the eternal values of a Kingdom of God that is among us (SSD 284).

9) *Jesus* affirms the absolute value of personality and exhibits the social nature of the self as the definitive embodiment of the *principle of love* through *self-sacrifice* on the *cross* for the fulfillment of selves in the community of the kingdom of God. In his life he exhibits love toward both God and humanity, representing in a double movement God to selves and selves to God. Drawing on Wells's words, Niebuhr describes his loving personality as of "extreme gentleness and delicacy and of great courage, of the utmost tolerance and subtlest sympathy." While he rejects Wells's depiction of Christ as king, as "martial Captain of Humanity . . . 'risen and trampling victoriously upon a broken cross'" (*Aspect* 44), he portrays Christ as prophet, speaking "for God to men," and as priest, "speaking for men to God." His sacrifice on the cross is "the spontaneous expression of love, of a love so sublime that it includes the enemy as well as the friend." Through the cross he intercedes with God

the Father for the "reconciliation of men to God." This is not by propitiation, for "The God of Jesus is no destructive and angry potentate but the forgiving father of prodigal children." Rather he shows "how to trust in God"; "by His very act of trustfulness, He restores the lost relationship," and by establishing "a community of intercession," he "continues to intercede" (*JCI* 7-8).

At the end of his first period, Niebuhr speaks of this restoration within community in terms of revelation. In a statement exhibiting the above points, Niebuhr says that Jesus reveals the nature of the supreme good as this love which realizes selves in the "Beloved Community":

> The Christianity of the gospels doubtless contains the required ideal. Its purpose is not the foundation of an ecclesiastical institution or the proclamation of a metaphysical creed, though it seeks the formation of a divine society and presupposes the metaphysics of a Christlike God. Its purpose is the revelation to men of their potential childhood to the Father and their possible brotherhood with each other. That revelation is made not in terms of dogma but of life, above all in the life of Christ. His sonship and his brotherhood, as delineated in the gospel, are not the example which men are asked to follow if they will, but rather the demonstration of that character of ultimate reality which they can ignore only at the cost of their souls. The *summum bonum* which this faith sets before men is nothing less than the eternal harmony of love, in which each individual can realize the full potentiality of an eternal life in self-sacrificing devotion to the Beloved Community of the Father and all the brethren (SSD 278-79).

The Theo-Ethical Task of Liberalism

Within the preconversion context characterized by the nine themes of idealistic liberalism, the task of theological ethics for Niebuhr is to represent the ideals of Christianity, most especially the ideal reality of God, against the non-ideal reality of the natural and social world, and to penetrate the non-ideal with the ideal. Appealing to the spiritual value of sacrifice and social fulfillment, personality and love, the task is to gain adherence to this view and to enjoin to action. While upholding such ideals, we must criticize the inevitable compromise between ideal and real that issues from the never wholly successful attempt to incorporate ideals into an objective world constituted of bodies, nature, and impersonal civilization. The view that Niebuhr espouses fits thoroughly within the tradition of Protestant liberalism of the early twentieth century.[11] Flowing out of Kant's *Second Critique*, shaped early by Schleiermacher and later by Ritschl and Harnack, the Germanic tradition intersects in Niebuhr with the American religious currents of experiential and social thought. The result is his conclusion that theology is practical and the religious life moral, that theo-ethics deals with values and seeks to establish the kingdom of God on earth.

A Strain of Realism

While he believes that Christian ideals are continuous with our own best values and are at hand to be used by us to build the kingdom of God on earth, he does not embrace the more optimistic appraisal of human nature and cultural progress characteristic of much of Protestant liberalism. He explicitly rejects the Hegelian affirmation of divine immanence, the foundation of much of this optimism, both because its spiritualizing of life denies moral effort, the value of personality, the real conflict between human desire for freedom and the facts of causality, and because its conception of God makes him responsible for evil and for adjusting the order of events to human advantage.

While he mentions evolution with reference to Charles Darwin and Henri Bergson, he never utilizes evolutionary thought to buttress liberal optimism; nor does he posit Christian superiority over Judaism. Rather he describes sin as failure through compromise to attain the ideal, a failure ingrained in individual and institutional life (à la Rauschenbusch); he laments as well the destructiveness, capriciousness, and waste in the impersonal world (à la Royce, Wells, and Bergson). In the face of such inimical natural forces he affirms (with James, Bergson, and Wells), as we have seen, that God is finite.

There is, then, a strain of "realism," recognizing the negativities in our lives, nurtured by non-Christian philosophers, writers, and social analysts, as well as by liberal Protestants, running through Niebuhr's own idealistic liberalism, and this strain intensifies through the 1920s. This is evident in his initial approval and later criticism of Schleiermacher's engagement with modern culture. Niebuhr rejects what he takes to be Schleiermacher's subjective starting point in favor of theology attuned to the scientific method, based on empirical facts, and focused on its divine object (in accord with Macintosh's empirical realism). The intensified emphasis on realism is also evident later in the decade in his drawing upon Kantian dualism to combat both Hegelian monism and overemphasis on progress, so as to affirm the presence of the real in conflict with the ideal.[12] But this is still an idealistic "realism," as he defines God, self, and values as ideal entities opposed to the objective world.

Amidst his theological liberalism it is remarkable to discover yet another strand of realism, a radical socioeconomic critique. Articulating it within his liberal framework, he criticizes the foundations of capitalism in its economic oppression and excessive individualism, engages in analysis of class conflict, and advocates solidarity with the poor.[13]

Religious Language within Liberalism

Symbols are essential for the theological ethical task of representing the ideal entities of God and Christ. Picturing the objective ideal of God and the spiritual life of Jesus, they activate persons to incorporate the ideal into their behavior. A symbol's truth consists in its accurate correspondence to the ideal object it symbolizes; its effectiveness lies in its motivating the embodment of such values as non-resistance and submission.

The cross is a better symbol than the resurrection because it more accurately portrays the ideal reality of God's sacrificial love as exhibited in Jesus and therefore can better inspire us to a life of resignation: "it is from the symbol of the crucified, more than from that of the risen Christ, that Christianity has drawn its greatest ethical power" (*Aspect* 44). The better symbol is always the more concrete. The abstractions of science or eighteenth-century orthodoxy do not reach people and have therefore contributed to "the alienation of the working classes from Christianity." Only concrete "symbols," "not abstract concepts," could be effective "if emotions and will were to be touched"; symbols are uniquely able "to communicate their message to the hearts and minds of those that labor and are heavy laden" (*CIC* 16-17), encouraging a life lived in relation to the ideal.

Christian symbols are essentially concrete because they are urban and apocalyptic. In an argument against Bertrand Russell's claim that Christianity is irrelevant to modern industrial society because it was agrarian in its origins, Niebuhr insists that Christianity's origins were urban and therefore contain "urban symbols," such as "heavenly Jerusalem, cities of God." Its apparent irrelevance is due rather to its alliance with the wealthy class and its failure to find a language that will communicate to the workers that faith makes a difference in life. Christianity's apocalyptic "expectation of a new heaven and a new earth, of the removal of injustices and of the establishment of the Kingdom of God" has been replaced by a socially irrelevant "heaven and hell eschatology" (*CIC* 14 & 16-17) which will not communicate effectively with industrialized people.

Language has an important social function. It is the "medium of culture," and thus contributes significantly to the self-conscious identity of a people, providing both a context for growth and a delimiting boundary for the group: "Language, however, imposes its limitations on civilization; it is not only a means of communication but often a barrier to wider community" (SSD 121). The problem is the loss of a common language. Where there is a common language there is a common culture. But both within the church, evident in denominational fragmentation, and between the church and world, evident in the lack of success of the church to communicate with modern society, such a common language has been lost:

> modern heirs are without a common language; the joy of the great community has been lost in the bickerings, rivalries, and misunderstandings of divided sects. The accord of Pentecost has resolved itself into a Babel of confused sounds; while devout men and women continue devoutly to confess, Sunday by Sunday, "I believe in one, holy, catholic Church."

The divisive influence of non-ideal social forces is visible both in the world and within the church itself:

> [in] the successors of the Reformation, the surrender of Christianity to national, racial, and economic caste-systems becomes even more apparent. Here the ideal of brotherhood has not only yielded to the principle of nationalism but has suffered the latter to exploit it in the interests of parties and of rulers until at times the church has become a mere appendage of the state. . . . Here the races confess the same creeds, engage in the same forms of worship, nurture the same hopes, but do so in divided churches, where white and black find it easier to confess than to practice their common sonship to God. Here rich and poor meet in their separate cathedrals and conventicles that each may achieve salvation in his own way and that their class loyalties may not be violated by the practice of the ethics they profess (SSD 10-11).

While religious language illustrates the impersonal economic, political, and social forces at work, it also pictures ideals: "the duty" for a Christian is clearly delineated: "dealing with the present world in the light of our highest ideals and best insights." The highest ideal is represented in the gospel account of Jesus: "His sonship and his brotherhood, as delineated in the gospel, are not the example which men are asked to follow if they will, but rather the demonstration of that character of ultimate reality which they can ignore only at the cost of their souls." The ideal portrayed in Jesus is that of eternal love:

> The *summum bonum* which this faith sets before men is nothing less than
> the eternal harmony of love, in which each individual can realize the full
> potentiality of an eternal life in self-sacrificing devotion to the Beloved
> Community of the Father and all the brethren. The appeal of that ideal
> is unmistakable.

Religious language both points to the ideal and illustrates the compromise
the church is invariably involved in with the world; the symbolic
discourse of theological ethics seeks to bring "the social forces operative"
in the life of the church "under the control of the Christian ideal" (SSD
277, 278-79, & 272).

Symbols in this theological idealism are separable from reality, both
from the ideals to which they appeal and from the non-ideal forces they
illustrate and seek to subjugate. The ideal of eternal love can be
symbolically imposed upon, but is not present within, the social world.
Words and thoughts, separable from each other, are spoken of as forms
external to reality, as illustrations: the churches "in their thought-forms
as well as in their language have become illustrations of the different
national psychologies"; or as clothing: "Not only the words but the ideas
that seek to clothe themselves in these symbols tend to become
unintelligible to members of another cultural group" (SSD 132). This is
evident in a comment he makes in the Preface to *Social Sources* about the
book's beginnings. It took its origins in a course on "Symbolics." To
make sense of the differences and possible unity in the church, he found
he had to go behind the doctrinal and theological language to historical
and sociological analysis of the underlying realities:

> The present work is the outcome of a course in "Symbolics" which the
> author was called upon to teach some years ago. The effort to
> distinguish churches primarily by reference to their doctrine and to
> approach the problem of church unity from a purely theological point of
> view appeared to him to be a procedure so artificial and fruitless that he
> found himself compelled to turn from theology to history, sociology, and
> ethics for a more satisfactory account of denominational differences and
> a more significant approach to the question of union (SSD vii).

The subject of religious symbols does have its place in Niebuhr's
idealistic thought, but as is evident from such a point of view, it is not
central. Although symbolism makes its appearance as a subject in "An
Aspect of the Idea of God" in 1920, it then all but disappears until 1929
when it reappears significantly in "Christianity and the Industrial Classes"
and *Social Sources*. The profound alteration in conviction at the end of
1929 which transforms Niebuhr's theo-ethical method will also change his

understanding of religious language and move it from periphery to center, although this will not become explicit until the end of his life.

Philosophical Idealism: The Cosmic Egoism
of Richard Dehmel (1863-1920)

The work in Niebuhr's two early academic treatises, except for a few criticisms, is basically descriptive, so that it is difficult to say what he made of Dehmel and Troeltsch. What we can see is the context within which he was working at the time and the concerns with which he was wrestling. While there are significant differences between Dehmel's romantic and Troeltsch's monadological idealism, there is nevertheless a common core. They are both concerned with the problem of the individual, its relations to other realities in life, and how to embrace the real while affirming the ideal. And they both find their final solution in some sort of nondualistic mystical union with the divine.

Espousing the life of aspiration--of ceaseless conflict, struggle, and union through unfettered love--Richard Dehmel, the leading turn-of-the-century German poet, embodies in his lyrical poetry the journey from narcissistic to universal egoism. The central problem for Dehmel, as Niebuhr presents him, is the nature of the individual. Within his lyrical subjective idealism Dehmel transposes the spirit/nature conflict into the opposition of spirituality and sensuality within the poet's own life. The problem of the individual is then how to hold these antitheses together.

Niebuhr delineates three stages in Dehmel's subjectivism. He moves from a life of self-expression, to a life of union with the female other, to a life of artistic creativity through which he is united in erotic love with the spirit of the whole world. All the relativities of existence, death and time, duty and desire, good and evil, pain and pleasure, are transcended in this cosmic oneness. The problem of the individual is solved by transcending it, by expanding the self to union with the whole through an act of resignation to the creative workings of the whole within. Through this union Dehmel discovers the holiness of all things and the eternal richness of each present moment. Yet this does not mean a cessation of dynamic activity; the cosmos is evolving endlessly towards greater completeness.

While Dehmel believes he has united idealism and realism, Niebuhr comments at the end that the poet has never gotten beyond the subjective realm:

Thus Dehmel has transcended individualism but he has never achieved nor sought to find a view of life apart from his subjective sphere. The egoism born of hope and youthful ardor has passed thr[o]u[gh] the sea-change of love--yet spiritualised [sic], purified, glorified tho[ugh] it be, it remains not less an individualism because its "I" is all the world and its happiness a cosmic joy.

Nor have his lyrical flights allowed him to confront the grim realities of life:

There is a temptation of the realistic mind to bring against such an ecstatic flight of thought, as his which we have sought to trace, a harsh indictment, calling back the soul to grim realities that thinking dare not change. Or some might say: "He is creating a world in his head which might be admirable if God had made it."

Yet it is not apparently the lyricism itself to which Niebuhr objects, for he concludes the thesis with his own lyrical flourish:

Not only a thinker who broods upon his mountain--Dehmel has come down as Zarathustra did to be a prophet to his people, the prophet of the will to the deed. His hand is a gnarled and willing tool of creation and his spirit, forged to steel, is ready for the bidding of the world's duty. His is the brave heart that does not shun the wonderful and perilous adventures we call life. He reveals himself to us as a poet of the free soul, in love with woman, life, and the beautiful, wild world.[14]

This "beautiful, wild world" of Dehmel's cosmic egoism is a far cry from the moral seriousness, social concern, and belief in the external objectivity of ideal divinity of Niebuhr's theo-ethical idealism. The theological task in Dehmel's idealism is not the representation of ideal reality but participation in it, for the purpose, not of loyalty to God and caring for humanity within the kingdom of God, but of erotic union with the sacred whole. Within this context religious symbols furnish pictures, but neither of ideal reality nor non-ideal forces. Rather they are objectifications of Dehmel's own subjective world and thus portray aspects of the poet's own self, frequently in the form of dialogue. While Dehmel offers no useful insight on the form and function of religious language, it is suggestive, given Niebuhr's later exploration of the poetic in religious discourse, that his first academic treatise is on a poet.

Ernst Troeltsch (1865-1923):
Historical Relativism, Absolute Conviction,
and Union with God

Troeltsch, according to Niebuhr's doctoral study, confronts the relation between nature and spirit in terms of the relativities of history and the absoluteness of religious conviction and experience:

> [In philosophy of history] all of his various interests met and in it he sought for the solution of the problem which concerned him more than anything else, the problem of the antithesis between the relativity of all historical entities, so of Christianity, and the absoluteness of conviction with which the value of such historical entities might force itself upon one (*ETPR* 219).

Every historical moment is conditioned by various factors--economic, social, political, scientific, cultural, religious--and is relative in its value to the whole of history.   While there are various rational patterns discernible in history, they rest upon the irrational, "a wide, dark mass of the purely actual and living," whose relationship to the rational "cannot be rationally determined."   Historical method thus can only deal with probabilities and not absolute certainties.

In the face of such complexity Troeltsch advocates a realism that will affirm the actuality of the irrational as well as the rational. Troeltsch, Niebuhr remarks, is eager to combine:

> an anti-rationalism, which recognizes the limits of rationalism, with rationalism and so to arrive at a view which incorporates all proved rationalism into a fundamental "irrationalism."   He defines this combination as "a reanimated, broad and deep realism, a living intuitive sense for facts, a complete surrender to the not yet rationally analyzed life, a feeling for the impossibility of ever analyzing it finally and down to its last remnants by means of reason, or of making rational construction out of it."[15]

His is a relational realism insofar as it recognizes history as a richness exceeding rational grasp that we dwell within.   Nature and history, our facts and norms, are all cultural concepts which are embraced by and emerge from an underlying "complicated movement of life."   The self as an isolated subject is itself an abstraction from this larger lived whole, for in actuality it is part of this comprehensive and sustaining life:

This sort of realism means 1) that all concepts of the natural sciences are working hypotheses; 2) that all concepts of the historical sciences are transformations, systematizations and concentrations of a much richer reality of facts; 3) that all isolations of the subject and especially of the conscious subject are only artificial abstractions from a continuous racial consciousness (*Gattungsbewusstsein*) and from a subconscious life which flows into some sort of unity with the physical; 4) that all our culture and religious ideals are emanations out of a complicated movement of life which no kind of research can completely illuminate; 5) that the whole realm of rationally clear facts and norms in nature and history is embraced by a much broader realm, a wide, dark mass of the purely actual and living; and 6) that the relation between the rational and the non-rational or "irrational" cannot be rationally determined (*ETPR* 214).

While affirming a relational wholeness, Troeltsch rejects a systematic wholeness that obscures the particularity, irrationality, and complexity of this actual whole. Drawing upon Adolf Harnack's speech over the bier of Troeltsch, Niebuhr says:

Broadness of outlook was coupled in him with keen appreciation for the peculiar character of each individual fact. Harnack has paid tribute to "the respect and tenderness" with [which] Troeltsch "took hold of every living thing," and to his scorn for "the violence of the rationalist and the mischief wrought by the systematizer. He felt himself removed by a broad and deep gulf from all those who have no rest until they have changed every living object into a simple and petrified thing and have robbed it not only of its charm but of its life along with all of life's tensions and self-contradictions."[16]

Even while rejecting a final systematic wholeness, Troeltsch nevertheless insists on seeing each part in relation to the whole; as Niebuhr says: "Every formulation of a normative standard will therefor[e] need to be made upon the basis of the whole process of history and not upon the basis of an individual event, relative to the whole" (*ETPR* 49).

The solution for Troeltsch to the uncertainties present in this realistic acknowledgment of historical relativism is a two-fold affirmation of: a "historical a priori" and a "religious a priori," or what he also called a "metaphysic of the spirit." The first Niebuhr describes in this manner: even though "all our values are relative to our historical situation, yet they are absolutely obligating within that situation." There is, then, a quality of absolute obligatoriness within every moment of history. This is so because there is a correspondence between structures of historical being and the human mind. The historical a priori thus links together both thought and being, and value and being. It is undergirded by a religious a priori: these correspondences occur by virtue of the knower's mystical participation as an individual monad in the life of Absolute Spirit--

> the problem of the relationship of the a priori to reality can be solved, Troeltsch holds, only by a metaphysics which discovers the source of the a priori and of the content of experience in the living union of the individual human monad with the divine all-life. History appears therefor[e] as the unfolding of the divine reason (*ETPR* 102).

History is the unfolding of divine reason because God as Absolute Spirit is the source both of history's rationality and apparent non-rationality. Knowledge of both aspects of history is possible because God unites them within his being and is the source of the correspondence of mind to reality, inasmuch as "The forms of reason . . . are the inner relations within the Divine Spirit," and because humans participate in the Spirit:

> The source of the a prioris, of the rational, as we have seen, must be found, Troeltsch thought, in some secret alliance between human reason and reality. And this secret alliance, he explained, as the identity of human monads with the Divine All-Life, whence flowed the absoluteness of all imperatives. This Divine All-Life, however, is also to be regarded as the source of all the nonrationality of the world, of all the brute material which reason seeks to penetrate and to transform. The forms of reason arise in the mind as it contemplates its object because they are contained in the object but their spontaneous origin and their obligating character is due to the fact that they are the inner relations within the Divine Spirit which embraces the whole of concrete reality. . . . Form and content, reason and non-rational material are united in the Absolute and because of that union, and because of the participation of the finite spirits in the life of the Divine Spirit, it is possible for them to discern the rational in the non-rational and to maintain the absoluteness of the rational (*ETPR* 217-18).

Troeltsch's mysticism is of "the active presence of the Absolute Spirit in the finite" (*ETPR* 266) which Niebuhr associates with Hegel, Schleiermacher, Leibniz, and Malebranche (*ETPR* 266). He notes, however, an ambivalence in Troeltsch's attitude towards mysticism. Sometimes he roundly rejects it as individualistic, socially impotent, disregarding of the symbolic and mythic conditions of worship and action, and irrelevant to the origins and founders of religion. Yet he clearly embraces mystical participation in the Absolute and on occasion speaks of the founders of religion as centrally drawing on such resources. Niebuhr explains this apparent contradiction in terms of Troeltsch's rejection of extreme mysticism--represented by individualistic and socially impotent visions and ecstasies--and acceptance of a mild mysticism--the experience of the presence of God which impels to action.[17]

History for Troeltsch means relativism, but it also means revelation. He speaks of our knowledge of God through mystical participation in terms of revelation: that comes by "the divine initiative," presenting us with "new visions and ideas about God, the world, and man and about the purposes of God with respect to the world and man," and yet as well manifesting "God's revelation of himself in human hearts and lives . . . , awakening men to a new and higher quality of life, breaking down the barriers which the sense of guilt would otherwise set up, and making a final breach with the egoism obstinately centered in the individual self" (*ETPR* 137-38, 155, & 232-33).

Apart from his study of Troeltsch, Niebuhr does not speak of revelation as divine initiative or self-manifestation until his conversion. While in his other early writings he uses revelation in various ways--as the provision of an object in history to be studied for the benefit of ethical and religious life, the stimulus to the rise of a new religious movement, and the presentation of an ideal to be realized[18]--none of these make it central as it will become in his conversion. Nor does he link faith with historical revelation elsewhere in his liberal period. Faith is understood here in Troeltsch as the "intuitive participation in the process of the Divine Being's inner movement" and thus as an "inward personal experience and a personal attitude" resulting in "a feeling of inner certainty and clearness" (*ETPR* 254-55).

Niebuhr's most extensive exploration of symbol and first mention of myth in his liberal period are in his study of Troeltsch. Myth and symbol are indispensable for Troeltsch--in mystical knowledge of God: "the content of the intuition is expressible only in symbolical form"; in religious life: "symbols and myths . . . are the condition of all social action and worship in religion"; in history: "an historical essence is symbolical"; and in reason: "Troeltsch recognizes the dangers of myth without logos, but the dangers of a religion of logos without myth are no less apparent to him" (*ETPR* 65, 114, 240-41, & 115).

They are indispensable as the media of revelation and of faith as the experience of God: myth "denotes the whole representation of religious experience or of revelation in the inadequate form of ideas--inadequate because symbolical, the ideas being the memory-images of the media through which the revelation has come rather than of the object of the revelation." Myth pictures symbolic ideas which are the images of the media through which the revelation comes. This picturing is an imaginative activity providing aesthetic attire for the revelatory intuition: "A productive experience or revelation presents itself to the bearer of the revelation in an abundance of new visions and ideas. . . . In the production of these ideas naive imagination is at work, giving to the intuitively apprehended revelation a naive aesthetic expression in which old and new elements are combined." As with Dehmel and Niebuhr's own idealistic theology, the representative function of religious language separates symbol from reality, even here where it is indispensable for our knowledge. While the impact of Troeltsch's view of myth and symbol is evident in Niebuhr's increasing interest in religious language in 1929, he is nevertheless skeptical about the importance of myth. Speaking of Troeltsch's difficulties with monadology, Niebuhr says:

> At one point he concedes that it may be a myth, as the Christian doctrine of the self-revelation of God is a myth. . . . However such an assertion by this constantly questioning and never dogmatic philosopher need not be taken too seriously. The doctrine of participation evidently represents the idea which was more or less constantly in his mind and which is essentially connected with the mysticism he desired (*ETPR* 154-55 & 269-70).

While Troeltsch thinks myth is indispensable, Niebuhr does not see any reason for taking it too seriously for the moment.

Niebuhr's dissertation, though a descriptive study, gives some hints of his judgment about Troeltsch. He says that whereas Troeltsch is usually presented and criticized as a philosopher of relativism, this is but a negative point alongside two other positive affirmations: the absolutely obligatory valuing or conviction of the historical a priori and the mystical participation in God of the religious a priori:

> There are three elements in this discussion of the truth or value of religion and these three elements are present to a more or less pronounced degree in all of his writings. The one is the idea of the relativity of all historical values, and so of religion, the other is the a priori and imperative obligation which such values impose upon us, the third is the presentiment, the intuition, the direct inner experience of the Divine Life. Troeltsch, indeed, seems to have emphasized the first of these elements in his final volume, and it is as a relativist that he appears to be generally interpreted and criticized as he was formerly criticized for his rationalism. However, insofar as relativism represents the negative side of his thought and in view of his insistent emphasis upon the a priori character of religion, upon its independence and causal inexplicability and, finally, in view of the constant trend toward a metaphysical interpretation of a priorism marked in his "Historism," it

is impossible to escape the conclusion that the emphasis, for Troeltsch, was really placed upon the second and third elements.

It is the second of the three points that Niebuhr finds most important in Troeltsch's work:

> Instead of regarding Troeltsch's philosophy of religious history therefor[e] as the philosophy of relativism, it may be regarded as the philosophy of complete obligation. Christianity is not only the sufficient religion, it is the imperative religion; it is our Fate (*ETPR* 262-63).

The third term, the monadological solution, in its effort through the principle of participation to hold together the rational and irrational, the absolute and the relative, Niebuhr finds an unsatisfactory compromise:

> Troeltsch's discussions of this metaphysical background of his thought are too sketchy to permit us to decide to what extent it solved for him the numerous antinomies of his philosophy. It almost seems as if he carried the dualism of rationalism and anti-rationalism, of relativism and absoluteness, of pluralism and monism only a step further back. Troeltsch's philosophy remains the philosophy of compromise.

Kant's effort to overcome these dualisms, Niebuhr believes, is the most promising: "The greatest conception of a mediation is to be found in the Kantian doctrine." But this too ends in contradiction: "But just for that reason it is ambiguous in more than one way. Every attempt to combine the antithesis leads to irremediable contradictions although the combination must be attempted anew ever again." Yet even as he rejects Kant, who will become an important but finally inadequate means to develop the relational view after his conversion, Niebuhr uses a Kantian distinction, affirming the practical over the theoretical, in suggesting a direction for further thinking: "Practically the two sides are held together in theism, but theoretically they can never be harmonized" (*ETPR* 270, 216, & 217).

Seeds of Relationality

In Troeltsch Niebuhr has encountered relational possibilities in historical relativism, personal conviction, and mystical participation in God; explored themes of revelation, faith, value and being; and noted affirmation of the indispensability of myth and symbol--all of which will emerge in his own creative configuration out of his future conversion.

Niebuhr is deeply influenced by Troeltsch's relativism and realism--
by his affirming history's particularity, complexity, actuality, and
irrationality; its intelligibility yet transcendence of any final systematic
grasp; its essential relating all particulars to each other as parts of a lived
whole; and its being an emergent part with nature of that whole.

In Troeltsch's historicism Niebuhr finds the distinction of inner and
outer, although not explicitly predicated of history, which he will use in
developing his relational view of inner history. Niebuhr exhibits an
ambivalence in Troeltsch, however, as he both identifies and distinguishes
inner and outer. Niebuhr says: "For him everything depends upon the
participation of the monads in the All-Consciousness, by virtue of which
'nothing is outer and nothing is inner.'" Yet he also distinguishes outer,
characterized by causality, from inner, explicable by a non-causal
ontological principle. As Troeltsch says:

> I believe also that the whole higher psychical life with its reference to an
> un-sensual reality demands ontological explanation by means of
> independent principles. The whole doctrine of the purely causal and yet
> wholly phenomenal process of all the parts of consciousness appears to
> me to be an unjustified transference, nowhere verified by reality, of the
> doctrine of cause from "outer experience" to "inner experience" (*ETPR*
> 266 & 123).

In Troeltsch Niebuhr also encounters the distinction between
observer's truth and "actual value-relations":

> The essential character of an historical complex is the value which it
> possesses and which is immanent within it. The primary question is not
> as to the value of an historical individuality from the viewpoint of the
> observer, but as to the actual value-relations which, in human history,
> have served to individualize complex reality into wholes possessing value
> or meaning (*ETPR* 241-42).

While in *The Meaning of Revelation* Niebuhr will link outer with the
observer's point of view and inner with lived relations, Troeltsch does
not. For Troeltsch, a critical idealist, the actual value relations are
objective; for postconversion Niebuhr, a postcritical relational realist, they
are personal.

Troeltsch speaks of actual value relations as if they are a historical
complex existing independently of selves relating. In the passage above
the "value-relations" are not involvements and connections of selves but
a "complex reality" which the value relations "individualize" into
objective "wholes possessing value or meaning." Such an objective

complex of value relations is known objectively: the conceptual forms by which we know such perceived valuational complexes are "the inner relations of the Divine Spirit," which can be observed "objectively." Niebuhr quotes Troeltsch as saying:

> The conceptual forms which are contained in perceptual reality and which human thought extends and completes are the inner relations of the Divine Spirit which embraces the whole of concrete reality. In this way the burden which the theory of validity had to carry is lifted from its shoulders and that which seemed to be the artificial product of men reveals itself as perceivable reality which is at the same time, like all reality, penetrated with meaning, idea and law. Real observation and thorough, deep going investigation can penetrate, objectively and ideally, into the real connections of all reality.[19]

While the issues of historical relativism and realism appropriated from Troeltsch will emerge reconceived in Niebuhr's conversion, he never will accept the objectivistic correspondence theory of truth based on idealism's mystical union with the Absolute. Instead, he will come to speak of inner history as relations to reality which selves are committed to and enact, which are known by being in them and drawing them into articulate form through a creative imaginative grasp from a particular perspective. Such knowing by being in relations to reality has a bodily dimension, as becomes evident when Niebuhr uses Santayana's "animal knowing," whereas Troeltsch sees the body primarily in a "critical" way as obstructing knowing. And such knowing by imaginative drawing out from lived (unconscious) relations has a linguistic dimension, evident as Niebuhr comes to present language as constitutive of reality, rather than correspondent, and to speak of inner historical knowing of God inhering only in grammar of the first person.[20]

Rejecting all forms of idealism in his conversion, his realism articulates a relational rather than monadological human-divine immediacy, which will become an action model of responsibility (a relational rather than unitive, ethical rather than cognitive, mysticism--apt, even though he would never call it that, insofar as mysticism means direct experience of the divine). What he finds as central in Troeltsch and what will be central to Niebuhr's thought is neither relativism nor mysticism but personal conviction. From his conversion point of view, he will reconfigure Troeltsch's relativism, realism, and divine immanence, as well as his talk of revelation, value and being, faith, and myth and symbol. For the moment Niebuhr encounters these relational possibilities in Troeltsch from within a liberal dualistic idealism. Yet the seeds are there, ready to send out their relational roots.

CHAPTER TWO

NIEBUHR'S CONVERSION:
THE EMERGENCE OF RELATIONAL REALISM

Committed to the dualism of idealistic theological and ethical liberalism, while exploring two forms of mystical idealism, Niebuhr undergoes a conversion from all forms of idealism (dualistic or unitive) to a relational theological ethics, which he calls at the time "religious realism." This conversion will issue in the five major relational motifs of his mature work--value, history, faith, feeling, and the culmination, responsibility.

Niebuhr's Conversion and Relational Thinking

In late November, 1929, Niebuhr, then Dean at Eden Theological Seminary in Illinois, travelled to Drew Theological School in New Jersey to lecture on "Moral Relativism and the Christian Ethic." Fresh from the publication of his fullest expression of idealistic liberalism in *Social Sources*, he journeyed in this address beyond the theological and ethical world of his origins into a dramatically new and different milieu.[21] Unheralded, the radical shift of perspective this lecture embodies is not acknowledged by Niebuhr then or later, although he does speak in his autobiographical essay of a decisive change in his thinking that occurred between 1930 and 1935 (*Ref* 74). It is a deep change: bearing on commitments in his personal relations to and understanding of God, affecting every aspect of his thought, and transforming his modern idealistic liberal dualistic framework into a relational perspective.

The postcritical meaning of his conversion is not realized until the end of his life. The shift at first is from idealism to realism. He jettisons idealism's spirit/nature dualism and begins to develop a relational view of being in contact with the real. He does this, however, under the shelter of the subject/object dualism of "critical" thought. At first he talks of a shift in focus from the subjective to the objective, from idea to actuality and from the human to the divine. Yet he insists on their relatedness. Later, creating space within a historicized Kantianism, he develops the relational character of the self's knowing and being in connection with society and God by interpreting the subjective as "inner history," while retaining the dualistic framework that separates natural phenomena as nonrelational objects measured by science. Only at the end of his life will he realize the postcritical potential of his conversion by including natural phenomena and scientific knowing within his relational perspective, in *Radical Monotheism*, and by explicitly abandoning all forms of "critical" dualism in *The Responsible Self* (see 82-83).

During the early 1930s he refers to his new perspective as "religious realism" and then in 1941 as "critical realism." His first use of the earlier phrase occurs in July, 1930. In "Can German and American Christians Understand Each Other?" he speaks of the desperateness of our situation "if we must continue to confuse our ideas and formulas with the reality we seek to express in them," and then says: "The way out of the impasse appears to lie only in a realism which will apprehend in all their stubborn actuality the facts of history and the fact of God." In Germany and America there is arising simultaneously "a new leadership which is blazing the path of religious realism." He has in mind in Germany especially Paul Tillich, for whom:

> One of the keynotes of this realism is emphasis on the apprehension of God in the present and the desire to understand history not by means of an impossible attempt to transplant ourselves into some remote past but by a resolute effort to wrest from contemporary experience its ultimate significance and revelational value (*Can* 915 & 916).

In a symposium on religious realism in 1931, Niebuhr makes clear that his shift from ideal to real is a shift from subject to object:

> But all of these movements of religious realism are united by a common interest in maintaining the independent reality of the religious object. Hence they represent a movement distinctly different from nineteenth century liberal theology which found its center of gravity in the idea of the ethical value of religion. Though realism shares this ethical interest and accepts many of the critical results of liberalism, it has shifted the center of interest from the subject to the object, from man to God, from

that which is purely immanent in religious experience to that which is also transcendent (*Realism* 419).

He now speaks of Karl Barth as well as Tillich as examples of German religious realists. But he continues his criticism, begun the previous year, of Barth's theology of crisis for its "complete separation" of "absolute and relative," "God and man," which is "inimical to its realistic interest." In beginning with the object, Barth fails to find a way to the subject, from God to man, thus ending in "Kantian dogmatism" and "authoritarian dogmatism." He begins to be critical of shortcomings in Tillich's realism, as well, even though finding it much more fruitful than Barth's. Tillich holds back from full involvement in the real, in dealing with human nature: he "continues to attend primarily to the functions of the mind, and to seek truth by defining their norms rather than by turning to an objective world with which the mind deals"; and with the nature of God: "What enters into experience for Tillich is never the Unconditioned itself but at best a 'Gestalt' of grace, some structure in which the transcendent becomes effective but in which it is not contained" (*Realism* 420-21, 422, & 425).

The overall differences between German and American religious realism are "in the analysis of religious and moral experience." While appreciative of the German critique of American theology's "optimism, monism, and rationalism"--its "anthropocratic tendency"--Niebuhr does not deny divine immanence, as the Germans do, but affirms the transcendent God's presence in the world:

> The independence of God from experience does not imply his remoteness from experience; the relativity of historical experience does not imply the absence of an absolute content or point of reference; the presence of evil in more subtle and pervasive forms than is usually granted by American realism does not imply the absence of the good (*Realism* 428; see *Moral* 10).

Barth and Tillich use realism to emphasize the separateness of divine from human realities, whereas Niebuhr's realism, while distinguishing them, affirms their inherent interrelatedness.

Niebuhr's conviction of divine sovereignty propels this movement from the subjectivism of ideals, from belief in the ideal reality of God maintaining spiritual values in opposition to the world, to the "stubborn actuality" of world and God, who is present in but "also transcendent" of "contemporary experience." Contrary to Barth and Tillich's dualistic conception, Niebuhr's understanding of divine sovereignty is relational.

From its origins in his radical conversion at the end of 1929 and its initial development as religious realism, divine sovereignty is expressed, in multiple ways, in the language of being in relatedness. The five major motifs of relatedness to being in Niebuhr's mature thought take their inception here. Four are visible in the Drew lecture, "Moral Relativism and the Christian Ethic": value, history, faith, and feeling; the fifth, responsibility, becomes visible in "The Social Gospel and the Mind of Jesus,"[22] an address given three years later, and only recently published.

Inherent in his conversion to divine sovereignty, a linguistic perspective in theological and ethical method will emerge at the end of his life in the affirmations that: language shapes and expresses being, the forms of our lives are constituted in language, and our lives can achieve integration through God evocatively present in religious language. As his theological ethics matures, Niebuhr explores religious language in its variety--as metaphor, myth, symbol, and dialogue. Within such linguistic richness he affirms our personal involvement in, interrelatedness of being with, and ongoing transformation by the mystery of being most fully manifest, for Christians, in the figure of Christ. By exploring the inauguration of these multiple motifs and linguistic concerns in his conversion we can understand the beginnings of Niebuhr's relational thinking.

The Inseparability of Value and Being

In "Moral Relativism and the Christian Ethic" Niebuhr explores the problem of historical relativism for theological ethics.[23] After rejecting dogmatism and rationalism as inadequate responses, he presents his own view that there is an absolute present in the relative which a person experiences as an "obligation to follow what he has found true." Our point of view is a matter of fate; we have been shaped by history. But this fatedness and the fact that many do not share our point of view do not lessen a person's sense of "obligation to make the best of his insight." The Christian must follow the Christian ethic not because "Christianity is the universally valid religion but from the fact that he is a Christian." "Christ is his fate" but while this viewpoint "imposed upon him by his birth at this point of history and under these particular conditions" is a "limitation," it is as well "an opportunity for discovery" (*Moral* 9-10).

Niebuhr has appropriated from Troeltsch the problem of relativism and what he interpreted to be his central point, a sense of absolute obligatoriness. Whereas Troeltsch explains this obligatoriness in every historical moment by placing it within idealistic correspondence of thought and being, Niebuhr rejects such cognitive identity and stresses rather the ethical personal, lived experiential dimension of commitment, both as what we have found true and as an unavoidable claim to follow it, to live out of it.

For Troeltsch the historical a priori, this affirmation of value, is grounded in a religious a priori, the participation of ourselves as finite monads in the inner life of God. While absolute value for Niebuhr, like Troeltsch, is present in every historical moment, unlike Troeltsch, Niebuhr grounds this value in neither correspondence nor mystical union but in relational being. At the end of his Drew lecture, Niebuhr lays bare this relational ground that lies at the heart of his conversion, in speaking of the divine "pattern of existence," "the absolute within the relative," and "the real within the apparent":

> Yet Christianity is not confined to this last attempt to fortify by argument its experience of an absolute element within the relative. It has the right to claim that its experience of the will of God is not only obligatory in form but also in content; that its claim to absoluteness does not rest only upon the character of human experience but also on the character of reality; that goodness does not depend upon human judgment but on the pattern of existence, or the will of God. The discovery of the absolute within the relative is the discovery of the real within the apparent, of the permanent character in changing relations. The discovery of this pattern of ultimate goodness has been the practical interest of that long process of trial and error which is set forth in the ethical experiments of all ages and races. The differences between these experiments give rise to the theory and practice of relativism, but the similarities are just as striking and testify to the absolute element present in the ethical life of man (*Moral* 10).

Goodness or value depends upon a pattern of existence or being. Indeed, there is a pattern in the world which is both a pattern of being and of value; this he calls the absolute and the will of God. While we experience absolute value in our sense of obligation to follow our fate, this value is not merely the product of experience or human value judgment, but rather inheres in being. Our experience of the absolute is obligatory in form as an experience of value to which to be true; it is obligatory in content as being upon which value is dependent. Form and content, value and being, are inseparable. They are inseparable in God, as his will is both pattern of existence and pattern of ultimate goodness. And they are inseparable in us: Niebuhr affirms, even while rejecting Troeltsch's mystical union, that experience of value is experience of being and that judgments of value and being bring God and self into intimate relationship. As a self has its own being in the world, it exists within and is dependent upon this ultimate pattern of existence and goodness, which is the real presence of God in the world.

Idealistic liberal theology separates value and being in its basic opposing of spirit and nature, ideal and real. God, whose domain is spirit, is not the creator of, nor responsible for, being, which is the result of natural processes. Thus conceived, the religious task is to permeate being as much as possible with the ideal. Both God and self can thus be principally defined apart from being. Niebuhr's thought becomes realistic and relational as he rejects this separation, linking inextricably value and being, spirit and the world. This linkage becomes increasingly clear in ensuing publications as he criticizes "modern attempts to define goodness as value without metaphysical basis" and affirms "no such radical separation between value and being" (*RelEth* 445 & *Value* 93).

Liberalism's separation of spirit and nature defines spirit specifically in terms of personality, imposing a set of values taken from one area, the personal, onto society, nature, and God, assuming no conflicts but continuity between the personal, social, and divine, all of which are subsumed within a harmonious system of values. But "that one can begin with the values of the individual and proceed to declare the values of society identical with them, or with the values of the human person and proceed to the values of God is more than dubious" (*Value* 108). Such proceeding from individual to universal is "unwarranted in view not only of the relativity but also of the conflict and tragedy of values" (*Value* 109). Against defining God and world in terms of the value of personality, Niebuhr affirms his commitment to divine sovereignty by calling for "the complete abandonment of an approach from values known as absolute prior to the experience of God" (*Value* 110).

In his autobiographical essay he speaks in the same way of his break from so-called liberal theology because "it defined God primarily in value-terms, as the good," rather than in terms of value and being. "Believing that good could be defined apart from God," it saw value as something humans could formulate and subsume God under, rather than recognizing the independence of value from selves, as ingredient in God's nature and therefore in being.

The answer for Niebuhr to relativism within this realistic conceiving of value is to affirm in the midst of our historical relativities the presence of God, which we experience both as obliging us to be true to our best lights and commitments, and as a relational pattern of goodness and being in our lives and world. While our understanding of such an absolute is always relative to our culture, it nevertheless is an understanding of that which is really there in our world. Our knowledge and experience are always incomplete, limited by our historical point of view, but what we encounter is not itself incomplete:

> All attempts to define this absolute factor will necessarily be incomplete, and all definitions will perforce be partly relative; but incomplete experience of the absolutely good is not experience of the incompletely good, nor is relatively true definition of moral reality a definition of a relatively moral reality (*Moral* 11).

Beginning with our experience of being, of God as a pattern in the lived world, value within Niebuhr's relational realism is much more personal than in Troeltsch's idealism. Rather than starting with a speculative principle of cognition and mystical participation, he begins with a fundamental relationship to ultimate value and being in our living. Troeltsch speaks of values in an objective mode as if they were axiological entities existing in historical complexes apart from selves and their commitments, whereas Niebuhr sees them as inhering in personal relations to being. He makes it clear in 1960 that his own change occurred fundamentally at this level of personal relations:

> And now I came to understand that unless being itself, the constitution of things, the One beyond all the many, the ground of my being and of all being, the ground of its "that-ness" and its "so-ness," was trustworthy--could be counted on by what had proceeded from it--I had no God at all. The change was not a change of definition of God but of personal relations to my world and the ground of the world, to the givenness of life, history, myself (*Ref* 72).

It is not that values are not relational for Troeltsch; they are, but they are the inner relations of the Divine Spirit present in the world, and not the relations between the being of a self and the pattern of existence within which it lives, moves, and has its being.

Niebuhr is more Kantian than Troeltsch. For all of his recognition of the limits of reason, rejection of speculative system, and affirmation of practical reason in the sense of absolute obligation, Troeltsch remains, as we have seen, an idealist. Niebuhr, on the other hand, embraces the sense of obligation apart from idealistic correspondence and mystical union. Previously in criticizing Troeltsch's idealism in his dissertation, Niebuhr appreciated Kant's "mediation" of the rational and irrational, and balanced a recognition that his theoretical attempt ends in "irremediable contradictions" with an affirmation: "Practically the two sides are held together in theism" (*ETPR* 216 & 217). What is meant by "practical" and "theism" is not explained. Now in his conversion essay we can see the meaning of both terms in Niebuhr's own sense of obligation in existing within the divine pattern of existence in the world. Like Kant, Niebuhr looks to a practical rather than theoretical resolution of our sense of the absolute, but goes beyond him with the postcritical affirmation both of the inseparability of content with form, being with value, and of the personal starting point of our fundamental commitments.

Troeltsch and Kant are obviously important figures for Niebuhr in his conversion with respect to value; there is a third major figure whose influence is much more in the background. It is impossible to assess for certain whether and to what degree Jonathan Edwards had a conscious impact on his conversion. While the language of Troeltsch and Kant is evident in "Moral Relativism and the Christian Ethic," Edwards's language is not. From his idealistic perspective in *Social Sources*, Niebuhr mistook Edwards's relational realism as a compromise mixing of ideal faith with the non-ideal world of bourgeois existence:

> A single line of development leads from Jonathan Edwards and his great system of God-centered faith through the Arminianism of the Evangelical revival, the Unitarianism of Channing and Parker, and the humanism of transcendental philosophy, to the man-centered, this-worldly, lift-your-self-by-your-own-boot-straps doctrine of New Thought and Christian Science. The common strand that runs through these various movements is the adaptation of the early faith to the changing attitudes of the bourgeoisie (SSD 104).

In fact, Edwards does not reappear until 1935 in "Man the Sinner," where he is drawn upon positively as Niebuhr uses him to discuss sin and free will.[24] Then in 1937, in *Kingdom of God*, in an extensive discussion of Edwards, Niebuhr presents him as affirming the same inseparability of value and being as was central to his conversion essay. Exhibiting a sense of deep kinship with him, Niebuhr describes Edwards's resolution of the problem of love in terms of this affirmation, that the "center of all being is their true good," that through a "sacramental sense of all existence . . . [he] sees the whole creation as an emanation of the divine fullness" (KGA 115-16). What he profoundly misunderstood in his earlier criticism of Edwards, he now embraces: the unavoidable presence of value in being, not as compromise, but as the sacramental sense of being, filled with divine presence.

Regardless of whether he drew upon Edwards consciously in his conversion, such a dramatic misreading of him, with whom he will later feel significant mutuality, suggests that Edwards's religious realism lodged deeply in Niebuhr, unsettling his idealistic liberalism. As we see his encounter with Edwards develop after *Social Sources*, it becomes evident that Niebuhr is much closer on the subject of value to Edwards than to either Troeltsch or Kant. A striking continuity runs from Niebuhr's identifying a pattern of existence and a pattern of ultimate goodness in 1929, through his explorations of Edwards's affirmation of the inseparability of value and being in 1937, to his impassioned and elegant identifying of the principle of being and the principle of value in *Radical Monotheism* (RMWC 32-33).

History: Relativism and Revelation as Pattern

Along with value, in "Moral Relativism and the Christian Ethic" Niebuhr affirms a second locus of the presence of the absolute in the relative, that of history and revelation: "The absolute within the relative comes to appearance at two points--in the absolute obligation of an individual or a society to follow its highest insights, and in the element of revelation of ultimate reality" (*Moral* 9). He has earlier used the category of revelation, but with different meanings and in a peripheral way. In his work on Dehmel he speaks of it as disclosure of the cosmic whole; in his theological idealism he speaks of it as the provision of an object in history which can be studied for the benefit of ethical and religious life, as a stimulus to the rise of a new religious movement, and as the provision of an ideal to be realized (see *Dehmel* 2, *TheoPsy* 48, *CIC* 13, & SSD 278-79). Now, from the perspective of his conversion, he draws upon Troeltsch's understanding of history as both relativism and revelation. As he says of Troeltsch, his was "the effort to find a position in which history might be overcome by history--the absoluteness of religious conviction be reconciled with the relativism of historical description" (*ETPR* 221). Now he takes up the task of exploring history to see if what is dissolved by it can be recovered through it.

Revelation is conceived relationally rather than objectively. No longer peripherally the presentation of an ideal, it is centrally the manifestation of ultimate reality as pattern of ultimate being and goodness in the historical world. By "pattern" he means a lived coherence within the history of selves. While Troeltsch sought the rational in the empirical, a rational structure knowable by objective cognition, Niebuhr is groping for a metaphor that will not make God an object, a thing, an entity, but a presence, power, pervasiveness--a permanence in our present existence personally related to, even if in largely lived rather than articulable ways. He goes on to say, in relation to Tillich, this "apprehension of God in the present" is the "effort to wrest from contemporary experience its ultimate significance and revelational value" (*Can* 916), and in response to Reinhold Niebuhr, "But God, I believe, is always in history; he is the structure in things, the source of all meaning, the 'I am that I am,' that which is that it is" (*Commun* 228). Much later he will say "the revelatory moment is revelatory because it is rational, because it makes the understanding of order and meaning in personal history possible. Through it a pattern of dramatic unity becomes apparent" (MR 17 & 109-10).

The will of God disclosed in revelation as a pattern of being and value in the world is transcendent because it requires change: to "the 'will of God' . . . men must needs adjust themselves"; and because the initiative rests with God: "goodness does not depend upon human judgment but on the pattern of existence, or the will of God" (*Moral* 10).

The paradigmatic locus of revelation for the Christian is Jesus Christ: "The supreme intuition and revelation of that absolute element, the Christian maintains, is given in the life and teaching of Jesus." Still evident here is the heritage from Troeltsch, in the talk of "intuition" of the "absolute," and of idealistic liberalism, in the phrase "the life and teachings of Jesus." Nevertheless, Jesus is the supreme manifestation of the pattern of existence and goodness in the world. Confirmation of this truth comes in the experience of humanity, Christian and non-Christian: "The verification of that revelation is to be sought in the experience of those individuals and societies whose lives are governed by this insight, and in the deductions to be drawn from the moral experiences of humanity outside of Christianity" (*Moral* 10-11). While there are profound differences in the experience of humankind, which give rise to relativism, there is also "a common underlying factor" to which the "empirical ethics of modern times," the "ethics of the great world-religions," and "Christian teaching" point--which is the will of God. Revelation in Jesus reveals something in being, the divine will as pattern, which non-Christians have had some glimpse of too. In the face of the relativities of existence Niebuhr affirms the universal presence of a relational absolute.

No doubt Troeltsch is a central element in the context of Niebuhr's changed thinking about history and revelation as he is about value and being. Troeltsch speaks of the divine initiative, the manifestation of God in human hearts, and of change in the recipient. Niebuhr embraces all of these, whether consciously or unconsciously we cannot say, since he does not quote from Troeltsch nor later acknowledge his influence on his revelational thought. Yet because he uses such phrases as "intuition" of the absolute, we can assume Troeltsch as a conscious influence, as he clearly is in focusing the problem of historical relativism (see MR x). What Niebuhr rejects is Troeltsch's theoretical perspective: revelation is not the presentation of new ideas garnered through mystical participation in the internal workings of the Divine Being.

There are other influences abroad in the land as well. Karl Barth had been making a stir in Germany and Switzerland throughout the 1920s. While Niebuhr may have begun to be aware of him earlier,[25] the first unequivocal reference to his "crisis theology" is in *Social Sources*. He explicitly agrees with Barth's affirmations of divine mercy, the forgiveness of sins, and the significance of the kingdom of God transcending human ideals, but criticizes him here and later for his dualistic split of God and world and consequent social irrelevance (See SSD 275-77; *Can* 916; and *Realism* 420-21). Barth's general stress on divine transcendence and revitalization of the category of revelation may have been influential, but Niebuhr's concept of revelation flowing from his relational conversion is significantly different from Barth's, and remains so.

Revelation is not a "bolt from the blue" (*Value* 111), but a manifestation in history of a pattern of existence and ultimate goodness. While Niebuhr says in the Preface to *The Meaning of Revelation* that he is combining Troeltsch and Barth, this should not be taken as an endorsement of any specific ideas of Barth, nor of Troeltsch for that matter, but rather of the general notions of relativism and revelation which the book combines. Niebuhr's respect for, and even close affiliation, though never identification, with Barth in rejecting idealistic liberalism is coupled with an ongoing critical perspective on him as indicated in his autobiographical essay. Troeltsch was a much more important influence than Barth on Niebuhr's use of revelation, and certainly on value and being, which was antithetical to Barth, although his interest may have encouraged Niebuhr's use of the category of revelation he found in Troeltsch.

Tillich becomes very important to Niebuhr after his conversion but there is no evidence that he knew of him prior to 1930.[26] Niebuhr finds Tillich more fruitful than Barth in 1930 because revelation for Tillich is "ultimate significance" that "invades my present" (*Can* 916). A year later Niebuhr describes Tillich as affirming a "self-transcending element" that is within "all reality." While he finds the realism of Tillich hopeful, it is not sufficiently realistic, for in Tillich, Niebuhr says: "it cannot be maintained that the Unconditioned itself ever becomes part of the religious experience. It remains transcendent; what enters into experience is the

sacred symbol" (*Realism* 422 & 423; cf. 425). Niebuhr feels a close
affinity with Tillich in his realistic modification of idealism, but for
Tillich it is only the symbolic reference to the ultimate that appears
everywhere in the world; for Niebuhr, whose realism is relational and
who therefore rejects idealism altogether, God himself is present.

While Tillich was the most fruitful advocate for religious realism in
Germany, Reinhold Niebuhr was a chief spokesman for it in America.
It is finally impossible to assess the interplay of life and thought between
brothers, but we can make judgments on their public pronouncements.
Reinhold Niebuhr was undergoing his own fundamental change at this
same time from idealistic liberalism to religious realism. But H. Richard
Niebuhr finds his brother, like Tillich, not realistic enough, denying the
presence of God in the world. In a dialogue between them in 1932
Reinhold Niebuhr writes: "My brother does not like these goals above
and beyond history. He wants religion and social idealism to deal with
history. In that case he must not state his goal in absolute terms. There
can be nothing absolute in history, no matter how frequently God may
intervene in it" ("Must We" 228). H. Richard Niebuhr, on the contrary,
affirms the presence of the absolute in history, not however as a realized
ideal, but as "the structure in things" (*Commun* 228).[27]

While Niebuhr is, no doubt, intimately affected by his ongoing
dialogue with his brother, the nature of his religious realism is from the
beginning relational rather than dualistic. Reinhold Niebuhr's realism
insists that the ideal can never be actualized in our non-ideal world, yet
hovers as the principle of love in Christ at the edge of the world calling
us to establish justice among its grim realities; Barth's realism affirms the
objectivity of God revealed in Christ; Tillich's realism faces the
negativities in being while affirming the reference of symbols in the world
to the Unconditioned beyond; and Troeltsch's realism embraces the
concrete complexity and irrational particularity of the world while
affirming a correspondence of thought and being through mystical union
with the Absolute Spirit. H. Richard Niebuhr's realism, in contrast to all
four, affirms in the actual being of our world and lives the presence of a
divine pattern. Supported by a convivial affirmation of religious realism
and appropriation of the category of divine revelation in history among
all these thinkers, Niebuhr, nevertheless, conceives revelation in accord
with his relational understanding of realism as the manifestation of God
as pattern of being and goodness in the world.

Faith as Trust and Loyalty

Faith is a third central theme in the conversion essay. Momentarily linked with value and history in Niebuhr's exploration of Troeltsch, faith appears separately before and after that point; then suddenly but quietly the three themes come together and become central in his own thought in the lecture given at the end of 1929--as if a seed planted in 1924 were beginning to germinate in the new soil of relational realism. Within the altered context, faith is neither the intuitive participation of the self in the Godhead, as in Troeltsch's critical idealism, nor belief in the ideal reality of God, as in his own earlier idealistic liberalism; rather faith is relational reliance on being, inseparably related to value as the pattern in history of the divine will disclosed in revelation.

Within this new perspective we can discern two aspects of faith, trust and loyalty, both oriented toward the will of God as pattern of being and goodness. While Niebuhr does not explicitly designate loyalty as an aspect of faith, he advocates an "unswerving loyalty" to "the absolute ethics of the will of God." He then goes on to speak of faith as a "conviction of the actuality of the . . . will of God" which is "trust in the actuality of God's love" (*Moral* 8-9 & 11).

Niebuhr uses the words trust and loyalty earlier--loyalty no doubt influenced by Josiah Royce. And he uses the word faith unconnected to either term.[28] In all these earlier uses, however, faith is related objectively to ideal reality and not relationally to the whole of being. Within the context of realism, he brings trust and loyalty together for the first time as the self's faith in God.[29] While this two-fold aspect of faith will only be developed systematically later,[30] in the years immediately following the conversion he speaks of trust, loyalty, confidence, and faith in general.[31] In all of these, inasmuch as faith is a relation to the actuality of God in the world, it brings us into touch with all of being, opening us to conflicts between beings and to the ongoing process of integration.

Influence is difficult to assess here. The category of faith is certainly present in his idealistic liberalism and in his work on Troeltsch. When Niebuhr discards his idealistic framework faith becomes central, as it did for his theological contemporaries. But he views faith differently from Tillich, Reinhold Niebuhr, and Barth for whom it is referential rather than relational. Faith refers to God beyond the world--spatially for Tillich as faith refers to the Unconditioned beyond finitude, temporally for Reinhold Niebuhr as faith refers beyond the present to the future of anticipated resolution beyond time, and transcendentally for Barth as God makes our language refer to him--rather than being a relation to God within the world. Perhaps Jonathan Edwards plays an important role here as well as with value, for his talk of the virtuous life of faith as the "consent to being in general" is closer to Niebuhr's realistic concept of faith than any of these others.[32]   But lacking direct evidence, it is impossible to say.

Feeling and the Religious Emotions

Concern for feeling and the religious emotions as a distinct subject of inquiry does not appear until near the end of Niebuhr's life, and then it is evident only in unpublished materials. Although only visible from this perspective of its later emergence, and its growing importance in the early 1960s, this relational theme roots in his radical conversion. Earlier he dealt with Dehmel's view of life as a passionate struggle toward erotic union with the whole. In his work on Troeltsch feeling is a consequent of faith as a "feeling of inner certainty and clearness" (*ETPR* 254-55) that flows from participation in the Absolute Spirit. In his own idealistic liberalism feeling motivates life. Christianity must seek to stir desire to follow the ideal. Through new movements of religious enthusiasm, feeling has been the means repeatedly to revitalize the church, and as the community of love it is the ideal for which Christianity strives.[33] Within the conversion, however, feeling and religious emotions are reoriented from stimuli of and adherence to ideals to a "trust in" and "conviction of the actuality of the holy, moral, loving will of God" (*Moral* 11). While not indicating its emotional effect, Niebuhr affirms as "loving" the pattern of existence and goodness, which he names the will of God.

Rooted in this reorienting of feeling from the objective ideal to the relational real is the affirmation of religious emotion evident in Niebuhr's teaching and lecturing near the end of his life: that feelings are fundamentally in touch with reality, that beyond our reasonings they can provide us knowledge of reality, and that the religious life made up largely of emotions is transformed through the ordering effect of religious language.[34] The presence of this concern in the conversion is almost entirely implicit so that it is impossible to locate influences. As it emerges into explicit interest at the end of the conversion period, it is, once again, Jonathan Edwards to whom Niebuhr is closest. In *Kingdom of God* Niebuhr writes that Edwards "was genuinely surprised at the display of 'religious affections' which followed some of his stiffly logical preaching." But conversions, Niebuhr notes Edwards saying, "bring an extraordinary conviction of reality" which they have "immediately felt."[35]

The Realism of Responsibility

The affirmation of God's presence as a pattern in existence, Niebuhr develops finally into his theological ethics of responsibility in which he conceives of God as the One action present in every action in the world. Here the self is principally neither obeyer of law nor striver after goals, but responsible agent, responding to the actions of the world upon it and the One action in their midst. While he uses the word "responsible" and "to respond" earlier,[36] it is without any special theological significance. In 1933 he begins to develop what will decades later become his central distinction between the ethics of teleology (pursuit of ends), deontology (adherence to law), and responsibility (response to actions and the divine action upon oneself):

> The mind of Jesus which is not to be found in the social gospel is the mind of a Jesus whose thoughts were directed not in the first instance to what man ought to do and in the second place to what aid he might receive from God in doing what he ought to do, but rather toward what God was doing and what man ought to do in the light of God's doing. God's doing--not what God ought to do in order that he might live up to the expectations men had of him--stands in the center of Jesus's mind. God for him is not the moral ideal but rather cosmic reality. He is the God of Job rather than the God of Plato. What God does is seen by him in the natural and in the historical process . . . (*SocGosp* 120).

Even though he has not yet found the language of responsibility to express this, so that he speaks of the self's response to what God is doing as an "ought" and calls Jesus, "the revolutionary Jew," a "strategist" in distinction from a "moralist" or "teleologist" (*SocGosp* 122), Niebuhr stresses God's doing things in the world and the self relating principally to this. Two years later marks Niebuhr's first use of the "responsible self" which eventually becomes the title of his posthumously published book. He works with the language of responsibility, however, in a largely tacit way until at the end of his life it emerges as a distinct motif culminating his career.[37]

The meaning of "religious realism" becomes clearest when Niebuhr finally conceives the problem of religion in the modern world as that of integrity in relatedness. Dwelling within a world of ongoing actions to which the self responds openly, or more likely defensively, we are confronted with the problem of integrating all of our responses to all of these actions so as to be a centered self. Only by opening ourselves in response to the One action present in all of these actions are we able to open ourselves to the entire community of being and thus move towards the integrating of all our responses (RS 139ff.).

While the word "integrity" is used throughout his early thought, it is construed within the idealistic framework as strength of character through adherence to, or in the case of his work on Dehmel, participation in, the ideal.[38]   In his conversion, evident in his recognition that modernity has a "disintegrating" effect, it begins to take on the meaning of bringing disparate elements together into a unity (*Moral* 4).   The result, as he will show later, is that we withdraw from the realm of being to some limited sphere of exclusive loyalty which will incapacitate us from integrating our whole self in response to our total ethos.[39]   While difficult, once again, to locate specific influences, the similarity of Royce and Edwards to Niebuhr's conception of an integrated life beyond limited spheres, in the total community of being, suggests they played important roles; perhaps G. H. Mead and Bergson were also important.   With regard to the motif of response itself it is difficult as well to say, except that it bears a significant resemblance to Edwards's notion of consent which similarly involves a dynamic relating to the totality of being in relating to God's being in the world.[40]

Relational Realism: A Linguistic Incipience

At the end of his life Niebuhr realizes the inherently linguistic nature of his conversion. Responsibility, begun to be distinguished as a third alternative in 1933, is presented in 1960 as itself a metaphor, joining the two terms of responsive existence and human life.[41]   Comparative analysis of this metaphor with others can illumine certain realities of self, world, and God because reality is embodied within our language. In *The Responsible Self* he compares the metaphors of "man-the-answerer" with "man-the-citizen" and "man-the-maker"; explores the nature and use of metaphor, symbol, myth, and dialogue for theological ethics; and develops a theory of meaning of religious language.[42]

Looking back over his past work from his explicit linguistic perspective achieved in responsibility, he acknowledges its implicit linguistic nature in a seminar comment:

> Thus as Niebuhr once remarked in a seminar on Theology and Language (1960), the Christian community seeks to apply the *symbolic pattern of Jesus Christ* to its interpretation of encountered reality. With this remark Niebuhr simply restated the problem of *The Meaning of Revelation*. He thought it necessary that theology should engage in reflections on language. Even *Christ and Culture* "might be written today from the

standpoint of language" (remark in the same seminar) (Hoedemaker 185, n. 50; his italics).

While the linguistic concerns emerging in his earlier writings are not often noticed when viewed, as usual, from a perspective preoccupied with history, once they are seen in his final work, they become evident in much of his earlier work after his conversion to religious realism. For instance, in the midst of his work on theology and history in 1941, he calls for the development of a theology of religious grammar that would, through the analysis of religious language, learn about our ethical lives and the presence of God in their midst:

> theology can attempt to state the grammar, not of a universal religious language, but of a particular language, in order that those who use it may be kept in true communication with each other and with the realities to which the language refers (MR 18).

In the idealistic beginnings of his career Niebuhr in fact showed interest in religious symbols which reemerges in altered perspective soon after his conversion. In 1931, his appreciative description of Tillich's religious realism is critical of his concept of the relation between religious symbols and reality. For Tillich, symbol and reality are separable because the divine reality is not present in the symbols but is simply pointed to:

> In the religious act reference toward the Unconditioned is explicit, though it cannot be maintained that the Unconditioned itself ever becomes part of the religious experience. It remains transcendent; what enters into experience is the sacred symbol in which the claim of the Unconditioned becomes explicit and real, or in which the voice of the Absolute is heard through the mediation of the relative (*Realism* 423).

For Niebuhr, on the other hand, the absolute is present *in* the relative. Even though the year before he speaks approvingly of Tillich making "a resolute effort to wrest from contemporary experience its ultimate significance and revelational value" (*Can* 916), he has now come to see that for Tillich this means to encounter the references in our world to the transcendent, whereas for himself it means to relate to the transcendent itself in our world.

The implication, not drawn out until much later (MR 95-99 and RS 154-55 & 161), is that symbol and reality are inseparable, and that symbol does not simply point to a reality elsewhere but expresses reality embodied within it. Several years later in his contributions to *The Church Against the World* (1935), Niebuhr takes a step toward this view, although in no self-conscious way, when he speaks of the truth "hidden within symbols and myths" of Jesus Christ crucified which comes not primarily as a remembrance of things past but as "the recollection of a most decisive fact in the present situation of men" (CAW 616). The decisive fact is the presence of Christ in our present situation from whom we learn that we too are among the crucifiers.

The development of a major theology of language in responsibility from this linguistic incipience in religious realism shows the postcritical potential in Niebuhr's conversion. Rejecting the "critical" separation of theory and practice (RS 82-83), he finally sees theology and ethics as inextricable precisely because religious language is the medium both of knowing and action. All knowing forms the active self and all acting expresses interpretation of being in the world. When symbols point, they are separated from reality and function theoretically, as in Tillich's conceptual analysis of the structures of being behind language in *Systematic Theology*. When symbols embody and express, they are inseparably connected with reality and function simultaneously theologically and ethically, representing knowing and action together, as in Niebuhr's stating the grammar of the lives of men and women in community with the divine, manifest in the different forms of *Kingdom of God*, or in his comparing the different "root metaphors" (RS 151-54) of *The Responsible Self*. Where for Tillich the symbol's function is to point and its effectiveness is measured by the theoretical clarity of its correspondence to reality, for Niebuhr its function is to bring to expression and its measure is the lived (theologically known and ethically enacted) fittingness of its use.

This concern with religious language, becoming visible in 1931, is rooted with responsibility, beginning to appear in 1933, and the other four more obvious motifs of history, value, faith, and feeling in the conversion essay's relational turn towards being. Within the conceptual clarity achieved later in his writings on responsibility, we can see that each motif and the earliest language of religious realism is inherently relational for Niebuhr: expressive and transformative of the inextricably related being of self, world, and God. After his idealistic liberal understanding of religious language as picturing a separable reality, Niebuhr is silent about language in his conversion. Out of this silence gradually emerge both a relational understanding of language, as an embodiment of being, and a relational way of speaking of divine sovereignty.

CHAPTER THREE

DIVINE SOVEREIGNTY IN RELATIONAL PERSPECTIVE: THE REALISM OF IMMANENT PATTERN

His turn from idealistic liberalism to religious realism at the end of 1929 Niebuhr later describes in his autobiographical essay of 1960 as the coming of the conviction of divine sovereignty. While divine sovereignty is important from the 1920s on for his theological contemporaries, they develop it within a dualistic framework to shift attention from the subjective realm of human experience, central (as they understood it) for nineteenth- and early twentieth-century liberalism, to the divine object--or as Barth would say, from us as subjects to God as Subject who acts upon us as passive objects. Within this "critical" disjunction of subject and object, divine sovereignty is God's freedom from human and worldly entanglements.

For Niebuhr, on the other hand, divine sovereignty is articulated in terms of immanence, since transcendence is developed within a relational perspective. God's reality has its being in the world as presence and action that is universal in acting on and sustaining all beings, relating continuously to us and eliciting our re-actions, whether of fear, anger, ignorance, trusting acceptance, or loving engagement. Niebuhr's conversion to religious realism is the discovery that God, rather than an ideal individual outside the world, is pervasive being in the world present in inherent relatedness to all creatures, and that the self is absolutely dependent for its existence upon God who acts continually upon us towards our ongoing transformation and integration.

The Context of Conversion to Divine Sovereignty

In the previous two chapters focused on Niebuhr's early writings from 1920 into the 1930s, we have been following the emergence of a major theological mind as it passes beyond the origins of its dualistic idealism through a radical conversion into the relational realism of its maturity. There is a disarming quality of effortless grace about Niebuhr's books. Not engaging in polemic, they give the impression of thought beyond the fray of theological controversy and contemporaries' groping toward theological clarity. In his preconversion essays, however, much more of the formative process is evident, as he refers to a diversity of thinkers, not only theological but philosophical, sociological, economic, and literary: Karl Barth, Henri Bergson, Auguste Comte, Emile Durkheim, Jonathan Edwards, Sigmund Freud (evidently though not by name), Washington Gladden, Adolf Harnack, William James, Immanuel Kant, Lucien Lévy-Brühl, Lenin, D. C. Macintosh, Karl Marx, George Herbert Mead, Reinhold Niebuhr, Ralph Barton Perry, Walter Rauschenbusch, Josiah Royce, George Santayana, Friedrich Schleiermacher, Ernst Troeltsch, Max Weber, H. G. Wells, and Alfred North Whitehead.[43]

There is no doubt that, amidst these, his brother, Reinhold (whom he does not mention before the change), and Karl Barth (whom he does mention just prior [SSD 275-79]) are influential in his conversion. Judging from his criticisms of and divergent thought from both in the essays immediately following his shift, the influence is, however, more one of comradery in the shared venture of theological revitalization. He is in fact closer to Tillich, whom he discovers just after his conversion, but in clarifying the meaning of religious realism in the early 1930s, he makes evident their significant differences. Whitehead, although teaching at Harvard through the 1920s, is first mentioned only just before the conversion. His systematic philosophy never engages Niebuhr, though we shall see how certain of Whitehead's religious themes become important after conversion and remain so throughout his career.

While Barth and Reinhold Niebuhr, and other American, German, French, and English thinkers are all part of the context of Niebuhr's conversion, we conclude from our exploration in the first two chapters that the two most formative influences in his 1929 conversion are the German, Ernst Troeltsch, and the American, Jonathan Edwards. In his work with Troeltsch he explored the motifs of value and being, history, and faith, and in kinship with Edwards value and being, faith, feeling, and responsibility. Each motif becomes an expression of a relational understanding of divine sovereignty, starting with what he has found to be central in Troeltsch, the givenness of personal commitments and the absolute obligation to be true to them, and recognizing with Edwards, at least as he understands him later in the 1930s, the relational defining of these convictions and divinity itself in terms of being and the consent to being.

At the end of 1929 and on into the 1930s, divine sovereignty means, in terms of value, that goodness is dependent upon being, not upon judgments or desires, and that our commitments to the will of God are to this pattern of the world's being. In terms of historical revelation, it means that the absolute is present in the relative as this pattern of being and goodness manifesting itself in our lives and world. In terms of faith, it means that we exist in relation to this pattern, wrestling with it as enemy but coming by grace to call it companion as well. In terms of feeling, it means the conviction that in this pattern of being and goodness is love which can elicit a felt sense of reality through religious affections. And in terms of responsibility, it means that God is a cosmic reality acting in the natural and historical world, eliciting the self's integrity, and manifesting through religious symbols fittingly used the divine presence in the world.

While the influence of Troeltsch is much more evident, the similarity of Niebuhr's new perspective to Edwards's theology is much greater. In all but the motif of history there is a close kinship as both thinkers see divine sovereignty as comprehensive of value, faith, feeling, and responding--all fundamental modes of relating to being. As for history, while Niebuhr has been much more influenced by Troeltsch than Edwards, he never accepts the speculative framework of monadological idealism within which Troeltsch develops historical relativism and absolute obligation, but rather develops history within a realistic framework more like Edwards's view of an immanent God who as being in general elicits our consent.

In elaborating God's sovereignty through multiple motifs, it is as if Niebuhr is adhering to Edwards's injunction that "the thing may possibly be better understood, by using many words and a variety of expressions, by particular consideration of it, as it were by parts, than by any short definition" (*End* 340-41). While there is no recognition at the time of Edwards's presence, Niebuhr later makes it quite clear how important he has become. In 1937 he speaks of the *Kingdom of God* as hopefully a "stepping stone" to the work of some later "Jonathan Edwards *redivivus*" (KGA xvi), and in 1960 he says that "in the thirties . . . religiously speaking I was, as I hope I remain, closer to Calvin and Jonathan Edwards" (*Ref* 73; cf. *CV* 105, n. 1).

Niebuhr's new perspective emerges most fundamentally, therefore, from a context of encounter with the relational thought of both Troeltsch's historicism and Edwards's theological realism.[44] But we can also be sure that the context of Niebuhr's conversion is much broader than these two thinkers, however central they may be. No doubt important as well for someone open to the larger social setting, as Niebuhr was, were the cataclysmic events of World War I, hoped by many to be forgotten in the economic boom and soaring optimism of the 1920s terminated by the Great Depression in 1929. And with his theological generation he participated in recovering the tradition of biblical Christianity: "With the aid of my colleagues and students I turned back to the 'Great Tradition.' Edwards, Pascal, Luther, Calvin, Thomas, and Augustine became important. But that is the familiar story of the whole generation" (*Ref* 74).

Yet it would be a mistake to say that any or all of these influences were determinative. Such causal thinking would fail to take account of the imaginative process as both understood and exhibited by Niebuhr. The alchemy of his mind takes up developed ideas, unintended suggestions, phrases, images, and underlying directions, and transforms them into the uniquely creative pattern of his own thought.

It would also fail to understand commitment to first person grammar inherent in his realistic conception of divine sovereignty. What is transformative is not external influence but inward personal commitment. At the heart of his change, as we have seen, is his recognition of holding commitments, "what he has found true" (*Moral* 9), and his sense of absolute obligation to live out of these. Such commitments are not so much conscious choices as their ground; they are deep-lying convictions that are not consciously selected but given and received in the depths of self. In his autobiographical essay Niebuhr indicates this in saying "Since I came to that conviction or since it came to me . . ." (*Ref* 72; cf. 71). Ahlstrom comments about the personal as well as larger social and theological crisis of Niebuhr's change:

> Richard Niebuhr was obviously a participant in a larger movement and was acutely aware that the Thirties were a time of crisis in almost every sense of the word. There is no doubt that much Continental thought besides Tillich had its effect, not least of all that of Karl Barth. In any event, it will not do either to make Edwards the sole catalyst or to interpret Niebuhr as a mediator of Troeltsch and Barth, as is frequently done. What happened to Niebuhr was at once more general (a renewed appreciation for classic Christian theology) and more personal (in

answering my queries on this subject he referred to his own *Turmerlebnis* of justification by faith--his terms) (215).

Niebuhr's conversion, which he likens to Martin Luther's "tower-experience," goes on within a rich context of thought and destructive events of recent social experience, but it is obviously, and more fundamentally, a personal crisis in his life, issuing, as he says, in the transformation of "personal relations to my world and the ground of the world, to the givenness of life, history, myself"--a reorientation toward the relatedness of divine sovereignty in being. For "unless being itself . . . was trustworthy," Niebuhr concludes, "I had no God at all" (*Ref* 72).

Divine Sovereignty:
Pattern of Being in the First Person

In 1920 Niebuhr emphatically rejects divine sovereignty because such a God of "Providence" would, as "creator" of the "totality of nature," be the "responsible author of evil," and would, as one "present in all the accidents and futilities of life," be "pulling about the order of events for our own advantage" and therefore be denying our "[h]uman sense of responsibility and freedom." His objection is focused on such a view of divine sovereignty within the Hegelian assertion of pantheism and mysticism. Over against it he affirms the "finite" "aspect of the idea of God," in agreement with James, Bergson, and H. G. Wells (*Aspect* 40-44). In 1929 he turns from rejection to acceptance of this most basic of "personal convictions" that "being itself . . . was trustworthy" (*Ref* 71 & 72). While he does not speak of divine sovereignty in the conversion,[45] as he reflects on the subsequent decade in his still later autobiographical essay, he makes it clear that he now understands this fundamental transformation in those terms:

> The thirties were for me as for many of my generation in the church the decisive period in the formation of basic personal convictions and in the establishment of theological formulations of those convictions. The fundamental certainty given to me then (sad to say, not in such a way that my unconscious as well as conscious mind has been wholly permeated by it) was that of God's sovereignty (*Ref* 71).

Once again, while difficult to assess influences on Niebuhr, his view of divine sovereignty is closest to Edwards's; there is even a similarity in the turning after an initial antipathy. Almost exactly two hundred years prior to Niebuhr's conversion, in the early 1720s, Edwards turns from a previous repulsion at the "horrible doctrine" of divine sovereignty to a "delightful conviction" of the "being" and "beauty" of "God's sovereignty."[46] For Edwards, as with Niebuhr, sovereignty comes to mean that the basic agency of transformation rests with God and that such a God of grace is present in the world and our lives ("Personal Narrative" 59ff.). While we cannot determine the degree, if any, of conscious influence on Niebuhr's conversion, we know that already earlier in 1929 he has encountered the issue of divine sovereignty in Edwards and drastically misunderstood it from his idealistic perspective, taking it to be an "accommodation of the faith to bourgeois psychology" (SSD 104). And we can see a profound similarity between the new orientation expressed in the conversion essay and Edwards's view as Niebuhr will come to articulate it by 1937:

> It is noteworthy, however, that just as the early Quakers had kept their theory of the Christian revolution closely related to their faith in the sovereignty of God so the Evangelicals now presupposed or reaffirmed the rule of God as the basis of all they believed about the kingdom of Christ. Jonathan Edwards, the greatest theologian of the movement, comes to mind at once as one in whom faith in regeneration was solidly founded upon a supreme conviction of the reality of divine sovereignty. It would be difficult to find in all religious literature a more moving confession of loyalty to the kingdom of God than the one in his "Personal Narrative," or to discover more illuminating statements of the principle than those which abound in his writings. In his thought faith in divine sovereignty was the explicit foundation of the kingdom of Christ (KGA 101).

Niebuhr certainly elaborates his concept within a context of shared concern over divine sovereignty exhibited by his theological contemporaries, such as Barth, Tillich, and Reinhold Niebuhr. But he differs from them in two ways: by affirming God's transcendence through immanence as divine pattern in the world, and by insisting on the personal interconnectedness with this immanent pattern.

A definitive passage from 1931 uses much of the language of the conversion essay--revelation, historical relativism, will of God in the world; here Niebuhr differs from his whole theological generation that affirms God's transcendence by separating God from the world. Instead he calls explicitly for articulation of a theory of immanence, that will at the same time affirm transcendence.

> The chief task which faces theology in an age of disillusionment does not lie primarily in the religious interpretation of disillusionment, though this

has its important place, it lies rather in building upon the foundation of disillusionment--not by its denial--the theory of an immanence which is present and which yet must be attained, in making the transition from God the enemy to God the companion, or God the Savior. . . . [T]he transition may most promisingly be sought in three spheres, all interdependent--in continued wrestling with the problem of Jesus and the historical meaning of the revelation of God in history, in continued realistic analysis of religious experience and the search for divine reality in actual religious life, and in even more urgent effort to realize the eternal will of God, as we must see it from the relative point of view of the present moment, in some form of social and personal justice which will carry within it, as immanent, a revelation of the God who yet remains transcendent; which will be adequate to our own situation, but which will contain the absolute demand (*TheoDis* 21-22; quoted in Fowler 68).

He conceives transcendence by locating God in the world as pattern of being and goodness which exists beyond our ideals and unrealistic desires, and beyond the limited sphere of our valuing only parts of being. While in the world, such a pattern is never identified with any part of the world nor with the whole natural process. The "realistic strain" in his earlier idealism, that wanted to affirm the real, face negativities, and deny that God adjusts the world for human benefit, is now realized in the commitment to transcendence in immanence. To encounter God is to encounter the ultimate realities of the world; conversely, to face the world's realities, inimical as well as beneficent, is, if seen from a fitting perspective, to encounter God. The elimination of American slavery, for instance, he saw in his idealistic period as the result, to a significant degree, of the nonideal economic force of labor (*Alliance* 200); he now comes to see this historical change as the action of God, not separated from such impersonal forces, but working as this pattern through them (*Grace* 219). Redemption is no longer conceived as the result of human effort gaining adherence to and living lives in conformity with ideals, but as the consequence of divine action, for God, as being and goodness, is at work in the world regardless of human actions. Yet our moral responsibility is intensified, for if God is the pattern of being and goodness in the world, our relation to this reality involves responsibility to the entirety of the world.

Niebuhr's conception of divine sovereignty as transcendence through immanence is further distinguished from the views of his theological companions by its ineradicably personal nature. The conversion was a change "of personal relations," he writes in 1960, "to my world and the ground of the world, to the givenness of life, history, myself," and "not a change of definition of God" (*Ref* 71-72). The conviction is not simply about God, divinity's supremacy and initiative, but about his own relationship to ultimacy, his own faith in the trustworthiness of being. God is a relational term--as he will say later, "soul and God belong together" (RS 122). The meaning of the word "God" involves the speaker of that word, for God is the pattern in the world we participate in, and it is by virtue of this pattern that we exist as selves. When it does not express that personally constitutive relationship, the word "God" means something else, such as an otherworldly ideal or entity.

Incipiently linguistic, this relational view of sovereignty as divine immanence in our beings means that religious language must express this personal relatedness in the first person, both singular and plural. While it is only at the end of his career that he recognizes the linguistic dimensions of this postcritical conviction, he, nevertheless, begins to reflect in major writings after his conversion on the first-personal character of this conviction. In 1937, for instance, he writes: "yet truth which was not merely true by reference to some impersonal standard but 'truth for me' required for its apprehension as well as for its expression the activity of a whole man, of intellect and will, of mind and body."[47]

These reflections on the personal arise upon ground cultivated by a shift in writing style in his conversion from dominance of third person to use of first-person grammar. Hardly noticeable at first, use of the first person gradually becomes pervasive. At the conclusion of "Moral Relativism and the Christian Ethic" he shifts to the first person plural: "*we* are not free from the same necessity of trust in the actuality of God's love. . . . And in it at least and alone *our* moral and religious relativism must yield to the affirmation of the absolute" (*Moral* 11; my italics). In a number of subsequent essays of the 1930s, use of the first person is evident, such as in dialogue with his brother: "But God, I believe, is always in history"; as the "structure in things," God "overwhelms *us* as *our* enemy," just as the "violated laws of *my* organism . . . make *me* pay the cost of *my* violation." Finally, in *The Meaning of Revelation* first person speech becomes the common mode of theological discourse.[48]

Troeltsch may have had an influence on this. Niebuhr writes in his dissertation:

> In view of this fact the validity which *we* claim for Christianity or which *we* can find in Christianity is its "validity for us." . . . But the relativity of such validity does not . . . detract from its absoluteness, and its imperative claim upon *us*. Christianity may be absolutely valuable only from *our* viewpoint but for *us* it "is final and unconditional, because *we*

have nothing else and because in what *we* have *we* can recognize the accents of the divine voice."[49]

But Troeltsch does not catch the significance of this as he thinks within his impersonal, monadological metaphysic. Edwards writes in the first person singular, of course, in his autobiographical "Personal Narrative," but it is impossible to say whether Niebuhr had read that prior to his conversion.

There are a few uses of the first person prior to the conversion, such as: "Practically if not theoretically *we* accept the judgment today that *our* definitions of God's nature are conditioned by *our* need of Him" (*Aspect* 39; my italics; see *Alliance* 203). But these occur only in the plural, and thus have the feel of an editorial "we." In any case they occur within the dominant mode of third person speech where the subject is not "I" or "we" but "Christendom" or the "individual Christian" (SSD 284). His change from idealism to realism, from a finite to sovereign God, is a change in grammar, the full importance of which he only realizes at the end of his life within the theme of responsibility as he affirms the nature of religious language as first personal (RS 109-10 & 115-17; cf. RMWC 45).

Divine Responsibility for Evil

Conceiving divine sovereignty as the pattern of being in, rather than an ideal individual independent from, the world raises powerfully for Niebuhr the question of divine responsibility for evil. In his early writings he rejected divine sovereignty precisely for this reason, allying himself with James's and Wells's finite God who is not "the responsible author of evil" because "God is a part and not the whole," "the creator not of the totality of nature, but of the spiritual life," and "an eternal (i.e. unceasing) tendency making for righteousness" who is not "present in all the accidents and futilities of life except as the spiritual nature of the victims put him there" (*Aspect* 41 & 43-44). Now Niebuhr faces directly the consequences of embracing divine sovereignty: that God is responsible for, although not the cause of, evil. As the principle and power of being in the world, God is not an ideal tendency supporting what we want, but the ultimate reality of the world. Such reality threatens us and is destructive.

In the next published piece after his conversion essay, Niebuhr uses Whitehead's words to speak of experiencing God as "enemy"; "the soul struggles [with] God the enemy and God the ultimate reality" and not "with some man-made deity, some projection of the wish or the social whole" (*Can* 915). Destructiveness and mercilessness are in God: "The God of things as they are is inevitable and quite merciless," who brings about "revolutionary change which will involve considerable destruction" (*Grace* 219 & 220). The "destructiveness of the cosmic God" is his rule in history "as a driving, directional movement ruthless so far as individuals and nations are concerned, almost impersonal in its determinism" (*SocGosp* 12 & 22). God brings destruction upon us: "That structure of the universe, that will of God, does bring war and depression upon us . . . , for we live in the kind of world which visits our iniquities upon us and our children, no matter how much we pray and desire that it be otherwise" (*Can* 229). God is not some ideal of our desiring, a projection of a wish fulfillment, but a structure of the world. Niebuhr starts with "God's action not within himself but in objective, natural and historical events" (*IsGod* 954).

But God is not only enemy; he is "companion" as well. Following Whitehead, Niebuhr sees that "[r]eligion . . . is the transition from God the void to God the enemy, and from God the enemy to God the companion" (Whitehead 16), but he does not want us to make that transition too quickly and thus risk obscuring the enemy quality of God: "but access to the companion may be too cheaply purchased to be real when it is not gained by way of the void and of the enemy" (*TheoDis* 16). In the destruction is God's judgment, but in the judgment is God's redeeming. "But this same structure in things which is our enemy is our redeemer; 'it means intensely and it means good.'" The good that it intends is fulfillment or love, but not as we would wish--"not the good which we desire, but the good which we would desire if we were good and really wise." This means that history shaped by the divine structure is the means to human fulfillment: "History is not a perennial tragedy but a road to fulfilment and that fulfilment requires the tragic outcome of every self-assertion, for it is fulfilment which can only be designated as 'love'" (*Commun* 229). Thus it is that God acting through impersonal forces eventually "eliminated slavery in spite of abolitionists" and that "the actual processes of history will inevitably and really bring a different kind of world with lasting peace." Even though the forces be impersonal "as machine production, rapid transportation, the physical mixture of races, . . . they are as much a part of the total divine process as are human thoughts and prayers" (*Grace* 219).

The "divine creative process" is both judgmental in its destructiveness and redemptive in its constructing, but these are the same process. Creator, judge, and redeemer are one and the same God. The divine process "has created fellowship in atoms and organisms, at bitter cost to electrons and cells; and it is creating something better than human selfhood but at bitter cost to that selfhood" (*Commun* 229-31). Jesus was able to unite

> in a true synthesis the fear of God and the love of God, the knowledge of God the enemy and the knowledge of God the deliverer. The manifestation of the rule of God in the events of his time calls not for repentance only but also for rejoicing. There is a bad time coming, there is also a good time coming. The two events cannot be separated from each other. The slayer may be trusted because he is the bringer of life. The life-giving Father, however, cannot be separated from the destroying judge. It is all one and the same process which damns and saves--not a Father who slays and a son who gives life, not righteousness which condemns and a love which redeems--but a God with one faithful working (*SocGosp* 13).

In a series of articles during World War II Niebuhr affirms the presence of God in the war. To deny this presence is "to become dualists who deny the fundamental unity of the world asserted in . . . radical monotheism," because they believe "there is an actuality in which God is not, and there are therefore situations and events in life which do not allow a rational, meaningful response on the part of men." This is, however, "the denial of God's universality and unity . . . that God is God" (*IsGod* 954). The war is God's judging but also his redeeming action. These two actions are one action because of God's vicarious suffering; the war is crucifixion and the cross is followed by resurrection:

> To recognize God at work in war is to live and act with faith in resurrection. If God were not in the war life would be miserable indeed. It would mean that the cosmos had no concern with justice. But if God were in the war only as judge, man's misery would be only sightly assuaged since before the judge all are worthy of death. To see God in the war as the vicarious sufferer and redeemer, who is afflicted in all the afflictions of his people, is to find hope along with broken-heartedness in the midst of disaster.

Such a view "looks in the midst of tragedy for the emergence of a better order than any which has been realized before. Nothing is regarded as beyond the scope of redemption." It also looks finally to the resurrection of the dead: "Even should death come to them hope wraps their broken bodies in fine linen, conserving what it can, preparing on Good Friday for an Easter miracle of divine action" (*WarJudg* 632-33). In the symbols of cross and resurrection we see "that the order of the universe is not one of retribution in which goodness is rewarded and evil punished, but rather an order of graciousness wherein, as Jesus had observed, the sun is made to shine on evil and on good and the rain to descend on the just and the unjust" (*WarCruc* 514).

God is responsible for destruction and evil, yet he does not cause it nor finally intend it. God "does bring war and depression upon us" but, Niebuhr goes on to add, "when we bring it upon ourselves." We bring it upon ourselves by violating the God-created structure of the universe: "That structure of the universe, that creative will, can no more be said to interfere brutally in history than the violated laws of my organism can be said to interfere brutally with my life if they make me pay the cost of my violation" (*Commun* 229). We violate this structure by our own self-interest which begets counter-assertion and results in war, whether military, economic, or verbal; such conflict is judgment. We are responsible for violations of God's loveful law of being, but God intends that there be destructive consequences for such violations; he intends judgment.

God is really destructive, really judgmental, in history, but he does not intend destruction for its own sake. Rather he intends the fulfillment and love of redemption; the order of the world is not retribution but graciousness. To see this our perspectives must undergo transformation, to see that God is not the lord of special providence administering to individuals' desires but is the lord of being, sustaining and supplying its basic needs.[50] God is not the cause of evil; we are when we violate the divine structure of things and when we misinterpret the cosmic process from our self-serving point of view. Nevertheless, God is responsible for it; as Niebuhr writes with Hebraic resonance at the end of his life, "There is no evil in the city but the Lord has done it" (RS 170). God is our enemy, but he is as well our companion, for this divine "doing" of evil "means intensely and it means good" (*Commun* 229), for it is the doing of "a God with one faithful working" (*SocGosp* 13).

Niebuhr's Relational View of God and
Feminist Theological Critiques of Divine Sovereignty

In tracing how Niebuhr's understanding of sovereignty of God differs from his earlier liberalism, we have seen as well how it differs from the turn to neo-orthodoxy taken by his theological contemporaries in the late 1920s and 1930s. Our claim that the emphasis on relationality distinguishes his view of divine sovereignty from Tillich's and Barth's must take account of the critique recently offered by Sharon Welch in *A*

Feminist Ethic of Risk--not only of Tillich and Barth but of Niebuhr as well. While much of her challenge focuses on *Radical Monotheism*, a work much later in Niebuhr's corpus than those we have used so far in tracing his ideas in their post-conversion formative stage, her concerns, along with those of several other feminist theologians critical of Niebuhr on this point, are crucial to address in our analysis of the meaning and fundamental significance of divine sovereignty as viewed from Niebuhr's relational perspective.[51]

Welch shows forcefully and insightfully how neo-orthodox theology conceives divine sovereignty in the mode of transcendent domination and how this issues in an ethics of control and conquest. Conceiving God as absolute power, neo-orthodoxy intends to relativize human claims to power, but in fact legitimates the absolute power of human imperialism (see Welch 117-19). While I find her critique of Barth and Tillich incisive, I do not agree that it fits Niebuhr.

She claims that Niebuhr valorizes absolute power by rendering God as exclusively of worth and all other beings as not valued in themselves but only in relation to God. She quotes Niebuhr as saying: "Radical monotheism dethrones all absolutes short of the principle of being" (Welch 116; RMWC 37). While Niebuhr does want to dethrone all absolutes, he does not, however, do this to set up God "the absolute" as an isolated substance. The passage she quotes occurs in the midst of Niebuhr's defining radical monotheism as "inclusive" of "the realm of being in its wholeness"--human and non-human, living and dead, organic and inorganic--which engages in a "wondering and not exploitative attention" to other beings. It dethrones all absolutes but--as Niebuhr goes on to say--"[a]t the same time it reverences every relative existent. Its two great mottoes are: 'I am the Lord thy God; thou shalt have no other gods before me' and 'Whatever is, is good'" (RMWC 37).

No doubt Niebuhr affirms a different reverencing of God than of the creature, but both are reverenced. The different reverencing is in relating differently to whole and part. He does oppose the reverencing of any part as if it were the whole--of which patriarchy is guilty--because this circumscribes the realm of being, all of which is valuable, and excludes and thus subordinates various parts; reverencing the whole involves reverencing all its creaturely parts.

Welch recognizes that for Niebuhr "other beings are valued," but she says, "they are not valued in themselves but are respected as holy 'because of their relations to the holy One'" (Welch 116; RMWC 53). She is literally correct: for Niebuhr nothing in itself has value--even though he says "every being is holy" (RMWC 53) or recognizes elsewhere "the 'givenness' of all beings having intrinsic value" (*Value* 116)--because all things exist in constitutive relatedness, and value inheres in that relatedness.   While Welch criticizes not valuing beings in themselves, I do not think she intends to deny that value is relational; rather, she objects to locating all value in God and conceiving the self as valueless except for its associations with (or in traditional language: imputations of righteousness from) the divine.   But he is not saying, as his neo-orthodox contemporaries do, that humans are worthless except as God, who alone has worth, bestows it upon them.

It is true that for Niebuhr this holiness does not inhere in a solitary self--as in the liberal tradition of atomic individuals having inherent rights--but exists in relationship to God.   Every being is holy because each exists in relation to everything else including the all-pervasive One who constitutes, sustains, and interacts with each creature.   The web of all beings is holy, and so are we as we participate in it, for worth is not a possession (owned by us or bestowed by a divine patriarch) but is rather an inherent aspect of relating.   While Niebuhr does not use the web metaphor, his affirmation of our holiness in relating to God, as well as the holiness of every being, attempts to overcome the "division between the holy and the profane" (RMWC 53), the dichotomy of modern culture that forever excludes some realm of being from worth and respect.

Radical monotheism is not in fact an expression for Niebuhr, as Welch avers, of "the principle of exclusivity" and the western "singularity of divine eminence" (Welch 116) but rather a manifestation of the principle of inclusiveness, evident in his use of contextual metaphors for God.   He does speak of God as "the One."   But this is not the eminent One, the "highest being" or "highest value."   As he says, God is beyond both being and value because God is neither a being nor a value but that by which all things have their being and value (RMWC 33, n. 7).   That is not only creation talk--that God has created creatures with being and value--but contextual talk--that God encompasses all valuable entities.   So also, in the language of responsibility, with "the One action" acting on me, it is immanent divinity pervasive throughout being.   An appropriate response to it brings one into accord with all being because the One pervades all being and is in touch with it.   To respond to God is to respond to all that God encompasses.

Welch sees that Niebuhr, along with Barth and Tillich, "are explicitly opposed to all forms of tyranny, human or divine.   They try to describe a divine power that fulfills essential human possibilities and criticizes human pretensions to absolute power" (Welch 120).   But they fail, she claims, because they valorize absolute power which legitimates coercive imperial power and undercuts the transformation of human life (Welch 116, 118, & 120). Even though Niebuhr reiterates Augustine's "whatever is, is good" (Welch 120; RMWC 37), this is belied, she says, because "the inexorable logic of absolute power . . . is destructive power. One can ensure the death of an enemy, but one cannot ensure the cooperation of another in mutually fulfilling and transforming work" (Welch 120).

Niebuhr does speak of the destructiveness of God, as we have seen, but not as the power of domination. His talk of divine destructiveness comes rather from his commitment to divine immanence and transformation. If God is present in the world acting on me in every situation, then God is acting on me in my dying as well as in my living. God does bring me to my death--not, however, as enemy triumphed over but as a transient but valued ingredient in the nature of things. Transformations, of which death is the last, are all destructive of their antecedent forms. Divine power is destructive--not, however, with the intention of domination but of redemption (see *Commun*), making us whole (see RS 155).

This talk of divine destructiveness also comes as an expression of Niebuhr's own experience. Speaking experientially (a feminist commitment), Niebuhr perceives "the nature of things"--in all its destructiveness, impersonality, otherness--as God and thus as divine threat to his life. He experiences God as enemy out to destroy him, but goes on to describe the miraculous change of orientation from God as threat to God as friend: "Now a strange thing has happened in our history and in our personal life; our faith has been attached to that great void, to that enemy of all our causes, to that opponent of all our gods" (RMWC 122). In this change he comes to trust, glorify, and love that power "out of which everything comes and to which everything returns" (RMWC 122).

Niebuhr is acutely aware that "this passing" (RMWC 122) includes death and that to trust it is to accept death. Welch links his emphasis on God as slayer with a "fear of change" (Welch 121), whereas Niebuhr is in fact describing his own change, in Whitehead's words, from God as the void, to God the enemy, and to God the companion. There is no doubt great pain, amazement, and uncertainty for Niebuhr in coming to trust in God imaged in this new consciousness--because it involves embracing the world and all those excluded parts of his being--but he passionately affirms the value of undergoing this change and affirming it. Moreover, he discovers in this change the "continuing imperative" (title of *Ref*) to change ongoingly: to relate to God immanent in all is to commit to life as transformation as God elicits new responses in every moment.

Welch discerns in Niebuhr's emphasis upon God the slayer a tragic sense of our lack of absolute power.

> The fact that our power is not absolute (we are conditioned by time, place, and the ongoing process of life) is regarded as a tragedy, not celebrated as the source of the richness, diversity, and novelty of life. . . . What I worship, naming it the web of life or the dance of life, he values as the source and "slayer of all" . . . with more emphasis on the slaying than the source (Welch 120-21).

To have such a tragic sense would be to contradict what Welch has seen clearly, that Niebuhr intends to dethrone all relativities that aspire to absoluteness. On the contrary, not only does he insist that we do not have absolute power, for we are all conditioned beings, but he maintains that not even God has absolute power in the sense (I think she means) of dominating others to accomplish one's own will. In the passage she quotes, Niebuhr laments the tragedy both of the divisions caused by religion and of "the twilight of the gods"--that we have placed our loyalty in things less than the whole which are therefore not "able to supply continuous meaning and value" (RMWC 121-22). While he may not be celebrative of "the richness, diversity, and novelty" of our conditionedness, he is affirmative of it; his positive embrace of historical relativism lies at the heart of *The Meaning of Revelation*.

Niebuhr's emphasis on the One as slayer is best understood within his historical context. An article Welch draws from extensively was written in 1943 in the midst of World War II. In it one can hear the tragic story of his generation--the unprecedented destruction of two World Wars. Niebuhr's preoccupation with death continues, however, throughout his mature years, although as we have seen, he does speak as well of glory and love. But this dour tone gives way right at the end of his life. His conversion is to being and his life-long struggle is for deeper trust in it; at the end of his life he writes "now we are falling in love, we think, with being itself" (RS 177-78). Here is the celebrative note Welch was missing. But in such affirmation Niebuhr never forgets that the dance of being is pervaded by uncontrollable mystery that not only engenders but also concludes life.

Seeing a dominating absolute power in his God, Welch concludes that Niebuhr negates finite existence as such. In the following remark she finds him equating "finitude and wrong" (Welch 121):

"It is a consoling idea," wrote Kierkegaard, "that before God we are always in the wrong." All the relative judgments of worth are equalized in the presence of this One who loves all and hates all, but whose love like whose hatred is without emotion, without favoritism (RMWC 123; in Welch 121).

Since he repeatedly insists that whatever is is good (see RMWC 126 and his tranformationist view in CC, especially 109-10), he cannot mean by the above to equate finitude and wrong. Whatever Kierkegaard may have meant, Niebuhr is using it to relativize all human judgments and to conceive God as free from favoritism: our views are "wrong" in the sense of being partial whereas God's is whole embracing all creatures without favoritism. While I would agree with Welch that Tillich--she says as a result of making this equation--does not believe "the kingdom of God can be manifest in history" (Welch 121), Niebuhr does in fact affirm the presence of God in, and not just beneath, history; in 1932 he says explicitly that the kingdom of God is being realized in history:

God, I believe, is always in history; he is the structure in things. . . .
[T]he kingdom of God comes inevitably, though whether we see it or not
depends on our recognition of its presence. . . . Man's task is not that
of building utopias, but that of eliminating weeds and tilling the soil so
that the kingdom of God can grow (*Commun* 229 & 231).

We have probed Welch's reading of Niebuhr because her important book, calling for communicative solidarity, has a resonance with his dialogical thought. It would be a mistake to be defensive on Niebuhr's behalf, who, more than anyone of the last generation, saw defensiveness as an essential ingredient in sin and who incorporated into his own thinking a self-critical, indeed repentant--what he called "confessional"-- attitude. I have attempted, nevertheless, to clarify Niebuhr's view of divine sovereignty in response to Welch's criticisms because of the fruitfulness of his thought for a feminist perspective and his closeness, in fact, to many of her most important commitments.

Linda Holler questions another important aspect of Niebuhr's thought in her critique of radical monotheism. In a trenchant criticism of Niebuhr's residual dualism, she shows how it denigrates feeling. She exposes the mind/body dualism in his handling of external history in *The Meaning of Revelation*, in which "value is objective because value-relations are 'independent of feelings of an observer'" (Holler 99). She goes on to suggest "What he needs, and I think wants to say is that value-relations are independent of self-centered projections . . . not independent of feelings" for "[f]eeling connects and discloses" (Holler 99). His devaluing of feeling is part of her larger criticism of radical monotheism, as she sees his affirmation of God beyond being and value as another undercutting of his relationality as he conceives God as a "self-in-isolation" who (quoting Niebuhr) "has [no] need of any being external to himself" (Holler 88; *CV* 112). She criticizes Niebuhr's shift in talk of God's relation to creatures from need to desire, as he goes on to say: "hence it may be able only to say that whatever is exists because it pleases God" (*CV* 112).

While Holler has ferreted out passages of Niebuhr's devaluing feeling and has shown with acuity its dualistic underpinnings--to which I would add another salient example in the Kierkegaard quotation above, cited by Welch (121), in which Niebuhr says God loves and hates without emotion--nevertheless, I think these passages should be seen within the full sweep of his thought. At the very end of his life, as he explicitly transcended dualism through the theo-ethics of responsibility, he realized the centrality of feeling to human existence and began a major exploration of it. This is evident, unfortunately, only in unpublished materials. He focused on it as a distinct concern in a lecture course, "Introduction to Theological Study," in fall 1960; connects "the realm of feeling" with "the symbolic layer" in his final "Christian Ethics Lectures" (March 15, 1961, p. 1); and taught his final seminar in spring 1962 on "The Religious Emotions." The most important exploration of feeling is the transcript of "Toward the Recovery of Feeling," one of his four Vanderbilt lectures in April 1961, entitled "Next Steps in Theology." He begins this lecture by affirming that true religion is "primarily an affair of emotion" (*Feeling* 14).[52]

In this light it is possible to notice Niebuhr's affirmation of feeling in his conversion essay and to see his investigation of love in *Purpose of the Church* (1956) as an important step towards reflecting on the religious emotions once unburdened by dualism. This sheds a somewhat different light on Niebuhr's shift from need- to pleasure-talk about God's relationship to humans. The passage Holler cites from "The Center of Value" (1952) is dualistic, but it also bears evidence of a modulating of this dualism. While the denial of reciprocal need between the divine and human is a rejection of relational involvement, Niebuhr in fact attributes pleasure and desire to God in 1952 which he had rejected altogether in that Kierkegaard quotation of 1943. Furthermore, Niebuhr qualifies his avoidance of need-talk by ending his discussion with openness to either: "But whether the relation is to need or to desire . . ." (*CV* 112).

Aware of Niebuhr's explicit attempt to recover feeling in the last two years of his life, the reader similarly can notice its undeveloped but essential relation to interpretation within responsibility:

> Such interpretation, it need scarcely be added, is not simply an affair of
> our conscious, and rational, mind but also of the deep memories that are
> buried within us, of feelings and intuitions that are only partly under our
> control (RS 63; cf. 97).

While encumbered much of his life by modernity's reason/feeling dichotomy, Niebuhr is freed for a major exploration of the religious emotions, which is, however, cut short by his premature death. No doubt Edwards's work on the "religious affections" has permeated his consciousness and been brought to focus in the space created by his own relational work with responsibility within which feeling can be embraced as responsiveness. We can be grateful to Holler for her incisive criticisms; at the end of his life Niebuhr, I believe, would have been similarly grateful.[53]

Catherine Keller similarly criticizes Niebuhr for his radical monotheism. She sees his promising relational thought "recoil" into an opposition of the One and the many:

> Only my relation to the single One establishes my unity in the flux. God
> is conceived as a unilateral force of unity, upon whom I can only be
> 'absolutely dependent.' Thus Niebuhr's monotheism defeats his own
> pluralism. . . . This is a oneness amidst but over and against the many,
> somehow apart from the many (Keller 181).

She recognizes "Niebuhr's desire for an integral in-gathering" but believes for him, as for Augustine, that "plurality itself is finally . . . demonized" (Keller 181).

I would agree Niebuhr is using words drawn from the patriarchal tradition of Western thought with mortgages to his own patriarchal past. One and many do sound oppositional; finding integrity only in relation to God does sound isolationist. But if the One is recognized as a contextual metaphor, as encompassing whole, and as immanent, pervasive throughout being, then it can be seen that the integrity Niebuhr seeks is the "truly multiple integrity" Keller affirms (181). To respond to the One as Whole--"web" in her words--is to respond unavoidably to all the parts of the whole.

The action of this immanent One meets me in the midst of the particularity in the pluralism of my situation. God's action is not generic but appropriate to the specific moment. As my situation changes, God's action changes, resulting in ongoing novelty in the divine-human interaction. Amidst the dynamism, intimacy, and relevance of this relation, God always acts to transform me towards universality--not towards the abstraction of generalizing thought, but the inclusiveness of otherness in being. I exist in multifarious relatedness with other creatures on many levels--physical, political, socioeconomic, cultural, and God's action on me is always within this larger "matrix" (RS 59), evoking my fitting response not only to God but God's community of being.

His approach is not either/or--either the One or the many--but both/and. The self amidst the multiplicity of relations to God and world is constantly being reconstellated as it integrates new actions and old ones taken up from within the new pattern of the present moment. Niebuhr would agree with T. S. Eliot: "The knowledge imposes a pattern, and falsifies,/ For the pattern is new in every moment/ And every moment is a new and shocking/ Valuation of all we have been" ("East Coker" sec. II). This integrity is not an atomic self subject to God but very much like the self Keller is imagining: elusive, open to the in-flowing world, personal in its continuity amidst the ongoing changes of each moment (Keller 188, 189, & 195-96).[54]

Keller faults Niebuhr for not having a metaphysics (Keller 181-82). While there is an important dialogue to be had between Niebuhr and Whitehead, Keller's philosophical mentor, Niebuhr eschews metaphysics because it usually means the objective rationalism of either Aristotelian or Cartesian dualism, which Whitehead similarly criticizes. Much more befitting a feminist perspective, Niebuhr starts from experience, not from any philosophical principle. As I have suggested elsewhere, starting from such a place can be rendered philosophically as postcritical or phenomenological.[55] Niebuhr starts from the self in its being--as responder: knower, valuer, truster, (late in his life) feeler, and speaker-- amidst its relatedness to world and God. Where Whitehead starts with the phenomenon of event as understood by modern physics culminating in cosmology of process and reality, Niebuhr begins with the experiential self culminating in ethics of responsibility. Keller has well shown how Whitehead can be a vital companion in a feminist dialogue. On the principle of both/and we do not have to choose between them, but I am suggesting that Niebuhr can be especially fruitful for this conversation because his ethics arise from the roots of relational thought of the experiencing self.

At the same time Niebuhr could learn something from Whitehead and Keller about the reciprocity of divine and human, for the explicit lack of which Keller rightly criticizes him. He never develops how God is affected by our responses, even though his view of divine immanence entails interaction. Nevertheless, he makes it clear how every responsible action occurs in the temporal process of memory and anticipation, and is affected by what has happened and what one expects to happen. In response to Whitehead and Keller, Niebuhr could affirm that this is as much true of God acting on the self from moment to moment as of the self acting on others and on God.

In a welcome collection of papers from a conference honoring Niebuhr at Harvard in 1988, Linell Cady similarly raises questions about his conception of divine sovereignty, seeing in "one strand" of it a relativizing and thus a denying of all human judgments and all human agency, which undercuts any efforts at political criticism and action. She notes however "another strand" irreconcilable with the first, that makes room for social critique by affirming the making of relative judgments to achieve relative justice (Cady 122-25). Based on this second strand she goes on to develop her own view of divine immanence, which is, I believe, similar to Niebuhr's.

While I see no evidence that Niebuhr insists on human passivity, by representing human agency as impeding divine agency, he does judge that making judgments is wrong. This is during war time, as Cady's quotations indicate. Niebuhr is concerned to address the self-righteousness of America and to affirm God's perspective as inclusive in reverencing all being and thus transcending our limited self-serving views. It becomes clear in the essays she cites that faith in divine power involves, rather than being irreconcilable with, moral response amidst the relativities of our existence. He says "A new sacredness attaches to the relative goods" (*Faith* 126) and in answer to his own question, "what will be the result for action?," says:

> No single answer can be given since the cross does not impose a new law on man. But one thing will be common to all actions which are based on such an understanding of war: there will be in them no effort to establish a righteousness of our own, no excusing of self because one has fallen less short of the glory of God than others; there will be no vengeance in them (*War* 515).

In 1943 he is concerned about self-righteous judging of the enemy that will lead to vengeance and so calls us away from all our human judgments to the inclusive love of God for all beings, especially our enemies. To deny these judgments is not to deny all moral discernment but is to move human action, as he will make clear in the language of responsibility, into the universal context of response to all being because God is immanent in all being so that to respond to God is to respond to the world. He thus affirms, as Cady desires, that "stressing the immanent power of Being in sustaining and ordering life makes it possible to see how human agency contributes to this activity" (Cady 125), and insists beyond this that as God acts on each one of us, so we must find our own fitting response.

Even if I am right that these four feminist critics of Niebuhr have misjudged his view of God's sovereignty, I believe their rejection of the phrase "radical monotheism" itself should be heeded. Even though Niebuhr uses "radical monotheism" relationally rather than dominatingly, it does represent his contemporaries' patriarchal conception of God as absolute power (as Welch has said), who is not engaged in feelingful interactions with feeling selves (à la Holler), who saves each self from the threat of the many by drawing it away to an isolated subordination to the One (à la Keller), and who is not immanent in the world (à la Cady). The word does not work as Niebuhr wishes it to in our present situation. He in fact went beyond it by talking of the "One" and "radical action" in his culminating relational perspective of responsibility.[56]

We are now ready to turn to the mature development of his thinking--to the theo-ethics of responsibility--having located its roots in his postcritical conversion, that affirms his personal connectedness to all being, divine and earthly, and conceives of divine sovereignty, not as transcendent and conquering, but as immanent and interactional.

PART TWO

DECISION-MAKING IN THE RELATIONAL ETHICS OF RESPONSIBILITY

The word *responsibility* . . . gives us a new symbol with which to grasp and understand . . . the actuality of . . . human existence. . . . Our task . . . is to try with the aid of this symbol to further the double purpose of ethics: . . . to . . . "Know thyself" and to seek guidance for our activity as we decide . . . and otherwise bear the burden of our necessary human freedom.

What is implicit in the idea of responsibility is the image of man-the-answerer, man engaged in dialogue, man acting in response to action upon him. . . . In trying to understand ourselves in our wholeness we use the image of a part of our activity; only now we think of all our actions as having the pattern of what we do when we answer another who addresses us.

Responsibility . . . inquire[s]: "What is going on?" . . . [For it] the *fitting* action, the one that fits into a total interaction as response and as anticipation of further response, is alone conducive to the good and alone is right.

Such interpretation, it need scarcely be added, is not simply an affair of our conscious, and rational, mind but also of the deep memories that are buried within us, of feelings and intuitions that are only partly under our immediate control.

Actuality always extends beyond the patterns of ideas into which we want to force it.

We shall be concerned . . . with the style, or with the form, that comes to expression in specific actions. We shall address ourselves to the question about our *being* in the first place rather than about our *doing*, though it is certain that in human existence being arises out of doing as well as that doing manifests being.

(RS 47-48, 56, 60, 60-61, 63, 67, & 149-50; his italics)

CHAPTER FOUR

POSTCRITICAL ETHICS OF BEING:
CONTEXT AND PROCESS OF DECISION-MAKING

Conversion from liberalism to the relational realism of divine sovereignty transforms Niebuhr's ethical reflections. Having considered his conversion--its antecedents, influences, and orientation--we turn in this second part to inquire into his maturity: a relational ethics of responsibility. What is the ethics of a relational divine sovereignty--of living beyond the dualistic separation of God and world; of living in commitment to God as relational presence, not as transcendent structure or action independent from, even though intervening in, the world, but as immanent pattern of being and value in depth and mystery of the world; of living as a relational self, not as self-contained individual isolated from other encapsulated entities, but as interconnected with the world? Beyond the "critical" options in ethics of subjectivism (the ethics of internal desire or will) or objectivism (the ethics of conformity to external standards of goal or law), Niebuhr's theological ethics of responsibility offers a "postcritical" social ethics of creative inherent relatedness.

Niebuhr was working on A Christian Ethics of Responsibility when he died. Like his great American predecessor, Jonathan Edwards, he did not live to see completed what he considered his major work, even though he had been lecturing on it at least since the early 1950s. The term, "responsible self," as we have seen, goes back to *The Church Against the World* of 1935, while the thematic concern is latent in his conversion, emerging first into public view in "The Social Gospel and the Mind of Jesus" of 1933. What we do have to work with principally is the posthumously published *The Responsible Self* of 1963, supported with various unpublished literary remains from the 1950s and especially early 1960s.[57]

Being and the Nature of Ethics

In these final reflections on responsibility, founded upon his conversion commitment to divine pattern in being, he defines the nature of ethics in terms of being, understanding, and action. Ethical reflection begins by attending to the being of the self, to the "actuality of . . . human existence." Not abstract nor individual, the self's being is relational: "the self is fundamentally social, in this sense that it is a being which not only knows itself in relation to other selves but exists as self only in that relation." Central to our relational being is agency: "these are the reflections of a Christian who is seeking to understand the mode of his existence and that of his fellow beings as human agents." "A being in charge of his conduct," the self is agent within a dynamic interactive web of relationships: for "a modern psychology, a modern study of society, a modern history . . . the pattern of thought now is interactional." Not only moral life but "[a]ll of life" is relational, or as he says, "has the character of responsiveness" (RS 48, 71, 42, 48, 57, & 46). We exist within a matrix of relations, a world, in which other beings act upon us and we respond to those actions. Niebuhr's ethics begins with actual being as human agency in a relational world.

Our responses as agents to the actions upon us flow from our deeply-lying commitments and understanding of "What is going on?" We seek to understand the dynamic nature of our self and the world of complex interactions within which we act. We seek to "interpret" the other's action, what it is, what is intended, and the sphere of action, what other actions and intentions are at work. Interpretation is inherently linguistic: discerning the words, images, symbols, metaphors, myths at play in the given situation is crucial for grasping a sense of what larger and deeper "dialogue" of "challenge and response" we are living within. The "symbol of responsibility" itself carries us into "the depths of our mind as we grope for understanding of ourselves and toward definition of ourselves in action" (RS 60, 46, 56, & 48).

Ethics seeks not only to understand our being in its responsive agency within the world but to guide us in our action:

> Our task . . . is to try with the aid of this symbol [of responsibility] to further the double purpose of ethics: to obey the ancient and perennial commandment, "*Gnothi seauton*," "Know thyself"; and to seek guidance for our activity as we decide, choose, commit ourselves, and otherwise bear the burden of our necessary human freedom (RS 48).

This twofold ethics is theological because what we find through the use of religious symbols, metaphors, stories within the actions upon us in a given situation is a divine action and intention. In every circumstance the One acts upon us eliciting transformation of self and society. If we respond well to this divine action, in our response to all the other multifarious actions upon us, our action is "fitting," appropriate to God's intention and to all the other actions within the relational matrix of being; our self then is one, an integrated wholeness.

Niebuhr's ethics of divine sovereignty is not focused upon decision-making, as is much of existentialism, but on being; not upon the metaphysics of objective being, as is classical Aristotelianism, but on personal being, mine and ours; not upon justifying moral deeds or stands, as is much of Anglo-American ethics, but on interpreting self and world, and acting accordingly; not upon explicit ideas, beliefs, or principles, as is much of western theological ethics, but on actions, on our largely unconscious commitments shaping our actions in response to the actions upon us, and on patterns of divine action present in our existence; not upon conformity to external principles, such as obeying a law or striving for a goal, as is much of Protestant and Catholic ethics, but on creativity of interpretation and sensitivity of action; and not upon violent overthrow, as is much of revolutionary ethics, but on socially transformative action.

Niebuhr's affirmation of God as present in the world acting immediately upon us issues in an ethics that is, therefore, phenomenological--attending to the actuality of our present being in the world; existential--guiding us in our present existing as we act, decide, and live from commitments and in freedom; hermeneutical--drawing attention to the act of interpretation in our living; theological--interpreting and responding to the divine action and intention amidst our present being in the world of interactions; and transformative--changing self and social existence towards inclusive and deeper embrace of being in all its diversity. Because Niebuhr rejects subject/object dualism that separates God and world, turning our ethical reflections away from the world toward an external source of meaning, we are calling his ethics "postcritical," as they return our thinking to the world we indwell as persons, in the depths of which we find the source of meaning emerging in our responsive living.

Investigating Niebuhr's ethics, we invariably want to ask several questions. Throughout his ethical reflections he has little to say specifically about what we ought to do. There is much of great worth about the nature of self and God, but to what extent is his ethics a helpful guide to action? In *The Responsible Self* he systematically distinguishes his ethics of responsibility from the two classical perspectives of the West, Aristotelian teleology (goal-oriented ethics) and Kantian deontology (law-oriented ethics). Is Niebuhr's ethics a genuine third alternative, and if so, how? In developing a postcritical or relational ethics--phenomenological, existentialist, hermeneutical, theological, and transformationist--how does Niebuhr articulate his social ethics as Christian? Finally, what impact does his ethics, committed, as it is, to the social nature of the self, have upon our life together and upon forms of social oppression, and thus what relevance does it have to liberation thinking?

Examining what kind of guide to action his ethics provides, we will focus in Chapters Four and Five of Part Two on decision-making--its context, process, and principles. Even though he never presents a systematic discussion of decision-making, we can consolidate his various remarks and conceive certain aspects, beyond what he said, by imaginative development from his principles and in accord with the trajectory of his thought. Throughout we will contrast his with the two classical positions to answer the second question about the originality and integrity of his ethics. In Chapters Six through Nine of Part Three, we will consider how such relational postcritical ethics is socially transformative and Christian.

The Context of Decision-Making

Beginning with the being of the self as agent, Niebuhr characterizes our existing as actions. Unlike most existentialists, however, his attention is directed initially not to the actions we perform but to those enacted by others upon us. Our acts are always responses to prior actions on us. This means that to be a self is to inhabit a world. Like Merleau-Ponty and Heidegger--and one could mention historically, Schleiermacher and Edwards--self and world go together; the Cartesian beginning with an isolated self is rejected from the outset. But unlike his philosophical contemporaries' more ontological and epistemological perspectives, Niebuhr develops his postCartesian beginning point in the ethical mode of action.

Existing within a multiplicity of actions upon it, the self is relational: to be is to live in response-relations to whatever is acting upon us. Our responses are relatings to specific actions but also to the different levels within which actions occur. As selves we exist in relation to the physical, chemical, biological, psychological, socioeconomic, political, scientific, cultural levels, each of which is acting upon us in particular, although not necessarily noticed ways, all the time.

These realities are both spatial and temporal. The context I inhabit in the present extends from wherever I am and, however circumscribed the sphere of my concern is, through increasingly comprehensive spheres outward to the entire "community of being" (RS 86-89). My context extends beyond individual interests, family, nation, humanity, the living, to the entire community of being, cosmic and cultural, for each of these is acting upon me to which I am responding. My context also extends backwards to the beginning of time and forwards towards its end, the beginnings and endings of my individual time, my people's time, the time of the human race, of life, of the earth and universe itself, as I respond in memory and anticipation to the actions upon me, to what has been wrought and what is aborning.

The principle metaphor or synecdoche he uses in *The Responsible Self* for the nature of this world of interaction is the linguistic one of "dialogue." An action upon me is like a word said to me in conversation to which I answer. The self exists in triadic relation to itself, society, and nature. Each word has its meaning within a conversation, and each conversation is seen as a part of a larger "continuous dialogue" (RS 80). Actions do not strike us as isolated atoms but in relations: as part of other actions occurring on the same level, as one level among many levels, as part of the totality of being, and as a moment connected with past and future moments within the full sweep of cosmic time.

As in a conversation where much remains tacit, unsaid or unsayable, our interactions are largely unconscious. The multiplicity of actions upon us are much too complex to be able to attend to all of them, or even most of them, consciously. We respond to them on various levels simultaneously and therefore tacitly. The triadic relation to nature and society in which the self exists implies a tacit awareness of one while focusing on the other; shifting attention from one to the other changes awareness of that which was focused on from explicit to tacit. In an unpublished remark on Polanyi's perspective on physical movement, Niebuhr recognizes this tacit awareness (without however using Polanyi's word "tacit") present in the skill of a bicycle rider.

> If you want a scientific account of how a man rides a bicycle read Michael Polanyi's *Personal Knowledge*: he knows something about a bicycle rider the bicycle rider himself doesn't know. The bicycle rider does not proceed in a straight line nor remain in a perfectly vertical position. His progress is marked by an almost infinite number of variations of the wheels to right and left and by a constant balancing of his body through small inconspicuous shiftings of weight. If the variations of the wheel or of his balance become extreme in one direction

they must be compensated for by extreme variations in the other
direction, and when the corrections become overcorrections there is
catastrophe. So it is with the life and thought of men (*Future* 6-7).

Under the ongoing impact of countless actions upon us, living our
lives is a continual "balancing" through "inconspicuous shiftings." We
are not, however, determined by these impacts, but respond to them.
Response is a personal act; even though mostly unconscious, it is not
mechanistic.   We respond out of tacit commitments, not external
conditioning. Niebuhr was loath to tell others what to do: "No man can
tell other people what is right and wrong" (*CE[YCE]* January 4, 1952, 1;
Grant 30). One reason he would not provide answers to others' specific
ethical problems is that conscious ethical decision is grounded in the
individual's tacit commitments. Only individuals can discover what
decision is appropriate to their commitments.

Since the self is viewed as existing in relation to the entire
community of being, the scope of ethical consideration in decision-making
is necessarily very broad. We can imagine that what many might agree
would be right for an individual could appear different in expanding
contexts. Self-defense we consider an individual's natural and legal right
and have extended this right to the larger sphere of the nation when
threatened by external forces: most argue it is right to go to war to defend
one's country. Yet the long history of animosity or previous friendship
between the two nations might make one hesitate about violent action at
this moment of friction which would only perpetuate rather than alter
present hostilities between the two nations. Within a still larger sphere
one could conclude that even though individuals and nations have a right
to defend themselves against attack from without, in a nuclear age such
defense is suicidal and a threat to the continuation of humanity as such.
Ethical reflections are certainly complicated by Niebuhr's interaction
model, but to be responsible, we must consider the different spheres and
total context of our being.

While the context is universal, it is at the same time particular.
Decisions are made in response to the specific configuration of multiple
actions upon us in a given moment within the various spheres. Our
decision, if fitting, is a response to an immediate complexity. If God is
acting upon us within every set of actions upon us, we must also respond
to this specific divine action as present in this moment's complex of
actions.   Unlike rationalist ethics whose abstract principles can be
insensitive to a particular circumstance; existentialist ethics, such as
Bultmann's, whose God encountering our consciousness demands the
same thing on each occasion; and Reinhold Niebuhr's ethics whose God

is absent from the given situation except as upholding an impossible standard of love demanding our own sinful pragmatic compromise to establish justice--H. Richard Niebuhr's has God acting in a way that works through and fits the particularities of the situation and the self involved.

Universal and particular are not in opposition for Niebuhr. Inasmuch as God encompasses the totality of being, the action of the One is always in and through the historical particularities of the immediate moment and total context. God's particular actions can become symbolic providing a pattern to guide our other actions, as is most centrally evident in Jesus's actions. But fitting decisions are not made simply in response to such general patterns but to God's particular action upon each of us in a given moment. The consistency of God's actions upon me does not rest in my general principles but in God's actuality continually acting upon me. The ethical intent for Niebuhr is to act in a way befitting the context, yet we cannot conceive it in its full complexity. But we do not have to, since we achieve universality not through intellectual generalizing but through specific response to divine action, which is universal. Niebuhr is interested not in an abstract conceptual, but relational, universality which extends beyond conceiving.

Not that Niebuhr refuses to articulate general principles; he does, as we shall soon see. But his focus for decision-making is upon the particular divine action in the moment's configuration of actions within the universal context of the world's and God's being. Burton Mack, distinguishing the particular wisdom of the Cynic sage from the general wisdom of Plato and Aristotle, gets at a similar view of concrete universality. He argues that Jesus exhibits the Cynic's "metis" by conjuring up specific situations through parables and making fitting response to them instead of articulating abstract principles of class logic under which particulars can be subsumed.[58]

In Niebuhr's stress on particularity we find another reason why he will not give others answers to their specific ethical issues. I must not only respond out of my own commitments, I must respond to the One action that confronts me in a given situation. The context for Niebuhr is, therefore, complex. It involves multifarious and multilevelled actions upon us; moreover, it requires the agency of the self relating to these actions through tacit commitments understood as ingredients in an ongoing dialogue between self and world, and self and divine actions. The response is to the particular and through it to a relational universal, not to an abstract, conceptualized principle. While ethical decisions should take account of general laws and goals, which deontological and teleological ethics focus on, these are not the criteria but guides to help us understand and respond to what God and the world are doing to and with us in each given situation.

The Process of Decision-Making

If all response is rooted in tacit commitments, then conscious decisions emerge from such unconscious connections: they are emergent gestalts which we discover.   Making a decision is an unconscious integrative act which draws together "hidden references, allusions, and similes which are in the depths of our mind as we grope for understanding" (RS 48) which emerge in consciousness as patterns giving shape to those commitments in relation to the issue at hand in the given situation.

While Niebuhr does not speak of decisions as "gestalts," he is aware of the process of creativity as described by Gestalt psychology and uses "gestalt" interchangeably with "symbolic form" (RS 151 & 175). Given his affirmation of unconscious commitments and formation of patterns, the word "gestalt" is appropriate for the decision-making process. Decisions are often pictured as a selection between options but this is a stage late in the process, since the options have been recognized as they emerge into focus from the network of tacit relations and interactions. The "critical" picture represents the selection process as objective, ideally divorced from biasing inclinations. For Niebuhr, however, all conscious decisions originate in tacit inclinings hidden in our unconscious connectedness to being and in our orientation within these interactions. Rejecting the dualistic portrayal of decision-making as impartial by detachment, he works with decision as patterns emergent from personal commitment and creativity within the unconscious web of relations. Impartiality is a function of scope--how inclusive is the context of my considerations?--not of deracinate thinking, plucked up from the root system of our being committed in the world. Imagining Niebuhr's view of the process of decision-making on the basis of his various ethical reflections--beyond what he may have said explicitly--we can discern four elements: embodiment, attention, interpretation, and speech.

i. Embodiment

If response is rooted in tacit commitments, then decision-making begins in and from the body. Such unconscious relatings within the web of being are not of the conscious mind but of the lived body--not the body as object of scientific analysis but the body which I am as I live in interaction, responding beneath noticing to all the actions upon me from moment to moment. Niebuhr speaks in his final "Christian Ethics" lectures of "me in my body" (*CE[RMK]* February 22, 1961) and says that "man must be understood in terms of embodied, concretized projects" (*CE[EBK]* February 22, 1961). In *The Responsible Self* he says: "it is *I* who am in or with this body, that *I* have this body, that this is *my* body." While he is saying this in the process of locating a transcendent dimension in which the divine radical action relates to the self, he does this by making a distinction between the objective body, "biological events" which are "actions that constitute elements in my body," and the personal or lived body, "*my* body." While we respond to actions on both, it is only responses to actions on my lived body or body in the first person that "are responses to the radical action by which *I am*." He goes on: "I am so intimately related to my body that the life of the body and my being seem almost inseparable." Nevertheless, there is "no way of moving from the impersonal statements" about mind, body, or emotions, "that thinking is going on, or that living is in process, or that feeling occurs, to the conclusion that therefore *I* am. Only if I posit the self can I refer this thinking, living, feeling to myself" (RS 109-10; his italics). This self that is posited is the agent but elusive self of the lived body, not a transcendental ego or abstracted conscious mind separated from the body. But we cannot reach that self by deduction from the objective biological body. If we do not begin with the dimension of the embodied self, we will be left only with a selfless body and the idea of a transcendent bodiless self. It is this personal body that is involved in the "constant balancing" and "small inconspicuous shiftings" (*Future* 6-7) of skillful accomplishment and our more general living.

While Niebuhr is here speaking of the body as root and agency of the enacting self, no doubt under encouragement from phenomenology (see Keiser, *Recovering* 53-56), he has earlier reflected on this personal body. In *The Meaning of Revelation* he has already recognized the distinction between "an explicit act" and "the implicit movements . . . in the body" (MR 167). He speaks of the body thinking in these implicit ways, as a tacit reliance in our bodies on the world and on our own capacities to make sense of the world, in Santayana's words of "animal faith": "Without this animal faith in a dependable external world we literally would not live as bodies. . . . By faith, by counting upon persistent factors in our environment we live as bodies and with our brains think out this common world" (MR 79). He speaks of the body situating the self, locating it in its hereness and nowness, so that "the questions about the origin, the meaning and the destiny of the self" are "[t]he question why I am I, in this here and now, conditioned by and dependent on this body" (MR 91). He says that pleasure and pain and other affections are "states of the soul" that occur in our personal body without whose involvement nothing happens, a personal body which is both individual and communal:

> Pain and pleasure here are not physical states primarily; what is important about them is that they are *ours*; they occur in *our* bodies, directly or sympathetically, and so become joys and sorrows of the self; they are states of the soul. Nothing happens without the participation of our bodies, but the affections of the soul come to us through and in our social body almost as much as in our individual structure (MR 98; his italics).[59]

Even though Niebuhr does reflect from time to time on the body in *The Meaning of Revelation*, these expressions of the lived body are amidst other expressions of the objective body separate from the self. In defining outer and inner history, he distinguishes "what happened to the cells of a body or the story of what happened to a self" (MR 60). Groping towards the lived body, but not yet having transcended Cartesian dualism's opposition of objective body and subjective self, Niebuhr affirms the embodiedness of the self not primarily through body-talk but in the language of society and history. Thus, in *The Meaning of Revelation* he speaks not of the lived body but of "our social body" (MR 98) and of "lived history"--"History as Lived and as Seen" (MR 59): "In *our* history all events occur not to impersonal bodies but to selves in community" (MR 65; his italics). Through discussion of inner history he shows how we are imbedded in social existence and time.

In *The Responsible Self* he continues to affirm our indwelling relations to others and to remembered and anticipated time (see RS ch. 2 & 3), but moves this beyond Cartesianism by affirming among these relations the responsiveness of self, their triadic nature, and the imbeddedness of self not only in space and time but in language: our "responses are imbedded. . . . The sentences in which I state my value-judgments are parts of paragraphs, the paragraphs of chapters, the chapters of a book" (RS 124). While all of these presuppose the embodiedness of tacit relatedness and while he has been working explicitly at conceiving a lived body, he, admittedly, does not go very far with it. Nevertheless, embodiment is an important element, even if not developed extensively, in Niebuhr's view of decision-making.

ii. Attention

Decisions as emergent achievements from unconscious rootage of our lived bodies begin to take shape through acts of attention. While in the Robertson Lectures he calls this "awareness": "this awareness is more or less that of an intelligence which identifies, compares, analyzes, and relates events" (RS 61), in the Earl Lectures he says the dialogical mind "attends" (*Earl* II. 23, in Grant 74). To begin "to inquire: 'What is going on?'" (RS 60), I focus on the problem at hand. As I do so, I begin to grope unconsciously for the appropriate backgrounds against which to consider this problem. Having initiated the tacit integrative process by focusing on the problem, I can nurture it along by shifting my attention to: the particular configuration of the moment in which the problem is lodged, the different spheres of action (especially the totality of interaction), the specific divine action upon me, and the ethical guides I sense are relevant to the problem--such as moral and religious principles, images and stories of ethical action, goals I aspire to and laws I feel obliged by, the advice of friends and the historical wisdom of the ages. As I shift my attention, as it were within a dialogue, between these various aspects back and forth between them and the problem at hand, they are brought into unconscious and incipient conscious connection with each other and oriented to converge on the problem. I thus move towards a pattern befitting the various aspects that will emerge into consciousness as the decision.

iii. Interpretation

The third ingredient in the process is the act of interpretation. We interpret "what is going on" (RS 59-68) within the moment's complex of actions. Before we consider general laws or goals, we try to make sense of what is happening. What is occurring and what does it mean? What is the intention behind the actions of others upon me? How are their intentions shaped by memory and anticipation? If they are obeying a law or striving for a goal, what is intended by the law-giver and the goal-setter and what do the agents understand as intended? As I arrive at a decision, I anticipate what the others' actions will be, even as I remember what it has been, or what I think it has been, in the past. And I do so within my own community, depending upon my shared interpretation with my own people of such actions coming from such agents.

As I respond to a present set of actions, I rely upon or alter my underlying interpretation of the total context of my being and of these actions. Is the community of being and the sweep of cosmic time alien, a threat, an obstacle, an irrelevance, an affirmation? Is there within it One action, one divine intention, bearing down upon me in every situation? If so, is it life-giving or death-dealing, to be feared, ignored, or welcomed?

While interpretation has its conscious aspect, it is significantly an unconscious action.

> Such interpretation, it need scarcely be added, is not simply an affair of
> our conscious, and rational, mind but also of the deep memories that are
> buried within us, of feelings and intuitions that are only partly under our
> immediate control.

Whether explicit or tacit, it is "in no mechanical way" a "reaction" but the "action of a self." It always relates things, always senses things as parts of wholes: "we interpret the things that force themselves upon us as parts of wholes, as related and as symbolic of larger meanings" (RS 61-63).

Grasping something always as a part within a larger whole, interpretation is inherently relational and symbolizing. We hear sounds and take them to be words; we see parts of color and light and grasp them as a whole image; we encounter particular resistances and in them feel wholes that are shapes. While Polanyi speaks of attending tacitly *from* the parts *to* the whole, and thus of a "from-to structure" (*The Tacit Dimension* 10-16), Niebuhr does not utilize this language: yet at the very end of his life he makes the same point, when he says of the dialogical mind: "It hears words and meanings in the sounds; see[s] images in the colors, the light and the shade; feels shapes in the resistances."[60] Interpretation is a largely tacit process of achieving a gestalt, a whole which patterns ingredient particulars.

As such, it is an act of creativity, an act different from teleological and deontological ethics applying a goal or law to the given situation. Grasping something as a part of a whole is different from applying a general form to a particular situation. Interpretation takes the particular more seriously by starting from it, attending to it and working from it tacitly towards a whole of which it is a part, toward a gestalt. Application of general forms begins, rather, with an act of explicit cognition that conceives a general form. There is, however, a creative relating and patterning of parts in wholes going on in the tacit dimension of awareness before we ever reach the level of explicit knowing.

iv. Speech

A fourth aspect of the decision-making process is speech. Interpretation is a linguistic act; it draws upon images, metaphors, symbols, myths, concepts, principles as it interacts--understood through the metaphor of dialogue--with the set of actions upon it in order to achieve gestalts in words. The unconscious integrative activity of interpretation is therefore prelinguistic; it reaches towards explicit articulate forms. In his culminating Earl Lectures he makes this and the previous two aspects of the decisional process evident when he says the dialogical mind

> receives signs, *attends* to them and *interprets* them with the aid of images, symbols, theories, concepts; but these were learned in previous encounters and mediated by social *language* (*Earl* II. 23, in Grant 74; my italics).

What good are words in making decisions? For teleological and deontological ethics they represent the goal or law to be applied to the given situation. They depend therefore upon a referential or correspondence view of the nature of language: my words correspond to the general forms and refer them to the issue at hand. By contrast, if words are gestalts emergent from the tacit integrating of parts into wholes, they do not have their meaning in the act of referring to some form. They, rather, have their meaning as forms of life,[61] as patterns creatively forming various ingredients known unconsciously, as wholes constituted of tacitly grasped parts. As life forms they have their meaning in use as they are enacted by a language-user, who depends upon the tacit parts and creativity that sustain the whole. And they have their meaning in relating: both as a pattern in itself, in which each part relates to every other part making up the gestalt words, and as the pattern connects to the context within which the words function. Linguistic acts are performative, contextual, and personal (MR 96 & 141). Rejecting a copy or correspondence theory, Niebuhr says an image or symbolic form both "grasps and shapes reality." It is an "art of knowing" through which self and reality interact (RS 161; cf. 152 & 156).

Words as forms of life play a crucial role in decision- making, for they are essential to discovering the fitting choice. As we attend to the challenge within its context and interpret what is going on, we need words that will take us into the *depths*. Words can open us to what is going on beneath consciousness by articulating, giving verbal shape to, various actions impinging on us. They can express the wholes those parts are symbolic of, what they really mean.   And they can activate appropriate tacit commitments the right decision will depend upon. Certain kinds of words--images, metaphor, symbols, synecdoches--are especially apt in eliciting such depths, which is an important reason why Niebuhr is preoccupied with them in the culmination of his thought at the end of his life.

Words as we enact or live them also extend us into the *breadth* of context.   Symbols and myths conjure up various backgrounds as we endeavor to interpret the challenge.   Since the right decision will be sensitive to the context, both immediate and ultimate, within which the actions bear down upon us, certain words are indispensable that can activate and orient us within such contexts.

We not only need language to respond to what is really going on within the total situation, we need it as well to discern the *divine action* in each event.   Since each situation is unique, however similar to other circumstances, God's action upon me in each situation is specific.   To make a choice, words are indispensable in order to articulate such specificity and to give conscious shape to what God is doing and intending in the depths of the multiple actions upon me.

Symbol, myth, and metaphor that discover depth, breadth, and divine action in a given challenge are, of course, *religious language.* Whether recognized as such or not, religious language is, therefore, indispensable to forming decisions.   Teleological and deontological ethics overlook the significance of religious words in the process of decision-making, focusing as they do on cognition rather than speech, on the general forms of goal or law rather than the actual texture of the given.

Decision based on religious language is a social act, issuing, to be sure, from a person but from a person in dialogical relatedness:

> It is not in lonely internal debate but in the living dialogue of the self
> with other selves that we can come to the point where we can make a
> decision and say, "Whatever may be the duty of other men, this is my
> duty," or, "Whatever others do, this is what I must do." Were it not for
> that first clause--"Whatever others think or do"--the second could not
> follow.

He goes on: "decisions are not individualistic . . . [for] without companions, collaborators, teachers, corroborating witnesses, I am at the mercy of my imaginations."   The dialogue within which I decide is temporal, filled with the remembered and expected as well as present companion, a "compresent":

> What makes the moment of crisis, the critical, decisive present, so pregnant with meaning is not the fact that the self is alone here with the responsibility of decision, but that there is someone compresent with it. . . . Every "Now" is a historical "Now," in which a historical self is compresent with a historical other and historical companions--that is to say, it is a present filled with memory and anticipation though these are focused in present decision (CC 245 & 247-48; cf. RS 94-95).

Talk with the living and dead is indispensable for decision-making as we seek to find out what we must do by comparing our interpretation and commitments with others. In conversation, literal and metaphoric, we clarify and corroborate our choices in their depth, breadth, discernment of the divine, and religious foundation.

Language of the Biblical Ethos

The Bible for the Jew and Christian is the fundamental body of language that enables reaching depth and breadth, and discerning divine action--that informs decision-making "as the book of the great dialogue between man and God in which what God has said to men is recorded as well as their answers to him and his replies to their answers" (CES 11). A witness to the divine-human dialogue, it draws us in, teaching us the vocabulary and grammar of this conversation, how to speak and therefore to live in this manner of taking up reality and responding to it. Through its symbolic forms, metaphors, stories, and other linguistic modes, it is an "aid" for selves to "tell each other what life and death, God and man, are *like*; but even more . . . gives form and meaning to their experience" (RS 154; his italics). Dwelling in the biblical language, we are informed by it. Its life forms become patterns for a participant who "consciously or unconsciously--apprehends, interprets, and evaluates his fellow man" (RS 155) and environing world. As we attend to the actions upon us, it inclines us to select certain aspects for our focus. As we interpret them, it provides us images that can pattern various parts into wholes, that can suggest which wholes the parts symbolize. It shapes our interpretation of context, indeed provides a background against which or from which to make sense of what is going on. The biblical background for both Jews and Christians is "an ethos of universal responsibility" (RS 154, 155, & 168). It extends our responsiveness to the timefull community of being, even while drawing our attention to the particular texture of the moment's actions.

Beyond its evocative quality that opens us to the depths and its comprehensiveness that carries us to the furthest reaches of being, biblical language offers us words to articulate the divine action upon us; it enables us to discern what God is doing and what is fitting for us to do in return. While teleological and deontological ethics search scripture for the explicit forms of goal and law, and then use these to determine decisions, Niebuhr begins with the particular situation and the as yet undiscerned action of God upon me within it, engaged against the biblical background fraught with interpretive possibilities for fitting action.

Rather than a cognitive form, the divine actuality precipitates our fitting response: "God . . . [is] the source of all moral requirements and . . . [is] the highest value" (CES 15). Niebuhr's ethics is distinctive because of his relational view of divine sovereignty. Ethics begins with divine presence rather than with an idea about God, with the divine acting upon us rather than with an explicit structure commanding or luring.[62] As action rather than idea, the divine presence has already made its initial impact upon us beneath explicitness, and must therefore be articulated in order for us to understand what it means. The importance of the Bible is thus not to tell us what to do nor to justify what we have done but is to provide a rich linguistic whole within which we bodily dwell, from within which we can attend, through which we can interpret, by which we can speak in order to create action befitting the moment's complex of actions, divine and worldly.

In this chapter we have focused on the context and process of decision-making. Within the biblical ethos for Niebuhr, scripture is language which helps us discern what is going on and what God is doing in what is going on; it does so both by illumining the context and by informing the process of ethical decision-making.

CHAPTER FIVE

PHENOMENOLOGY OF THE MORAL ACT:
PRINCIPLES OF DECISION-MAKING

Moral principles in Christian ethics are usually conceptual abstractions from the Bible or philosophical structures. For Niebuhr they are drawn from a phenomenology of the moral act engaged from within a cultural horizon of biblical, philosophical, and theological ideas and attitudes. Having explored the context and process of decision-making, we turn in this chapter to the principles issuing from describing aspects of what is going on rather than from reasoning that refers to structures external to the particulars of the lived world. Rather than presenting a general category under which to subsume the immediate situation, relational ethics will enable us to discern what is there in its particularity within the concrete circumstance and patterned whole of which it is part.

In our exploration we will identify six principles. Fittingness and the immanent action of God are the two fundamental principles of relationality, connecting self inherently with encompassing context and present divinity. Four subsequent principles delineate aspects of relatedness: integrity, self-transformation, freedom, and need-meeting. Appropriating a phrase Niebuhr used at the end of his life, we call this a "phenomenology of the moral act,"[63] in order to stress the reflective nature of his ethics as description of the lived self inhabiting a situation.

Fittingness: An Aesthetic Dimension in Ethics

While there is no one place where Niebuhr discusses all six principles, fittingness is undoubtedly central. In contrast to the two classical positions of teleology and deontology which ask "What is my goal, ideal, or telos?" and "What is the law and what is the first law of my life?," he asks "What is the fitting?":

> the three approaches may be indicated by the terms, the *good*, the *right*, and the *fitting*; for teleology is concerned always with the highest good to which it subordinates the right; consistent deontology is concerned with the right, no matter what may happen to our goods; but for the ethics of responsibility the *fitting* action, the one that fits into a total interaction as response and as anticipation of further response, is alone conducive to the good and alone is right (RS 60-61; his italics).

While hints of the fitting can be found in Aristotle, Stoicism, Judaism, and Spinoza (RS 57-58 & 167-71), Niebuhr develops it as a third genuine alternative to the good and the right of classical ethics.

Fittingness, according to the *Oxford English Dictionary*, means what is proper, appropriate, suitable, adapted, adjusted, agreeable, becoming, harmonized, answering to something, satisfying, serving one's turn, corresponding to something else, balancing, being of right measure. To these Niebuhr adds yet more: "[t]he fitting, the suitable, the correspondent, the consentaneous, the congruous, the meet" (*RSMS* ch. 2, 21; in Grant 77). It means, therefore, a sensitivity and responsiveness. It is not a class category, like law and goal, that subsumes particular situations under general forms that can be clearly and comprehensively conceived, but is a relational term that functions in the midst of a complex interaction, an *ethos* that expresses an adequacy of relating beyond the reach of conceptual power.

A central paradigm for this is dialogue: "An agent's action is like a statement in a dialogue" (RS 54). In a conversation we respond in an appropriate manner to what is said to us. We speak to what has just been said and to what we take it to mean. Suitable responses are multiple, not just one. Yet there are limits; we are aware when someone responds in an unbecoming manner. But we cannot lay out the limits beforehand; it can even be difficult to say afterwards what limit has been violated, yet we can sense it with confidence. As we respond in dialogue, we do not usually work according to explicit concepts. Expression has a natural ease that does not get directed by conscious deliberation. No doubt ideas do occur as we talk, but our talk has its own flow that means more than its concepts. It means more in the way we say things, the backing we give to our words, the sounds and rhythms of our speech, the kinds of words we use as clear or ambiguous, simple or rich, and in the energy and intention with which we speak. Appropriate response in conversation engages these various aspects. We may agree with the concept a person is affirming and yet respond in ways counter to other aspects, or we may disagree with the idea and yet be in harmony with these other aspects, or we may respond in kind with some and counter to others in varying combinations. In dialogue it is not that ideas are absent, but that so much more is occurring in the total meaning of the moment.

Similarly in moral decision-making, it is not that goals and laws are not being thought about, but the fitting decision must include a responsiveness to the many aspects of the situation. While there are certain elements we can make explicit for consideration, there are many others, as in a conversation, of which we are not explicitly aware and yet to which we do make responses more or less suitable.

Dialogue is a whole made up of many different parts. At the end of his life Niebuhr speaks of dialogue in terms of part-whole. Statement and response are parts of the larger whole and only have their meaning in relation to each other:

> The fitting . . . reply to a question is one which so relates itself to the latter that the two parts of the dialogue form one meaningful whole. . . . A statement is meaningless for all those who do not have in mind the question to which it is an answer. When we try to understand the work of an author we do not make much progress unless we are able to say with some precision what the problems or the questions are which he is endeavoring to answer. Thus the fitting action is one which so meets alteraction that the two together form a whole in which the two parts derive meaning from each other. They are suited to each other; they correspond (*RSMS* ch. 2, 21; in Grant 77).

The fitting is therefore a sensitive relating to a whole within which we are participating and to which we are creatively contributing. The fitting moral decision is a gestalt embodying and emergent from this whole.

The life situation that becomes a paradigm for the teleologist is the builder constructing a boat or technician making a machine according to an idea or blueprint, and for the deontologist is the politician acting according to and administering the domain of rules or laws. For the responsibility ethicist--or *cathekontic* ethicist (after "the category to which the Stoics gave the name of the *kathekonta*,' that is, of 'things meet and fit'"[*RSMS* ch. 2, 20; in Grant 80]), or what we might call the *metic* ethicist--it is dialogue, or other forms of challenge and response, such as emergencies and times of suffering. Just as a speaker challenges us to respond so do these other situations. Such a moment

> cuts athwart our purposive movements. It represents the denial from beyond ourselves of our movement toward pleasure; or it is the

frustration of our movement toward self-realization or toward the actualization of our potentialities. Because suffering [or "emergency"] is the exhibition of the presence in our existence of that which is not under our control, or of the intrusion into our self-legislating existence of an activity operating under another law than ours, it cannot be brought adequately within the spheres of teleological and deontological ethics (RS 60).

Yet precisely in such challenges the identity of a self or of a nation is shaped; "[y]et it is in the response to the suffering [and emergency] that many and perhaps all men, individually and in their groups, define themselves, take on character, develop their ethos." He gives as examples:

The emergence of modern America out of the Civil War when measures were adopted in response to challenges that the founding fathers had not foreseen; the welfare-state decisions of the New Deal era in reaction to depression and the entrance of the nation into the sphere of international politics in reaction to foreign wars despite all desire for isolation.

These he sees as "evidence in the social sphere of the extent to which active, practical self-definition issues from response to challenge rather than from the pursuit of an ideal or from adherence to some ultimate laws" (RS 60 & 59).

But how is fitting response learned? Goals and laws can be taught explicitly, but fittingness is more caught than taught, the way language is learned. While there are times when the meaning of words or grammatical formations are made explicit, much of language is learned through an unconscious process of appropriation and achievement. The young child learns to use words among mature speakers, sensing a meaning beyond the sound, achieving a whole through use of parts. So also in moral decisions, even though Niebuhr nowhere speaks of learning as ethical, the paradigm of dialogue suggests we learn ethical fittingness as we learn linguistic fittingness, catching among mature choosers how to be similarly sensitive; although not without explicit reflection at times on various elements, most of the time such learning happens by doing within community. Given the relational, ethos-inhabiting, *metic* quality of fittingness, a further reason should be clear why Niebuhr will not tell others what they should do in a specific situation. The principle of fittingness tells us how, not what, we should decide; we choose fittingly within a whole that we are aware of and respond to largely on the tacit level. Abstract goals and laws can offer guidance as articulations of some of our basic commitments but they cannot express nor work from the living whole of the moment within which we participate and search for a fitting response.

The principle of fittingness gathers up the various ingredients we have discussed in the process and context of decision-making. Arriving at the fitting choice as an emergent gestalt involves embodiment, attention, interpretation, and speech as we seek an agreeableness of our action with the actions impinging on us, their universal spatial and temporal context, and the divine action acting upon us.

By making the fitting central, Niebuhr has located an aesthetic dimension in his ethics, for the fitting as a relational pattern is an aesthetic reality, discerned in, acted toward, and embraced for its intrinsically valuable patternedness. Like Jonathan Edwards, who develops a relational ethics in "the cordial consent or union of being to being in general" (*The Nature of True Virtue* 99), Niebuhr conceives ethics as centered in the consentaneous union of fitting relations, but unlike Edwards, who explicitly uses the category of beauty for God in connection with developing his relational ethics, Niebuhr nowhere acknowledges an aesthetic aspect of his ethics.

He is not, however, without reference to beauty. In 1937, he speaks of similarities between the religious and the aesthetic in terms of their comparable independence from rather than subordination to the ethical and their embodiment in the concreteness of actuality rather than in the abstraction of ideas. Referring to Rudolph Otto's definition of the religious in terms of the holy, he says "religion is not dependent, directly or indirectly, upon ethics, but is an independent valuing function of men, akin in many ways to the aesthetic function. In man's religious relation to the world the value of the holy appears, as the beautiful appears in the aesthetic relation" (*Value* 94; cf. RMWC 51-52).

Moreover, the religious and the aesthetic are not focused upon an idea, whether of God or of the beautiful, but upon actualities that have the characteristics of deity or of beauty:

> The abstract idea of beauty is neither beautiful nor real. It cannot be made incarnate by paying attention to it; attention must rather be given to those characters by virtue of which a work of art becomes, or is recognized as, beautiful . . . ; so in the case of deity. The idea of deity does not have the value of deity; it is no more worshipped than the idea of the beautiful is aesthetically valued or the idea of goodness morally preferred. Moreover, a being is found to have the value of deity not as a separate quality but by virtue of those characteristics which enable it to fulfill the need for deity (*Value* 113-14).

While he does not say what the characteristics of the beautiful are, he does say that the "value of deity" is for beings who have the "character or constitution . . . which corresponds to a need" (*Value* 113), and that this religious "actual need" is for lived meaning: "The religious need is the need for that which makes life worth living, which bestows meaning on life by revealing itself as the final source of life's being and value" (*Value* 115).   Such meaning is encountered in the concreteness of "religious experience" and cannot be analyzed "by reference to values known and regarded as absolute prior to the experience" (*Value* 115).

While Niebuhr never acknowledges it, we can see that the religious for him is not only similar to, but has within it, an aesthetic dimension: implicit in his thought is the aesthetic appeal of the fitting. Beauty is a pattern of interrelatedness of intrinsic worth that solicits our interest. A fitting action is similarly a relational pattern--as responsive to the multifarious and many-levelled actions and to the divine action upon it within the matrix of its being. It has intrinsic worth since a pattern of response in a given moment is of value in itself and does not exist as merely instrumental to some other value.   And it has an allure: the possibility of a fitting response in a given circumstance elicits our efforts at discovering it, and the completion of a fitting response engenders a feeling of well-being.

It also puts us in touch with actuality, which Polanyi, with whom Niebuhr felt such affinity at the end of his life, identifies as an indispensable function of beauty in the scientific quest for truth: "the intellectual beauty of a theory is a token of its contact with reality." He calls it a token of reality because "[i]ts appreciation has universal intent, and bears witness beyond that to the presence of an inexhaustible fund of meaning in it" (*Personal Knowledge* 145 & 201). Beauty is a token of reality because we feel in our responses to it, through our senses and beneath conceptual grasp, the many tacit strands of our being which are brought to articulate focus in the explicit pattern. To be in touch with these integrated strands through a conscious gestalt engenders a sense of reality and provides the basis for further patternings of these relations in the future. The fitting action is, therefore, an aesthetic ingredient in his ethics as a pattern with inherent meaning and value which draws us to it, eliciting our integrative activity to create it and engendering a deepening sense of contacting what is actual.

Still more deeply hidden within his implicitly aesthetic ethics is the erotic. Niebuhr has nothing to say about the erotic and seldom mentions desire. When he does it is usually negative (see *CV* 102-03 & 112; *RS* 60) because he sees a disjunction between wishes, desires, and ideals, on the one hand, and the structure and actual needs of the being of the self, on the other (see *Value* 113). Nevertheless, there is a potentiality for developing an erotic dimension in his aesthetic ethics because shifting ethics from obedience to responsibility opens up the whole question of desire anew. Conceiving action with an aesthetic dimension offers an alternative to the dualistic (Greek, medieval, and modern) hierarchy of reason imposing form on the formless energy of desire. Unlike the strain of dualism in Christianity, in Augustine and since, in which desire (understood as energy that is chaotic or moved by an inner dynamic that will not conform to the right standard, or to any external standard) is inherently subversive of reason, desire within responsible action has a potential to be understood as manifesting the deepest levels of existential need and relational fulfillment. Moral evil is not located in the flawed self's pride, disobedience, or passion, nor in a lost goal or lost faculty of reason. Rather it is located in unfitting relations: to being--as a reduced sphere of action; to oneself--as divided, dis-integrated; and to God--as unresponded to through ignoring, distrusting, compart-mentalizing. It is distorted patternedness.

In shifting from obedience to responsibility Niebuhr has rejected any ethics of conformity to external principles and affirmed the capacities and needs of existential being. Responsiveness for Niebuhr is energy, and this energy is both relational and patterned. The effort within ethics of responsibility in general, and decision-making in particular, is not to control formless or wayward energy by imposing an external form of law or goal, but is to find and to cultivate the appropriate pattern amidst the environing interrelated actions. Virtue is passionate inasmuch as it is action, but the passion is not meaningless or misguided motion in need of form bestowed by dominating agency; rather it is inherent passionate patternedness. So also with the body: it is not set in opposition to mind and the moral self but is a sphere of passionate patternedness extending beneath consciousness. Like postcritical philosophy and contemporary feminist ethics, meaning for Niebuhr is immanent in the situation and does not need external authority to impose order. Evident in his conversion to a relational divine sovereignty, the ultimate authority is divinity immanent in the world acting on us in inter-responsivity in every situation. While Niebuhr nowhere glimpses this erotic potential, it is implicit in his relational ethics.[64]

Divine Immanent Agency: Particularizing Intentionality

The basis for fittingness and all other principles of moral action is the intentional agency of divine immanence. God's "intention [is] present in and beyond and through all finite intentions"; "there is no action in the whole extent of actuality in which the universal intention, the meaning of the One beyond the many, is not present" (RS 170). Within the interactional weave of each moment, God acts on each self with a particular intention. Unlike Bultmann's general mandate, that Christ always commands us in every encounter to respond with openness to the immediate future, Niebuhr speaks of God acting on us in every moment in a way that is sensitive to us in the particularity of our situation. The divine action "contains and transforms, includes and fashions, every particular" (RS 164), "rejoices in its creations," and is "wholly affirmative of what it brings into being," for humans and natural entities "have a meaning derived from their place in that divine action, which hates nothing that it has made but wills it to be and to be whole" (RS 166). This wholeness is not sameness but is variegated according to each's configuration of relations as it fits from its place within the whole:

> it is only an old, though deeply established, prejudice which will lead us
> to believe that there is only one fitting answer to the question, one ideal
> solution of the problem, one right relationship. "God fulfills himself in
> many ways lest one good custom should corrupt the earth" (RS 162-63).

While this divine intention can be understood as a statement in an ongoing dialogue demanding response (see RS 56-57, 64, 77, 80, 97, 151, 160, & 173), Niebuhr speaks principally of it in the language of action. Perhaps he does this to avoid misunderstanding that the divine word is not a literal, audible word but the divine presence bearing in upon each of us whose intention we need to attend to and interpret.

The self acted on by God in its particularity is a relational self so that in its living it exhibits larger patterns. The self "is not an isolated event but symbolic in his particularity of something general and constant. In the other I meet not a composite other but yet something general in the particular" (RS 77). In his discussion of conscience and rejection of G.H. Mead's "generalized other" (which he had earlier accepted[65]), he affirms what he calls "constancy in . . . interaction." The self lives "in responsive relations to Thou's who on the one hand display constancy in their actions toward the self, and on the other live in constant response-relations to other Thou's and It's" (RS 77). These constancies are lived patterns enacted--what he calls "ethos" or "mode of interpersonal interactions" (RS 77 & 79)--not ideas conceptualized. To attend to these patterns is to be drawn beneath concepts to a tacit level of actual particularity, although it becomes the basis for subsequent conceptual generalization.

The divine action engages us in our relational particularity, making us aware of this "universal in the particular" (RS 88), that ultimately the largest pattern we live within is the all-encompassing "One context" or "One realm" (RS 125, 140) in which "[w]e live and move and have our being" (RS 140; cf. 44, 88, 153). This is not an abstract conceptual generality of divine governance, to which we are to conform, but the all-pervasive actuality of God engaging each of us through immediate contact in the concrete present to which we are to respond.[66] We can, of course, make explicit the pattern we understand we are living and what we understand God is asking of us, but the principle we generalize arises from the given situation we are in as impacted by the divine.

Ethics "does not proceed from a known or defined universal to the particular as an earlier rationalism did, but moving toward the particular it seeks in it the pattern that is verifiable by other knowers" (RS 88). Niebuhr focuses our attention on the "presence" of the divine actuality beyond our knowing: "How or why these events fit in, it does not yet know. So far . . . it accepts the presence only of One action in all actions upon it" (RS 125-26; cf. 171). Our attention is not drawn away from the actual reality to a general law or goal inhering in our tradition. We must wrestle with the immediate action to interpret what it means rather than sorting through our set of principles for the right one to apply. This struggle is always within a community of "other knowers" so that understanding will involve articulate patterns communicated by and communicable to others. But the focus is on actuality rather than ideas.

The universality of the divine intention means, therefore, the divine actuality pervasive throughout the one ultimate context and it means the various universal things befitting our particularity. For instance in the Hebrew Bible, Niebuhr says: God intends to do good to Joseph through the particular intentions of others to do evil, and God intends to purge, chastise, and reform Israel through the Assyrian invasion (RS 169). For us, he says, God intends to transform our interpretative framework so that we can come to see and affirm such things as life embracing death, renewal after destruction, resurrection rather than entombment, and "the glory of all being" (RS 142-43).

Niebuhr's foundation of commitment to divine immanence not only enables him to grasp particularity but a radical sense of novelty and creation's goodness. If we focus on conceptual generalities, we miss the newness of each present moment's novel configuration of actions:

> the self as one which is so determined by the conventional views . . .
> that it cannot respond . . . except in ordained fashion and with
> conventional symbols is . . . an abstraction from the actuality of our
> existence. It must ignore for the sake of its dogma all that is personal
> and all that is novel . . . (RS 81).

Each moment is new. The application of general concepts to the present does not catch or exhibit such newness. Attending to God's "universal intent" (RS 88) in the particular does.

The goodness of creation for Niebuhr is in the concrete mesh of the moment in which the novelty inheres. Not simply good because God generally created and liked the original order, the very "isness" of every particular is good. He quotes Augustine, saying "whatsoever in any degree is, is good," and shows that Augustine affirms the goodness of every part "severally" but the greater goodness of those parts "altogether" as wholes (CC 210; cf. RS 125). To draw back from the particularizing agency of God to a general divine governance or source of the human condition misses this goodness in the concrete. The creation is indeed good if God is acting in the concrete texture of the given. If God only governs the world from afar through general rules, it would appear that even God cannot stand it in its particularity or at least does not consider its concreteness of crucial importance.

At the center of this principle of relational ethics is the God-human relationship. All action is a response to the universal God immanent in each time and place with a particular intention. To respond suitably to this particular action on me is at the same time to find a response appropriate to all the other actions upon me in the web of being here and now. To move away from the particular to a general rule of governance is to lose our contact with the actuality of God, the center and source of Niebuhr's phenomenological ethics, the origin for all elaborated ethical principles, the point from which all decisions emerge.

Integrity: Maturing Inclusiveness

"A small seed of integrity" (RS 139) exists within each one of us. It fructifies and grows into maturity through response to this One action. Acted on by a multiplicity of actions on various levels, the self experiences its fundamental problem in being a self as one of unity: "How is it possible to be *one* self in the multiplicity of events and of one's interpretations of them?" The self is fragmented so long as it tries merely to respond on each level to the different actions, for there is only the psychological self, the social self, the economic self but not an underlying integrity. But in responding to the One acting in all these impacts on me, I become "I"; I become one. This is because the One action is "One intention" which is "One context." The divine intention acting on me pervades the total context, which is the community of being. To respond to God in the moment is to fit in that moment into the universal context. Yet "[h]ow and why these events fit in, it does not yet know" (RS 121 & 123-26; his italics). We experience universality in relatedness without being able to conceive it.

This principle of lived integrity enables Niebuhr to embrace ambiguity and opposites. Life is much more complex than any one conceptual scheme can handle. The fact that we can encounter universality beyond conceptual coherence means that elements rationally irreconcilable can be embraced within the divine intent and our response to it, without our knowing how. One reason why the western tradition has employed ends and laws is to organize our lives into rational wholes, to sort out and choose between alternatives. But for Niebuhr apparently exclusive options can be lived amidst and responded to because we are not following rational concepts that exclude part of the real but are responding to a universal presence acting on us.

Our ethical action does not issue for Niebuhr out of striving for what we do not have (goals) nor out of conforming to that which we are not (laws), but flows out of who we are, out of our own self, out of our integrity, that is, out of our "central self" (RS 115) responding to the divine action that fits us into the universal society of being. We can call this "character," as Stanley Hauerwas does (see *Character and the Christian Life*) and say the ethical act flows from our fundamental character, or we can say it flows from the fullness of our being, from our maturing responsiveness to the divine action within all of being. While Niebuhr does not use the word "fullness," it is apt because our response to God dislodges us from our narrow spheres of living and opens us out to the entire world so that we respond within and from the richness of being. Evident at the end of *The Responsible Self*, he speaks of "falling in love . . . with being itself" (RS 177-78).

Integrity is both an action we perform--integrating the disparate elements of our lives into an inclusive whole--and the resultant state of being--the comprehensiveness and coherence of our being, borne of a maturing sensitivity to and embracing of life's ambiguities. Integrity is not the dualistic principle of "either/or" but the median or centrist principle of "both/and" (see CC 40, 120, 129, 149, & 233). Informed by this principle we choose in an inclusive manner, embracing the polarities and contrarieties of existence, not merely adhering to one option in opposition to all others. As we choose inclusively, we are opened to more of being, enabling a complexifying that achieves a greater maturity from within, which we will activate in the next moment of choice.

Unity for Niebuhr is the basic problem of the self, but this is not an exclusive unity, the development of a single principle or characteristic; rather it is a relational unity. Integrity does not deny the multiplicity of selves within but affirms their interrelatedness, constituting a living whole. Without integrity we are fragmented as a bundle of selves reacting to one and another action upon us, adhering exclusively to one part of being and then another. As the seed of integrity grows within, however, we experience these parts embracing each other--whether spirit and matter, mind and body, universal and particular, reason and feeling, divine and human, and the diversity of all the concrete specifics in our personal lives. Not the singular adherence to a law or pursuit of a goal, and adamant refusal of (what then appears as) compromise, but the inclusive embracing of being in all its diversity and otherness, resulting not in the singleness but fullness of the self is the meaning of this ethical principle of integrity.[67]

Self-Transformation: Embracing Change

In that each new moment brings a novel configuration of particular actions upon me, each of my responses changes and hence I am changing. In that I respond to God acting upon me in each new interaction, I am constantly being drawn out of my narrow confines to respond in a way fitting to the total context of my being and to whatever new thing God is enacting within the interrelational network. Responsible existence is therefore continuing transformation. While being stretched to the universal over and over again, I am also drawn from my abstractions about God and what I ought to do back into the world. In his eloquent conclusion to *The Meaning of Revelation*, Niebuhr shows how our ideas of God with respect to unity, power, and goodness are "painfully transformed and all religious behavior transfigured" in "permanent revolution." In each case our abstractions are shattered by entrance into the concrete. We conceive of God as the "one unconditioned being," "the one beyond the many," but are transformed by discovering through revelation that God is rather "the one who acts in and through all things, not as the unconditioned but as the conditioner" (MR 182 & 183).

So also with power and goodness. The power we had attributed to God we believed exceeded the world, but we discover rather that "[h]is reality and power is the reality and power of the world." The goodness we had thought was something to be adored in itself and something to be appealed to for protection; but we discover rather that the goodness of God "is the simple everyday goodness of love--the value which belongs to a person rather [than] the value we find in an idea or a pattern; it is the goodness which exists as pure activity."

Transformation means not only "permanent revolution" (MR 186, 189, & 182) but what we can call an ethics of incarnation. We are drawn away from our transcendent ideals back into the world where God is active. The ethical act that is responsive to God and fits the total context transforms us, making us a more integrated self, com-prehending more of the entire community of being. A relational, rather than dualistic, incarnationalism, Niebuhr's ethics affirms neither an idea incarnate in our lives nor a God only present in Jesus, but the divine presence active amidst our fleshly and changing existence. We are not only integrated in ourselves and into the entire world; we embrace the changes in ourselves and world as the grace of God, as that in which God is acting on us.

Freedom: Reinterpreting Our Context

Freedom exists in our responsiveness and therefore in relation to others; freedom and limit occur together. "Our freedom presupposes and anticipates action not subject to our control." Our freedom is not to initiate action nor to control it but is to respond to the other actions upon me. Yet freedom is not simply in the agency of re-acting but lies centrally in interpretative activity. Niebuhr defines it as:

> the question of the self's ability in its present to change its past and future and to achieve or receive a new understanding of its ultimate historical context. If these two modifications are possible, then reinterpretation of present action upon the self must result, and a new kind of reaction, a response that fits into another lifetime and another history, can and will take place (RS 173 & 101).

Freedom is a matter of change, not of initiation nor of absence of restraint or limit. It is change not of things (technological power) nor of other people (political power) but of ourselves, the power of self-transformation by reinterpretive response. We can change, or have changed in us, our interpretation of past and future, and thus of our entire temporal environs. Through these changes we can change our present being as we understand anew the actions upon us in the present and what responses fit in. Freedom lies, therefore, not principally in conscious decision-making but in interpretation, yet not so much in conscious analysis as in lived understanding embodying tacit and explicit response.

Freedom lies in reinterpreting our social and personal past. Study of our social past is the "reconstruction of a past which is still in us, in conscious and unconscious ideas, and in complex associations of emotions with those ideas." He goes on to speak of such changes in American racial and international history:

> Insofar as the reinterpretation of our past has led us to some new understanding and acceptance of the past actions of and upon our groups, our present encounters with each other as North and South, Negro and white, have been guided by somewhat new ideas. Every nation with similar social recollections of past animosities, with a similar inherited complex of emotional and personal attitudes of group to group, seeks, I believe, to move toward freedom, toward freshness and fittingness in present interaction by similar reconstructions of its past (RS 103).

Freedom lies in "freshness and fittingness" in our relationships, conscious and unconscious, not in independence from relations.

So also in our personal lives, freedom lies in "reconstructing our personal past." Analytical psychology has offered important insight into this process:

> How deeply our unconscious as well as conscious memory affects our reactions to other persons in our present; what images of ourselves we carry with us as a result of past encounters reaching back to the day of birth; how the feelings of dependence, love, and aggression, attached to those past meetings, modify our interpretations of ourselves and others in the present--all this and much more has been brought to our attention by these psychologists. They have found that if present relations of selves to others are to be reorganized, if the responses of selves to others and to themselves in interaction with others, are to be made constructive rather than destructive, if they are to fit better into the total process of interpersonal life, then the past must not be forgotten but remembered, accepted, and reinterpreted (RS 104).

Not only can the past be changed through reinterpretation, so also with the future. We interpret and can reinterpret our anticipations of the coming of spring, of the energies and resources of our bodies, of the food supply and population growth, of economic development, of political needs short- and long-term. We invariably interpret the environments of our personal and social anticipation, and our interaction with them, thus shaping our present responses.

Freedom is not merely or principally decisional but is relational and linguistic. Because freedom is the relational action of reinterpretation, he speaks of it as dialogical. We understand response to past and future through the metaphor of dialogue. As a dialogue with past and future, we are able to make reinterpretative responses in the present that are free, that are responses originating out of our own personal creativity, that are reconfiguring past, future, and therefore the present, and that fit into the real situation we dwell within. To speak of the ultimate situation of our receiving and answering takes us most fundamentally into the mythic dimension of dialogue. Myths we live, much more than the myths we think about and consciously believe, express our sense of the whole in which we live, move, and have our being, our orientation to our total context. If, however, our mythic sense of the whole does not fit our true context, we must engage in reinterpreting our time and place by revising "the myth ['deep in our minds'], the interpretative pattern of the metahistory, within which all our histories and biographies are enacted."

The myth Niebuhr discerns us actually living within is "the mythology of death." We live most deeply as threatened by the alien world and death-dealing time. But we are unfree in this because our lived myth does not fit our real context, which for Niebuhr is "a history surrounded by eternal life." We must then engage in "the central work of revising our mythology of death into a history of life" through symbols that express "the conviction that we are surrounded in history by life and not by death, by the power of being and not by ultimate destructiveness" (RS 106-07). Through such reinterpretation we can attain--or be given-- freedom as the fittingness and freshness of response within the encompassing community of being and the divine intention coursing through it.

Need-Meeting: Responsiveness for Fullness of Being

Responding to the immanent divine action and multiplicity of worldly actions with a freshness and fittingness is to meet the needs of beings, to actualize the fullness of being. Within the language of value the "[g]ood is . . . that which meets the needs, which fits the capacity, which corresponds to the potentialities of an existent being." His definition of value, both positive and negative value, speaks of a "*good-for-ness* of being for being in their reciprocity, their animosity, and their mutual aid" (*CV* 103 & 107; his italics).

Within the language of responsibility this positive good-for-ness is that which is "producing good" and is "good for being" (RS 125). Amidst many values good for being, Niebuhr centers our ethical attention upon the greatest need: "serve that value which is in greatest need, not the highest value." Attending to needs in opposition to the Platonic perpetual transcendence of particulars, he says: "the transient is good; we shouldn't just deal with the eternal Ideas of Plato." There is a "difference between the fundamental and supernatural values: to bind up wounds before saving souls; to achieve order before justice." The greatest needs are concrete and now, the "values at hand."[68]

To attend to the present values in the particular moment involves an interchange of means and ends. In teleological ethics certain things, the transient, are always means to higher, permanent ends. While a bowl, a tree, or an animal can be a means to an end, they are also, for Niebuhr, ends in themselves. So also with humans: "we are all means to one another and all ends" (*CE[RMK]* April 28, 1961). Other people and other things can be means to my own end of self-realization. Yet they can also be values I pursue for their own sake, which, however, consequently realize myself. Moreover, my state of self-actualization has a goodness primarily for others and only indirectly for me. My actualized state may be a means to their own self-realizing ends or an end they themselves work to achieve. Making this same point in the language of value, he says: "In this situation every good is an end and every good a means" (*CV* 104-05).

Niebuhr will not tell us what needs to meet, for it is the particular felt needs in each new situation to which we must respond. We alone can interpret for ourselves what these are, what needs in the midst of a given interaction we feel are claiming us in the divine action upon us. Nevertheless, we can see that the needs beyond physical maintenance necessary for achieving fullness of being are comprehended by the principles of his phenomenological ethics. To meet needs, mine and others', is to live in fitting relations with other beings; to respond appropriately to divine Action; to mature into integrity; to embrace change in self and society; to give freedom to others and find freedom within by reinterpreting self and situation within a universal context.

Conclusion:
The Context, Process, and Principles of Decision-Making

The postcritical realism that affirms God's presence in the actual world issues in a phenomenological ethics of relationality. While some thinkers have defined Niebuhr's ethics as dispositional (see Yeager; Grant 26-27, 93-94, & 140-41, n. 22; and R.B. Miller 244 & 259)--rightly stressing a transformed self as the basis for responsible ethics--it should be evident that conversion must be understood as more than a change of an internal attitude or of a conception of God, and more than a one-time occurrence. Transformation is in every moment as God acts upon us. The dispositional characteristics in Niebuhr might better be taken as clues to an ethics of spirituality: the change we are confronted with and can undergo in every moment is to move from surface to depth in ourselves; in that depth to move from a narrow to inclusive context; and in that context to respond appropriately to the divine Action acting on us. Such changes are indeed a transformation of the way we are disposed and of what we are disposed towards, but the word "dispositional" sounds subjective--as if a change can occur in the self and then subsequently be applied to other realities. It does not adequately delineate the spiritual center of Niebuhr's phenomenological ethics: that we are constituted in our relatedness and in our re-acting to the divine Action.

Based on a phenomenology of our moral being in act--on reflection about the self that catches it in its dynamic activity within its inherent relatedness to God and world--Niebuhr's ethics works with context, process, and principles of decision-making in relational terms. Transcending the dualisms in "critical" ethics, his ethics understand that decision-making occurs in a context--an interactional matrix of the actuality of our being in relatedness, extending to the furthest reaches of being and time, yet connected with every situation within which God as universally pervasive actuality acts on each person with a specific intention befitting both personal particularity and social and cosmic totality. They affirm that decisions are the emergents of a process--gestalts arising from tacit commitments through the form-evoking activity of embodiment, attention, interpretation, and language use. And they recommend that decisions be guided by relational principles--responsiveness to God and world that meet relational needs, integrating, transforming, and freeing us in our being-in-relatedness toward actualizing the fittingness and fullness of being.

Here in Niebuhr's ethics of responsibility we do have a third alternative to the classical western stances of teleological and deontological ethics. While the classical views work principally on the explicit level of goals or laws, his embraces the nonexplicit complexity of self and situation in actual living: not primarily ideas in general but persons in the particularities of their relatedness to being; not reasoning but trusting, feeling, interpreting; not conformity to the prescribed through striving or obeying but creativity amidst the concrete through responding; not partial modes of time, future or the present, but the fullness of time past, present, and future; and not thinking about an external God, goal-setting or commanding, but experiencing and making sense of an immanent God.

Niebuhr's alternative lacks, however, the greater simplicity and certitude that comes with objective prescriptions and conformity to them. It throws us back upon our human capacities for making sense and finally upon faith, beneath all explicit knowing, by which we seek to understand what is going on and to act fittingly. And it calls for a spiritual discerning, to learn to sense how God is acting on me in what is going on and how to be appropriately responsive. Reflecting on the moral act in its relatedness as the basis for decision-making presents an ethics different from the rationalisms of the two classic views.

PART THREE

CHRISTIAN RESPONSIBILITY:
SOCIAL ETHICS AND STYLE OF LIFE

[In] defensive social ethics['] . . . destructive interactions of castes or racial groups in the United States and in South Africa . . . there is operative in the minds of the defensive group a deep fear of coming destruction. The future holds . . . only loss and descent, if not into the grave then *ad inferos*. . . . [M]en . . . try to do what they think is fitting, in order that they may maintain status . . . or . . . gather wealth or prestige or righteousness in order that they may be remembered, be not relegated to . . . nothingness.

[T]hat the world is being saved . . . from destruction involves the burning up of an infinite amount of tawdry human works, . . . the healing of a miasmic ocean of disease, . . . the making good of an infinite number of irresponsibilities, that [is] . . . not done except by suffering servants who often do not know the name of Christ though they bear his image. . . .

We were blind in our distrust of being,
      now we begin to see;
we were aliens and alienated in a strange, empty world,
      now we begin sometimes to feel at home;
we were in love with ourselves and all our little cities,
      now we are falling in love, we think, with being itself; . . .
for all this we are indebted to Jesus Christ,
      in our history, and
      in that depth of the spirit
      in which we grope with our
      theologies and theories of symbols.

(RS 99, 100, & 177-78)

CHAPTER SIX

JESUS CHRIST AS SYMBOLIC FORM

Rooted in his postcritical conversion to divine sovereignty, understood not in dualistic but relational terms, Niebuhr's work with responsibility provides a third alternative to the classical ethics of teleology and deontology, guiding life not by prescriptive conformity to ideals (whether goals or laws) but by personal creativity in touch with the fullness of the realm of being, the existence of one's own self, and the active presence of God. Now we turn in these last four chapters to ascertain how this postcritical social ethics of relational responsibility is socially transformative, concerned with liberation themes, and is Christian.

Interpreting the Christian Style of Moral Agency

In the Robertson Lectures of 1960, the major part of *The Responsible Self*, the only published piece of his culminating work on responsibility, Niebuhr tells us that he will not deal "with the subject of Christian ethics proper but with an introduction to that subject" (RS 4). Such an introduction will engage in ethical analysis of "human moral life in general" (RS 45). But the moral life in general is always approached from some perspective. For Niebuhr these are

> reflections of a Christian who is seeking to understand the mode of his existence and that of his fellow beings as human agents. The point of view is that of a Christian believer; the object to be understood is man's moral life; the method is philosophical (RS 42-43).

He explains that by "philosophical" he means the "nontechnical though widely accepted meaning of love of wisdom or understanding" (RS 42). Not intending to start from revelation, the Bible, or church doctrine, he seeks rather "the development of an instrument of analysis which applies to any form of human life including the Christian" (RS 45-46); while "my approach is not Bible-centered," he says, "I think it is Bible-informed" (RS 46).

Nevertheless, even though the Robertson Lectures are but an introduction, Niebuhr does offer a definition in it of Christian ethics proper: "The object of the inquiry . . . of Christian ethics [is] simply the Christian life" (RS 45). The subject matter of Christian ethics is the Christian life while that of Christian philosophy as an introduction to Christian ethics is human life. Both are perspectival. Niebuhr seeks in Christian philosophy an "understanding of our human life from a Christian point of view" and in Christian ethics an "understanding of Christian life only, from a Christian point of view" (RS 45). And both analyze being, understanding, and action of selves. The Earl Lectures, the Appendix of *The Responsible Self*, are focused on Christian ethics proper--he begins them, "we shall attempt to interpret the Christian life" (RS 149); in them he makes clear that Christian ethics also deals with the being of the self: "We shall address ourselves to the question about our *being* in the first place rather than our *doing*, though it is certain that in human existence being arises out of doing as well as that doing manifests being" (RS 149-50; his italics). In his last "Christian Ethics Lectures" he says on the opening day that the being he focuses on is the agency of the self: "ethics is the inquiry in which we use all our faculties to try to bring into it precision, rationality, wholeness in our lives as agents" (*CE[RMK]* January 30, 1961). But then he introduces a new note: concern with being as agency is not merely with action but with the manner of enacting, "with the style, or with the form, that comes to expression in specific actions" (RS 149). Christian ethics is, therefore, investigation of the Christian style of human life as agents.

The form of Christian being is one style among many of moral agency. Consonant with his relativism and ecumenicity he refuses to elevate the Christian way to supremacy because people "lack standards by which to judge their standards," but insists on a "nondefensive effort at self-understanding." "It may be Christianity represents a qualification of human practical existence, or at least of Western moral life, rather than a new and wholly different way of living" (RS 150). Christian ethics should therefore "not be a defense of the Christian life but an acceptance and understanding of the Christian life" (*CE[RMK]* February 1, 1961).

To explore the style of Christian life is to reflect simultaneously on its context or what Niebuhr calls our "ethos." In presenting his definition of Christian ethics at the outset of his last lectures he says: "Christians are people who live, act, and think in a certain world and a certain history. To reflect critically on the ethos is what Christian ethics are." He explains that by "ethos" he means our "reaction to and relation to the world" (*CE[RMK]* January 30, 1961). In this way he speaks of the phenomenologist's "lived world." He is thus setting out in his Christian ethics to imagine a phenomenology of Christian moral being that attends to the Christian style of life as agency within its ethos or lived world.

While Niebuhr's definition of Christian ethics as investigation of the agency and ethos of Christian being does not include a specific reference to language, the Earl Lectures clearly present Christian ethics as ineluctably linguistic. At the outset of these Lectures he speaks of approaching the agency of Christian selves through a symbolic perspective: "we shall attempt to interpret the Christian life with the aid of the great modern symbol of responsibility." Christian ethics, like ethical analysis of human moral life in general, is initially interpretative. To grasp the meaning of our being requires the aid of symbols, metaphors, synecdoches, and myths which give expression to and shape patterns in our existing. In Christian ethics we articulate the depth, breadth, and divine agency present in our form of life through the biblical symbolic form of Jesus Christ: "Christians in their interpretations of human life and in the administration of their own existences always employ the symbolic form of Jesus Christ--that is what makes them Christians" (RS 149 & 162). The Christian style of moral being is inextricably shaped by and expressed through the symbolic form of Jesus Christ.

Christology: The Symbolic Form of Jesus Christ

"Jesus Christ is a symbolic form"--so Niebuhr begins his culminating reflections on Christology in the Earl Lectures of *The Responsible Self.* Christians use this symbolic form to

> tell each other what life and death, God and man, are *like*; but even more he is a form which they employ as an a priori, an image, a scheme or pattern in the mind which gives form and meaning to their experience.

Through the life form of Christ Christians interpret, whether "consciously or unconsciously," all of reality: our relations to other selves, God, and nature (RS 154, 155, & 165; his italics).

As symbolic form, Jesus Christ, for Niebuhr, is the responsible self. Through the biblical portraits he images response to the human, worldly, and divine actions upon him in a fitting manner. Carrying over the central affirmation in his Christology from *Christ and Culture*, that Christ embodies a duality of relation for us to God and self ("He exists rather as the focusing point in the continuous alternation of movements from God to man and man to God" [CC 29]), he speaks of this now in the context of responsibility: "In him man is directed toward God; in him also God is directed toward men" (RS 163). Christ for teleological ethics "is understood as man, perfectly directed toward God as his end" and "as divine . . . that redirects men who had lost their relation to their end"; and for deontological ethics as "perfectly obedient to the Father" and as the "Word of God that redirects men who had . . . fallen into disobedience." Within the metaphor of responsibility Christ is both "the responsible man who in all his responses to alteractions did what fitted into the divine action" and "is also the one who accomplishes" "reconciliation of man to God" (RS 175-76 & 43).

By imaging Jesus as responsible self Niebuhr is clearly affirming the humanity of Christ. Jesus is a person like us who responds, with his human capacity of responsiveness, to all the actions of his environment acting on him. While fully human, divinity is also fully at work in Christ. Avoiding the Greek language of substance, Niebuhr affirms divinity as present in Christ in a way that reconciles us to God. In *Christ and Culture* he spoke of his own approach to Christology as that of a "moralist" who looks at "the virtues of Christ," as "excellences of character," that he both "exemplifies in his own life" and "communicates to his followers." Regardless of whether Christians "look to the Jesus of history or to the pre-existent and risen Lord, the virtues of Jesus Christ are the same" (CC 14-15).

This relational method enabled him to speak of the humanity and divinity of Christ without getting into a "mental cramp" (Wittgenstein) over whether God's substance was somehow in or mixed with human substance. Yet he makes it clear that God fills Jesus's being. In criticizing the liberal appropriation of love as the single virtue in Christ (in Harnack and Reinhold Niebuhr), he says: "It was not love but God that filled his soul" (CC 19). Within the action model of the ethics of responsibility, he is now able to say more precisely how God fills his soul: as ongoing divine action upon him. God is continually acting upon

Jesus; because he is open and responsive in a fitting manner, his responses are at the same time God's actions on us. The uniqueness of Christ does not lie in God acting differently towards him from other selves, for God acts upon Jesus as upon ourselves. Jesus is Son of God, but so are we--"By Jesus Christ men have been and are empowered to become sons of God"--when we respond openly and fittingly to divine action. Rather his uniqueness lies in the fact he is for Christians

> the one who accomplishes in them this strange miracle, that he makes them suspicious of their deep suspicion of the Determiner of Destiny. He turns their reasoning around so that they do not begin with the premise of God's indifference but of his affirmation of the creature, so that the *Gestalt* which they bring to their experience of suffering as well as of joy, of death as well as of life, is the *Gestalt*, the symbolic form, of grace (RS 175-77).

In short, Christians make an experiential claim about the divinity of Christ: that in him they have found the symbolic form of grace, the means of reconciliation. Manifesting his earlier relativism or relationism in adhering to experiential, rather than metaphysical, claims, Niebuhr denies the so-called superiority of Christianity. Others, such as Moses, Buddha, or Mohammed, may respond to the divine action so as to become paradigms for a whole people's way of being in the world. At the very end of *The Responsible Self* he asks about the effects of Christ: "could the same results have been achieved through other means? Are they being produced elsewhere through other means?" He answers: "That seems possible" and goes on experientially in the first person "nevertheless this one is our physician, this one is our reconciler to the Determiner of our Destiny" (RS 178).

Jesus is unique in that he is fittingly responsive to God and at the same time is the agency of our reconciliation. This double movement in Christ of self to God and God to self is central for Niebuhr to Christian ethics. Yet Jesus's life form as a gestalt of grace does not preclude the possibility of other forms outside Christianity having redemptive agency. Niebuhr's thought has here a richness for interfaith dialogue.

The Symbol-Based Principles of Christian Ethics

If we return now to the six principles of moral action earlier delineated, we find each is present in fullness in the symbolic form of Jesus Christ as responsible self. As we have drawn out these principles at work in Niebuhr's ethical reflections, so we group them into the so-called theological virtues: faith (fittingness and divine immanent agency), hope (freedom, transformation, and integrity), and love (need-meeting). While he does not use these three as an organizing principle in his ethics nor connect them with these six principles, nevertheless, he did attend to each of them, although unequally: working extensively on faith in the 1950s, considering love sporadically but coming to brilliant focus in 1956, and exploring hope fragmentarily but intensely at the very end of his life. Our combining principles and virtues will underscore the continuing presence of the earlier moralist approach--that investigated virtues as excellences of character, which now he is calling a phenomenology of the moral, and specifically, Christian life--and display how these three virtues are functioning each as a type of response within the culminating context of responsibility.

Principles of Faith: Fittingness and Divine Agency

With regard to the first principle, Jesus exhibits fittingness in his responses to the full extent of space and time. He acts within an "ethos of citizenship in a universal society" and an "ethos of eternal life." He acts in an environment that is "extending onward toward infinity in time as well as in social space" (RS 167).

But this responsiveness to the full extent of his situation is made sensitive and comprehensive by his fitting response to the divine immanent agency acting on him with particular intentions: Jesus "is the responsible man who in all his responses to alteractions did what fitted into the divine action." Jesus prays in Gethsemane, "Not my will but thine be done." He sees the will of God at work in the world and seeks to respond to it in every situation. But divine will is primarily action rather than commandment or imperative. "Will of God meant for him not only or primarily divine imperative but the divine action, carried out through many agencies besides those of men obedient to commandment. . . . The will of God is what God does in all that nature and men do." Jesus attends to the divine will as action: in nature--"every event from the death of sparrows, the shine of sun and descent of rain" he interprets as "signs of cosmic generosity"; in society--to all human events "he responds as having a meaning derived from their place in that divine action, which hates nothing that it has made but wills it to be and to be whole"; in limiting and destructive actions upon him--"Jesus acts as one who interprets them in the context of divine, of universal, action . . . as words in a divine sentence" in which the power by which they are done is given by God and the destiny he lives out is determined by divine will; and in the coming end of time--the eschaton he understands as the manifestation of God's present rule, "The actuality of the present is to become emergent" (RS 164 & 166-67).

i. Jesus's Response to God as Creator

Jesus's response to divine intentional agency is within a universal ethos. Niebuhr distinguishes three aspects of response to divine action: to God as Creator, Orderer or Governor, and Redeemer.

> If then we try to summarize the ethos of Jesus in a formula we may do so by saying that he interprets all actions upon him as signs of the divine action of creation, government, and salvation and so responds to them as to respond to divine action. He does that act which fits into the divine action and looks forward to the infinite response to his response (RS 167).

Responding to God as Creator, Jesus attends to the entirety of being--all creatures human, organic, and inanimate--as the realm of divine creativity. Trusting in God's present creative action, he affirms the goodness of being and loves particular creatures including his enemies. We so often fail to attend to the world around us. Musing on the experience of "passing by" in Nickolai Hartmann's *Ethics*, Niebuhr says "We depreciate by ignoring--other humans, nature, art." "Even in the intimacy of Yale Divinity School, we pass by; we know how much more it could be. I've been driving up and down Whitney Avenue for thirty years; most the time I pass by architecture, the dreams of man. Life is a gallery; we go through and pass by. We can't read each other with a passing glance" (*CE[EBK]* & *CE[RMK]* April 26, 1961). "The modern artist challenges us to give more than a passing glance. We can't read the creation with a passing glance--nothing: people, art, things, nature." We must undergo a "transvaluation of values," but Jesus exhibits what we can move towards: a life attentive to the environing world that "interprets all things as creation of a good will," rather than "evaluating the world in terms of myself," and that affirms with both will and emotions the "right-to-be-ness of his enemies" (*CE[EBK]* April 26, 1961 & *CE[RMK]* April 24, 1961).

"How do we come to an emotional knowledge of the goodness of being?" he asks; his answer: in the "sphere of *poiesis*." Just as the "poet by word brings to birth expression out of his refulgent genius," so we are drawn by God "out of his creation called into being by his word or Word," and are "being reconciled to the source of all being, creator of all things, sustainer of all life," as it "dawns upon us whatever is is good" (*CE[EBK]* & *CE[RMK]* April 26, 1961).

We undergo stages in coming to emotional knowledge of the Creator amidst creaturely goodness. The stages, Niebuhr remarks, are like coming to appreciate modern art. "Our first reaction to the modern artist is: he is out of his mind." "We look at the late Picasso's multi-profiled woman and first wonder about his sanity. It doesn't conform to 'good art'," such as that of Rembrandt or Praxiletes. "After this stage of rejection, then I resist my own interpretation of good and evil and believe that Picasso knew what he was doing." So also, "I don't know what God was doing when he made me but I accept it" (*CE[RMK]*, *CE[EBK]*, & *CE[RMK]* April 26, 1961). From rejection to acceptance we can pass on to affirmation, understanding, and wonder.

"Man [is], I am fearfully and wonderfully made. We are secrets in enigmas within puzzles, to paraphrase Churchill." Emotional knowing arrives at "wonder: knowledge not for control but knowledge for love of the thing." Kepler exemplifies this in speaking of the scientist "thinking God's thoughts after him"; Polanyi in insisting "no one should be a biologist unless they love animals"; and Sir Charles Sherrington in reflecting on "the mystery of mind and the wisdom of the body." The "religious part of his [Sherrington's] book" is not his "conclusion on natural theology," but "the central part in which he speaks with awe of beings" (*CE[RMK]* April 26, 1961).

The final stage of emotional knowing of the Creator is cultivation. Niebuhr rejects defining cultivation, and therefore culture, as either "the work of imposition of patterns of your own"--where, for instance, a "father makes his child in his image that he wanted" or where "in a garden we remake a tree so it is not like a tree"--or as restraint, where, for example, "[o]ur job is to repress the wild tendencies," "eliminating the weeds." Rather he speaks of cultivation as "tending." Referring to both Sophocles's "education as tending of the soul" and Barth's exegesis of the second creation story--"God made earth and heaven, sent mist to water the ground and man to cultivate the garden"--Niebuhr articulates his "theory of Christian culture": "We are to respond as creatures with eliciting tenderness to enable creation, and our fellows, to become themselves" (*CE[EBK]* & *CE[RMK]* April 26, 1961). Jesus as responsive to divine creativity presumably (Niebuhr does not make it explicit) exhibits each in their fullness: attending to all of creation, rather than passing by parts of it, accepting, affirming, emotionally understanding, loving (with an awe-filled love) particular beings in their isness, and cultivating all of creation--by a tender eliciting, eliciting tenderness, that enables creatures to become themselves.

ii. Jesus's Response to God as Orderer

Jesus responds to God as Orderer or Governor as well as Creator. "We are surrounded with many existences." While under Creator Niebuhr has focused on the goodness and cultivating of beings, under Orderer he focuses on their power, the way they pressure and limit us. If the pressure is felt as "support I realize it as cooperation," but much more often "[w]e experience action upon us primarily as suffering," as a "pressure finiting me." Amidst such pressures that restrict and threaten me, God is present as ordering activity. The social orders are not a static framework established by God at the beginning of the world but a present and ongoing ordering. "Creation is thought of as static; order was placed eons ago. Rather it goes on: we are being created, and new orders are created." To speak of God as Orderer is to speak of "an 'orderering,' rather than a description of an ancient order" (*CE[RMK]* May 8, 1961 & *CE[EBK]* April 28, 1961).

Amidst such pressures, which eventually bring him to crucifixion, Jesus responds to them while he responds in faith to the one present ordering action of God. He shows a "responding to all pressing, limiting powers as to respond to God." He responds in the complexity of "pushings and pullings" to "one ordering process" which is "one circumambient movement" (*CE[EBK]* & *CE[RMK]* May 10, 1961). For Jesus there is one "[c]ircumambient controlling movement which governs--not whatever is is right, but whatever is takes place in an order that is right, and whatever is will be put right."

> How does he respond to the limiting power: treason among followers, the government, all the finite agents? He says 'not my will, but thine be done.' He responds as one who is reacting to the government of God. . . . Everything is taking place within the realm of God.

Jesus stands within the Jewish prophetic tradition:

> Prophets are always asking Israel to do this--respond to finite agents as if God is the ruler. Jesus confirms this preaching of his predecessors; he practiced it thoroughly. . . . World government is here says the Jew, says Jesus Christ, and illustrates it in his action. The King rules now, even if his kingdom is hidden.

Jesus experiences the infinite in the finite, not as "predeterminism," which makes God fate, nor as "postdeterminism," which makes God absent from the now, but as "the co-temporal--in the way in which duration is in time, as in music (not succession, but as a whole). God is present as *durée*." God is present in past, present, and future as "the musician present in the play of notes; the author present in a continuity of paragraphs and chapters" (*CE[EBK]* May 10 & May 12, 1961). Jesus "sees infinite action that was compresence and overarched all finite actions. Like Joseph, 'You thought it for evil but God meant it for good.'"

The justice or righteousness of God is therefore immanent in the world. "Amid all injustices of finite men, in through with beyond is the justice of God." It is "distributive" or "balancing." "I am going to die; what is God's justice in my death? He is as much concerned with other generations as mine, and beings other than humans." And it is "educational in character. It elicits from the created being possibilities dormant apart from pain and suffering. Even Jesus Christ learned obedience. 'Whom the Lord loveth he chasteneth.' . . . True that sorrow, pain can embitter, but often enough it enlarges, sweetens life" (*CE[RMK]* & *CE[EBK]* May 12, 1961). Righteousness characterizes not only God as Orderer but as Creator who "brings forth potentiality" and, as we shall see, as Redeemer who is "liberating."

Response to the ordering justice of God for a Christian is paradigmatically presented in the self-denial of Jesus, for in him we see affirmation of the universal will of God, *metanoia*, love of enemies, and cross-bearing. Jesus prays "not my will be done, but thine be done." In this he exhibits a changed mind, responding adequately to the challenge at hand and recognizing that all power comes from God. "We are members of one another in God's order," the enemy being part of God's creation; thus we suffer for each other's deeds "borne as the cross, if it is borne with forgiveness and not resentment," showing that the "constructive can come out of the destructive" (*CE[RMK]* May 12 & 15, 1961).

Self-denial for Niebuhr is not dualistic, neither spiritual withdrawal from the finite forces acting upon us nor self-assertive physical restraint exercised by us over certain actions of others within a pressured situation. He disagrees with both Barth and his own brother. Barth in his "Letter to the Germans" said the church stands above the conflict between communism and capitalism; they are both bad. Reinhold Niebuhr said it was wrong not to choose between the two since one always has "to choose between two grays." Speaking from his conception of divine sovereignty, H. Richard Niebuhr says, we are "up against something whichever side we choose. We can't choose between powers. There is none good save God" (*CE[RMK]* May 17, 1961). "Dualism doesn't work; spirit and flesh are so intermingled." Rather we "need to respond in such a way as always to say 'Not my will but thine be done,' both when we are acted upon by finite forces, but also when we are positively acting and exercising pressure on others." Neither withdrawing nor asserting self,

> Jesus exercised a prophetic office in conflict between Pharisees and Sadducees, the upper and lower classes, Israel's conflict with Rome. Take the story of the man with the withered hand as illustration; he dealt with the strong who don't want the weak to be cured (*CE[EBK]* May 17, 1961).

There are times not to act, but to seek repentance.

There are times as well to act, but if we do act to restrain others we should do so in a way that accords with the principle of self-denial evident in the portraits of Jesus, which Niebuhr articulates as: "Any restraint on others which doesn't contradict our own will invariably becomes assertion of our own aggressiveness." This means that "restraint of others includes self-restraint, but also restraint from one's opponent and larger community." Hence

> Democracy's idea of checks and balances is a Christian concept. One cannot act responsively as one who is restrained only by his own conscience. . . . Sinners are restraining sinners. The society which restrains criminals is itself a criminal society.

We should "use the power we have without attempting to change the nature of our power before acting." And we should "affirm the value of the one we are restraining in the very act of restraint. . . . To will the destruction of another is irresponsible, such as in genocide or capital punishment" (*CE[EBK]* May 17, 1961). So also in war-making: "in war the desire is to restrain but not to destroy the individual, although individuals are destroyed" (*CE[RMK]* May 17, 1961). In all this, as Jesus exemplifies,

> responsibility is a continuing thing, not just one action. Christian pacifists I know are more interested in reconciliation and peace-making than withdrawing. Peacemaking rather than abstaining from war is Christian pacifism (*CE[RMK]* & *CE[EBK]* May 17, 1961).

Jesus exhibits this continuing responsibility of trusting in the divine power as co-temporal presence awork amidst the finite powers of beings acting on him. Whether cooperating with him or precipitating suffering, God is for Jesus the power eliciting "an order that is right"--balancing, educating, bringing forth potentiality, peace-making, and liberating.

iii. Jesus's Response to God as Redeemer

While God as Orderer focuses that aspect of Jesus's response to the powerful limitations in his life through self-denial that continually seeks out the divine will in each circumstance, God as Redeemer expresses the reconciliation in which Jesus lived and which he precipitates in the lives of others. Jesus exhibits that transformed consciousness whose "ultimate response to the inscrutable power in all things is one of trust" (RS 175) because "God is present in the world as Savior" (*CE[RMK]* April 24, 1961). Jesus's life is a "*Gestalt . . .* of grace" which works from "the premise" of God's "affirmation of the creature" (RS 175-76) and manifests a life of "liberation from sin and liberation from supernatural powers of evil" (*CE[RMK]* May 12, 1961). Jesus knows "that the world is being saved." Not only are self and world being liberated from sin and destruction, but he lives a grace-filled life that "feel[s] at home" in and loves "being itself . . . the city of God, the universal community of which God is the source and governor" (RS 177-78).

Jesus Christ not only images a life turned toward God as Redeemer but, both as "Jesus Christ in history and the symbolic Christ within," he is the means by which Christians are transformed. The church's efforts to explain this great work of reconciliation through various theories of the atonement are not satisfying insofar as they draw upon "questionable images of the ultimate rightness of God, or of the sources of human estrangement." The cross of Christ often seems to be "the great negative instance" which demonstrates that God is not love (RS 176). "We all understand the cross," humans suffering, the good destroyed, "but we don't understand the resurrection too well" (*CE[RMK]* April 26, 1961). While the theories of Christians do not adequately explain, nevertheless, their experience through Christ as the transformative "*Gestalt*, the symbolic form, of grace . . . turns their reasoning around." Then beyond the cross the resurrection can be embraced experientially by Christians as "a life-power that is not conquered" in the midst of suffering and death but which "[r]eality maintains and makes powerful," as God's "continuing Lordship." Resurrection does not replace creation or destruction but is joined with them as ways of divine manifestation, expressing the eternal significance of God's presence: "So we apprehend the way of God as manifested not in creation and destruction but in these *and* resurrection, in the raising of the temporal to the eternal plane" (RS 175-76 & 177; his italics).

In experiencing transformative grace we "are empowered to become the sons of God"; this transformation does not save individual souls "out of a perishing world" but redeems "those who know that the world is being saved," through burning up of the tawdry, healing of disease, forgiveness of sins, making good our irresponsibilities, and resurrecting the dead (RS 177). This is the action of divine righteousness, of a "liberating, freeing, redeeming God," who "suffers vicariously" as "seen in the cross of Christ" (*CE[EBK]*) May 12, 1961). Through many "suffering servants who often do not know the name of Christ though they bear his image," this work is carried on, bringing us to the realization of God's affirmation of the creature, which opens us "to feel at home" in the world and to "falling in love . . . with being itself" (RS 177-78). Response to God as Redeemer opens us to the entirety of creation, to dwelling in trust and love within the whole community of being.

We see, then, in the symbolic form of Christ a faithful attention to the divine intentional agency at work in every situation acting upon him, and a responsiveness that befits both God's intention and the environing world as he responds to the divine Creator, Orderer, and Redeemer. And we are affected by it, as this symbolic form elicits a similar fitting responsiveness in us. We not only see but are opened to it and transformed by it through the language of symbolic forms. This symbolic form both expresses and shapes our "sense of 'being in the world'" (*FaithNat* 101).

Faith manifest in these first two principles of responsible Christian ethics has deepened from its earlier meanings. Now in the linguistic gestalt of responsibility we experience faith more intensely and complexly in the depth of particularity and the breadth of universality. Faith has deepened from commitment to the intelligibility of the world and sense-making of it by revelation (in *The Meaning of Revelation*); through commitment as trust and loyalty underlying science and other ways of knowing, but most fundamentally as trust and loyalty in the principle of value and being as the One which integrates my being (in *Radical Monotheism*); to commitment as moment to moment tacit responsiveness (see MR 109-10; RMWC 16-17 & 48).

Faith's universal context has deepened from the world as a cognitive intelligible reality, locus of sense-making revelation; through the world as less cognitive but still conscious and purposive cause of loyalty for the

One, the realm of personlike faithfulness and integrity; to the world as the lived matrix of our responsive being.

In this context God is no longer only making sense of self and world through revelation, nor engendering integrity that comes through trust in the One and loyalty to its cause, the realm of being, but is acting constantly and complexly on us in our ongoing responsiveness in each particular moment. The symbolic form of Jesus Christ expresses both divine action and human response: it manifests divine action in three forms of intentionality as Creator, Orderer, Redeemer; it provides the paradigm for Christians of how to act responsibly; and it affects Christians in these three ways in the concreteness of their here and now.

Principles of Hope: Freedom, Transformation, Integrity

In the second set of principles present in the symbolic form of Jesus Christ we see evidence of hope in his embodiment of freedom, transformation, and integrity. Freedom as a fitting response achieved through reinterpreting our actual context is a manifestation of hope:

> In the life of the self, responding to action upon it in the present, freedom from the past or newness of understanding and movement toward more fitting response does not come through the rejection of the past but through its reinterpretation. In the curious existence of the I, as a being living in three tenses, the reconstruction of our past can be a large part of our hope for the future (RS 104).

While Niebuhr's discussion of change through reinterpretation explores the human self as such, not the symbolic form of Jesus Christ, nevertheless he does discover in Jesus the freedom of fitting response to divine action upon him within an appropriately interpreted total context. He asks whether this view of Jesus as the responsible self is a "fatalism" because response is always to "action not subject to our control" and ultimately to "the determining power, the One who acts in all the many" (RS 173). He answers that if this self's responses to the "determining power" is understood deontologically or teleologically, it can be seen, mistakenly, as fatalism.

In deontological "ethics of absolute human freedom," freedom lies in autonomy which initiates through self-legislating; response to actions beyond control appears as unfreedom as we are connected with and acted on by other agencies so that we cannot initiate but merely re-act. Or deontological ethics sees freedom paradoxically to lie in giving up all initiating activity in obeying the divine initiative; response in its agency and creativity appears then as the bondage of pride and self-assertion. In teleological ethics, freedom lies in setting or receiving goals and manipulating means to achieve them; response appears as unfreedom because we respond to actions beyond our "human mastery." Or teleological ethics uses "symbols of making and design" to understand the One as "the predesigner, the foreordainer of all that happens," then "nothing but fatalism could result from an ethics of response to God" as our responses are seen as already set as we "play out the roles" in a "predesigned" plan.

In contrast, an ethics of response to divine action is neither the absolute autonomy of self-initiation or the "pure resignation" of obeying a commanding God, nor the unencumbered setting of goals and manipulating means or role-playing a script of a foreordaining God. Its freedom lies, to be sure, in "free acts [that] take place in response to actions over which we have no power," but these acts are free because they are "truly *ours*" since "they are the consequences of interpretation," since they "fit the dialogue" of "our actual experience of life," and since "[o]ur freedom presupposes and anticipates action not subject to our control" (RS 172-73; his italics).

From Niebuhr's perspective Jesus's freedom is not of autonomy or resignation (individualistic and noncontextual), nor of human mastery (conquering the conditions of life) or of a predesigned machine, that "think[s] of the determination to which we are so subject as in itself invariant after the manner of a machine."

> [S]uch a Determiner of Destiny is not the One to whom Jesus Christ made his responses . . . [rather, Jesus's God] is the loving dynamic One, who does new things, whose relation to his world is more like that of father to his children than like that of the maker to his manufactures; it is more like that of the ruler to his realm than like that of the designer to his machines (RS 173).

Jesus's images of father and ruler fit the situation better than the symbols of fatalism. His freedom does not lie in control of the situation and the actions, divine and otherwise, that occur, nor of the actions that will happen in response to his actions, but lies in his creative discerning and sensitive answering to the "new things" the loving One is doing. Jesus's freedom is interpretative, dialogical, and timefull--understanding actions on him within the larger dialogue with God and world, presupposing past actions and anticipating new ones. Not freedom of control, whether domination of the outer world or inner spirit, nor freedom of subservience to divine domination or foreordination--but fitting response within a relational matrix is the freedom exhibited in the symbolic form of Jesus Christ.

Hope is manifest as well in transformation and resultant integrity. Reinterpretation of our context and the actions upon us is transformation of self towards integration that is fittingness. Fittingness is true freedom because it is the actualization of that "small seed of integrity" (RS 139) within each one of us which can bring us into touch and balance with the whole. In the symbolic form of Jesus Christ, Niebuhr discerns not only the responsible self but the agency by which "this strange miracle" is accomplished that we come to trust in God's "affirmation of the creature" and bring to all our "experiences of suffering as well as of joy" the "*Gestalt* . . . of grace" (RS 175-76). Such transformation integrates us as we respond to One action in all and dwell within one realm embracing all discordant elements.

Jesus Christ, as the gestalt of grace for Christians, embodies, elicits, and meets the hope, inherent in freedom, for transformation into integrity:

> the hope of that life of universal responsibility, of citizenship in the country of being itself, of reaction in all reactions to the God of grace, to the grace which is God--that hope is there, and there is rejoicing when the potentiality that has been put into life becomes for some brief moment an actuality. That this aspiration and hope has happened in human history and that it happens in individual life is for the Christian inseparably connected with Jesus Christ (RS 176).

Such hope for gracious dwelling in the country of being, in the fullness of integrity, reacting fittingly to the action of grace upon us is "the hope of glory." Glory is the fullness of fittingness, not merely my participation in it, but "the glory of all being" (RS 176 & 143). It is salvation, not merely of me, but of all humanity: "all things were made for redemption and resurrection" and it is "God's will eventually to bring all into knowledge of him. There is no reason ultimately to separate people into sheep and goats, for we live in hope of the eschaton when the world will be one in Jesus Christ" (*CE[RMK]* April 24 & May 15, 1961).

This theme was much on Niebuhr's mind in his last years. His last Christmas sermon was on "The Hope of Glory." He spoke of anticipation that "everything noble and good [would be] gathered up and brought to fulfillment." At the same time he spoke of a "hope of personal immortality: we shall be like Jesus Christ, full of grace and truth." But he goes on, we "can't have hope of glory without sacrificing all our little glories." In such sacrificing "we hope that we will hope again; we believe spring will be once more" (*Hope*).

He speaks in his last lectures on "Christian Ethics" of responsibility as the "ethics of hope." Hope is eschatological, not teleological:

> the eschaton is always more important than the telos, the end that is action of others upon us, rather than what goals should I set this side of the *finis*. . . . Christian ethics is of hope, not purposive striving after goals. It is hope, not purpose; our lives are directed towards the future which is in the hands of God.

The ethics of hope involves "disengagement" and "preenactment." Hope requires us to "disengage self from the world, . . . from little things that we become so involved in, . . . [to become] disinterested so we can see without so much involvement. When we suffer, we have to learn to objectify pain: there it is again; it's going on again." Hope preenacts the future: "I preenact the situation I hope for. The child in hope for manhood is an eschatologist not teleologist. He enacts manhood. He does now what he is going to do then." And so with response to God: "I expect to praise God but can't now, but by expecting I will come to the place where I do praise him" (*CE[RMK]* April 7, 1961). In both disengagement and preenactment the self discovers a largeness within itself in which it can embrace the whole of the moment instead of a particular aspect dominating the entire self.

That largeness is denied by the "ethics of action," to which he says: "Let's be serious about America and Western Civilization, but not too serious such that we seek salvation in politics." And it is denied by the defensive "ethics of postponement," which he represents in saying:

> It's horrible to die; my life's all I've got in this world. It's horrible to die at fifty, sixty, seventy; let me die at ninety, one hundred, one hundred and twenty. It's horrible for nations to die; don't let Communism [take over and thereby] become a part of the United States.

We do "preenact our deaths many times, but not eternal life" (*CE[RMK]* April 7, 1961). In a reinterpreted world sustained by the presence and future of eternal life we can preenact our deaths in this larger context and disengage from our narrow desire to hold on to our particular life and thus see our death within the whole. To the horribleness of dying he says:

> Death no less than life appears to us an act of mercy, not of mercy to *us* only, but in the great vicariousness of responsive and responsible

existence, as mercy to those in whom, with whom, and for whom we live (RS 144; his italics).

Such disinterestedness is not "not caring about the world, being uninterested in the world" (*CE[RMK]* April 7, 1961), but is finding the fitting place of our life and death within the whole.

Niebuhr's embracing death within life is perhaps no more poignantly expressed than in his writing to the widow of a Yale Divinity student who died from cancer. Niebuhr had been visiting him regularly in the hospital, until his own first heart attack disabled him for two months. After his brief recovery and the student's death, Niebuhr wrote to her:

> Since my conversations with Richard about hope--about what we hope for when the present life offers no hope--I have had to deal with that question for myself. I would now be in a better situation, perhaps, to communicate the kind of hope by which we live even in dying. In any case when I think of Richard, as I often do, I find my mood to be one of gratitude for having been privileged to know him, and assurance that all is well with him--not only in the sense that he is beyond the touch of this life's evils but in the sense that he is participant in the joy that lies beyond this life. I feel confident too that you will find reconcilement to your loss of your loved companion, not so much because time heals our wounds as because grace makes its presence known so that we become not only resigned to what we must accept but see Easter in our good Fridays.

He concludes his letter, alluding to Francis Thompson's "The Hound of Heaven" (which he had once remarked was his theology [*CE{RMK}* March 10, 1961]): "The Lord be after you."[69]

Yet Niebuhr's eschatological ethics is not principally of the salvation and glorification of the individual but rather of the whole, nor principally a focus on the future but rather on the present. The end does not bring a new reality but makes clear what is already present although only dimly perceived now:

> The divine rule, the divine action in all things, which now men only dimly perceive and understand in their encounter with creative and destructive events, will be clearly revealed at last, in the end. What is to become clear in the end, however, is not something new.

What is already present but unnoticed is the pervasiveness of divine immanence and thus the seed of integrity not only in me but in all the world, the potential fittingness of all being and us within it. In this sense

Niebuhr's eschatological ethics is both emergent and realized, affirming the present presence and future manifestation of divine grace in the world:

> It is now an emergency that is coming. The actuality of the present is to become emergent. God whose rule is hidden and whose rule will become manifest is ruling now, despite all hiddenness. Realized eschatology is realized theology (RS 167).

Responsible hope, which embraces the deaths of individuals and nations because encompassed by the life-giving gestalt of grace, is the hope of glory. This "hope of glory does enter into being." It "has happened in history and . . . it happens in individual life." "For the Christian [this is] inseparably connected with Jesus Christ." The hope of glory is the self's discovery "of the presence in him, of Jesus Christ" by which "the Christian addresses the Determiner of Destiny actually, not merely verbally, as Father." The hope of glory is "[w]hen he feels and knows himself to be a son of God, an heir in the universe, at home in the world." Glory does not take us out of the world but expands our context to its ultimate horizons and engenders in us a sense of circumambient life, a trust in the goodness of being, and an "at-homeness" (RS 176) in the moving matrix of mystery.

Principle of Love: Need-Meeting

The final principle is the need-meeting of love: by being good for being to actualize the fullness of being through meeting the needs at hand in the immediate situation. Christians learn the meeting of concrete needs at hand through the symbolic form of Jesus Christ:

> we are now concerned with the role of this symbol in the life of agents, who value and disvalue, who judge and respond to judgment, who decide, and react to decisions made about them. And there we note first of all how much there has entered into the moral language of Christians the figure of Jesus Christ. They know themselves to be Christians when they see their companions in need in the form of Christ; there echoes in their memories in such moments the story Christ told which ended in the well-known statement, "Inasmuch as you have done it to one of the least of these my brethren you have done it unto me."

Through this symbolic form and its narrative texture, they see the other as in need and that needy other as Christ. The needy neighbor and Christ are yoked metaphorically together so that each is seen under the aspect of the other:

> Symbol and reality participate in each other. The needy companion is not wholly other than Christ, though he is not Christ himself. He is a Christo-morphic being, apprehended as in the form of Christ, something like Christ, though another (RS 154-55).

Through Christ as metaphor the needy companion is related to as a Christomorphic being.

While Niebuhr speaks of need-meeting through the shaping power of the Christ symbol, he does not here articulate this in terms of love. Usually he prefers the Reformation language of faith to love, while recognizing the possibility of using this language: "You may wish to use the language of love instead of faith, and that is ok but I prefer Reformation language" (*CE[RMK]* March 15, 1961).

Issuing from his own conversion to divine sovereignty, he is in fact critical of liberalism's preoccupation with love. Whether in the thought of Adolf Harnack or Reinhold Niebuhr, he objects both to focusing on a quality of the self, the virtue of love, rather than on a relation to a reality, God, and to exalting love above all the other virtues, such as faith and humility, to the point of speaking of "the absolutism and perfectionism of Jesus's love ethic" (Reinhold Niebuhr, *Interpretation* ch. II; quoted in CC 15). Such idealistic talk suggests Jesus "commands love for its own sake" and that this love is

> that complete dominance of the kindly over the aggressive sentiments and emotions which seems indicated by the idea that in him and for him love "must completely fill the soul," or that his ethics is characterized by "the ideal of love" (Harnack, *What Is Christianity?* 78 ff; quoted in CC 15-16).

Beginning with this critique of love, he goes on in *Christ and Culture* to essay a brief inquiry into the nature of love. As he was changed by the realization that God is in the world and that being, shaped by this immanent divine principle and agency, is trustworthy, so he affirms that, although love is one of Jesus's significant virtues: "It was not love but God that filled his soul." Speaking of the infinite value of the human soul or of Jesus's love as "merely an illustration of universal benevolence" are abstractions Niebuhr rejects because "worth is worth in relation to God" and "Christ's love of men was . . . a decisive act of divine *Agape*." Selves are not valuable as isolated individuals, but have their value in relationship, chiefly to God; Jesus's love does not exemplify a universal, but is a particular act and attitude in relation to God. While liberalism saw Jesus loving humans and God with the same generic benign love, Niebuhr distinguishes Jesus's love of God as "nonpossessive *Eros*" from his love of other selves as "pure *Agape*" because Jesus loves God with human love but loves humans with divine love. Jesus "loves God as man should love Him, and loves man as only God can love" (CC 18-19).

In this Niebuhr is affirming the two natures of Christ, not in the substance language of Greek metaphysics but in the relational (which he here calls "moral") language of the virtue of love. Hence Jesus's love of God is eros involving adoration, gratitude, joy, and (in Edwards's phrase, which Niebuhr liked) "consent to Being," while his love of other selves is agape involving pity, giving and forgiving, suffering for and because of them, and calling them to repentance.

The love by which Jesus loves God is human desire; the divine love with which he loves humans is the power of being. Liberalism's identification of love and God--which Niebuhr opposes: "Though God is love, love is not God"--reduces the divine agency to a "universal benignity," whereas Jesus's love, for Niebuhr, is a love flowing with "the power who causes rain and sun, without whose will and knowledge not a sparrow dies, nor a city is destroyed, nor he himself crucified." This "transcendent power that to all men of little faith seems anything but fatherlike" is what Jesus loves with human desire and manifests in loving his neighbor. Jesus exhibits trust in and love of being in its ultimate power rather than love of "fatherhood," "oneness," or "of cosmic love" (CC 17-18).

In spite of his preference for speaking of faith rather than love, he goes on from this critical exploration of love to an entirely positive passage on love in *Purpose of the Church*, which James Gustafson calls "one of the most persuasive interpretations of the meaning of love in recent Christian literature" (RS 11). "What then is *love*?," Niebuhr asks here, and answers: "By love we mean at least these attitudes and actions: rejoicing in the presence of the beloved, gratitude, reverence and loyalty toward him" (PCM 35). He then launches into a description of love as relationality--as mutuality, as some feminists would name it today. These four qualities in both attitude and act are relational to, and primarily focused on, the being of the other: taking pleasure in it (rejoicing over, desiring, longing for, finding happiness and satisfaction in it), accepting and experiencing gratitude and wonder at the gift of it, without jealousy and competition, respecting and seeking to know it in its otherness, and wanting to sustain it even at the cost of one's own survival. Love does not seek to absorb or be absorbed by the other, to remake it in one's own image or to use it as a means to one's own advancement or to satisfy one's own curiosity or drive for power; love is not jealous nor does it violate the integrity of the other. Rather, love shares in, affirms, and enhances the being of the other in its isness, otherness, integrity, greatness, gloriousness, and loyalty to its own cause.

When such relational and being-affirming love is directed toward God, the problem becomes for the self how to love God from the particularity of its existence in its own concrete time and place: "in the fatefulness of its selfhood, of being this man among these men, in this time and all time, in the thus and so-ness of the strange actual world." And the problem is how to love God as the One Mystery--"the One on whom he is completely, absolutely dependent; who is the Mystery behind the mystery of human existence"(PCM 36)--from whom comes death as well as life, wrath as well as love, demands seemingly too hard to bear, and a world filled with animosity as well as friends; that is, how to love the power of being itself. When directed towards others, the problem becomes who is the neighbor I am to love. My neighbor is my friend and enemy, the one in need who is hungry, naked, imprisoned, ill, oppressed and oppressed by me, but also the one who ministers to my needs. My neighbor is also my companion past, present, and future, humankind as a whole but, more so, humans in their particularity. My neighbor is as well not only person but angel, animal, and inorganic being, indeed all that participates in being.

Neither of these discussions of love in *Christ and Culture* and *Purpose of the Church* are in the language of responsibility. They take no account of the beloved's interactive responses to the lover, nor do they open up the erotic dimension. There is, unfortunately, little talk of love in his culminating ethics. Yet love is implicit in Niebuhr's development of responsibility through Jesus as symbolic form. In all that Jesus does and is as a responsible self, he manifests this principle of need-meeting love as he responds in faith to God's particular actions upon him and dwells in fitting relations to all of being.

For Niebuhr himself, the importance of love in his culminating thought is nowhere more evident than in the conclusion to the Earl Lectures in which he speaks of love of self being transformed into love of being: "we were in love with ourselves and all our little cities, now we are falling in love, we think, with being itself" (RS 177-78). Over the years since embracing divine sovereignty, he has not only discovered within himself a trust in being but has awakened to the love of being itself.

Conclusion:
The So-Called Theological and Natural Virtues

Niebuhr's fundamental affirmation of our existence as relational response is significantly textured by faith, hope, and love. While the exploration of Jesus as symbolic form allows us to see Niebuhr's six ethical principles according to these three virtues, each principle, not only for Jesus but for the Christian, has all three virtues in it, which, though different, are mutually interconnected. Response to divine intentionality includes love of and hope in, as well as trust in, divine action. The love of being is interdependent with trust in divine intentionality and in fitting relations within the web of being, and with hope for the actualizing of freedom and transformation towards integrity. There is no love without trust in and loyalty to being, and without an expectant openness to the timefull dimension in which we meet the beloved. There is no faith in being without desire for being and an interpretive context of memory and anticipation. There is no hope without trust in being that can eventually realize what is hoped for, and without love that desires such fulfillment. As he says in the 1940s: "to have faith in something as able to give value to our lives is to love it. Without such love there is no faith. And to have faith is also to live in hope, in constant anticipation of new unfoldings of worth and meaning" (*Faith* 123).

Articulating these six principles of Niebuhr's ethics in terms of the three theological virtues is appropriate because virtues are excellences of character and therefore ways of living, and his phenomenological ethics seek to describe principles at work in our living. But these are not virtues in the traditional sense. In an essay on the three theological virtues and natural virtues written in 1953, he says that they "are not achievements or products of training, . . . not habits somehow established in the constitution of the agent, . . . [not] states of character" (*FHL* 152-53). Rather they are "relations which depend for their continuance on the constancy with which the objective good, to which the self is related in these ways, is given." Virtues are, therefore, "relations to other beings and particularly . . . relations to God" understood as both "gift and response"(*FHL* 152). Contrary to the traditional view, virtues "have the character of response rather than habits. As responses they are personal both on the side of the agent and on the side of the object, that is they are responses of a person to personal actions such as faithkeeping, love, promise" (*FHL* 153).

Defining both theological and natural virtues as responses and therefore as dependent upon their relation to the giving action (grace) of

God, he rejects the Thomistic distinction between natural virtues as achieved habits and theological virtues as divine gifts added onto natural habits:

> From this point of view faith, love and hope are not *the* theological
> virtues which may be added as gifts to achieved moral virtues--courage,
> temperance, justice and prudence--but the chief or most inclusive
> theological virtues among which one must also number endurance or
> patience (*hupomone* rather than *andreia*), self-control, righteousness, and
> humility (*tapeinophrosune* rather than *sophrosune*), not to speak of other
> kinds of gracious behavior. Insofar as the distinction between moral or
> achieved, habitual virtues and theological virtues may be maintained[,]
> the line must be drawn elsewhere than Thomas and his followers draw
> it. It lies between the habits which put one in the way of receiving the
> gifts and the gifts themselves. So the righteousness of man or justice
> may put one in the way of receiving the gift of divine righteousness,
> though not without the kind of pain that Paul experienced, and courage
> may put one in the way of receiving the gift of patience and endurance,
> though not without the conversion that a Peter had to undergo (*FHL* 152;
> his italics).

He thus rejects Thomas's conception of theological virtues as "superadded additions" and of natural virtues as merely human achievements apart from grace. But at the same time, while agreeing with them that there is no difference between natural and theological virtues, he diverges from Protestants who see them only as sheer gifts, involving no human activity, from a detached, i.e. transcendent, God. Rather, for Niebuhr they are "responses" humans make to the actions of God within an ongoing relationship. To respond to God is to have these virtuous capacities, which have been distorted, restored:

> They ["the three chief theological virtues" and "all Christian responses"]
> seem, rather to represent the restoration and the perfection to its true
> activity of a personal capacity for response which has been perverted.
> The love of God and of the neighbor in God are not foreign to man's
> nature or, better, to man in his natural situation. . . . The love of God
> is the restoration and perfection of a response which has always been
> present in misdirected or inverted form; this seems also to be true of
> love of the companion (*FHL* 153).

In living, all humans manifest love, faith, and hope--in negative, if not positive, form: love as desire for some objective good and as an emotional relation to the Ground of Being, usually manifest negatively as hostility; trust in communal relations and in the Ground, often exhibited as distrust; and hope as a dimension of "internal futurity," frequently experienced as anxiety over anticipated death. The presence of these principles, however distorted, in our living makes possible their phenomenological description as aspects of our actual relational being.

The theological virtues, as well as the natural virtues, are natural responses enabled by divine grace to function as intended. Therefore, we can describe the six principles inherent in these virtues as present in all moral life, even though we do not see them functioning fittingly except where restored through the grace of actualizing, liberating, fulfilling symbolic forms. For Christians this occurs through Jesus Christ. Niebuhr's ethics are Christian, therefore, because he sees the principles and virtues of the moral life centrally illuminated and reconstructed by the symbolic form of Jesus Christ. The texture of these symbolically informed virtues is nowhere more evident than in the concluding paragraph of his Earl Lectures where his pursuit of response and Christian responsibility culminates in the experiential and evocative expression of love, faith, and hope. Not only does he speak of falling in love with being itself, he speaks of the transformation of faith--"we were blind in our distrust of being, now we begin to see; we were aliens and alienated in a strange, empty world, now we begin sometimes to feel at home"; and finally of hope--"[Jesus Christ] is our physician, this one is our reconciler to the Determiner of our Destiny. To whom else shall we go for words of eternal life, to whom else for the franchise in the universal community?" (RS 177-78).

CHAPTER SEVEN

CHRISTIAN LIFE AS ACTION:
I. LIBERATION FROM SOCIAL DOMINATION

Liberation as Social Transformation

While Niebuhr seldom speaks of "liberation," throughout his mature thought he calls for "transformation" both of self and society.[70] His 1960 autobiographical essay, "Reformation: Continuing Imperative," he concludes, referring to Marx and the prophets, with this concern: "I also believe, with both the prophets and, of all men, Karl Marx, that the reformation of religion is the fundamental reformation of society" (*Ref* 80). Liberation from social oppression is rooted in spiritual transformation.

We come now to the most unreconstructed parts of Niebuhr's theo-ethics. The perspective of responsibility was rapidly emerging into maturity in the last years of Niebuhr's life but he did not live long enough to gather up his ongoing critical comments about social oppression and to rethink, as he intended, the social dimension of his thought from within the metaphor of responsibility. While there is no evidence his rethinking would have resulted in focusing on identification with the poor, there is a potential in his ethical principles and discussions, emerging from the relational roots of his thought, for developing other liberation themes: a systemic analysis of social oppression as part of his constructive view of selves in their relational being; a critique of subjects' dominating power over hierarchically subordinated objects; and a movement towards creating a context of fulfillment fitting for all.

We can say from the perspective of responsibility that the various forms of social domination--sexism, environmental exploitation, the Christian imperialism of anti-Judaism, war, racism (all dealt with in this chapter), and classism (explored in Chapter Eight)--are all forms of unfittingness, structured by dualism which dichotomizes and organizes the separate entities hierarchically into superior and inferior. We will gather up Niebuhr's critical comments and fruitful suggestions that bear on these forms of social oppression to show, not only his ongoing concern, but his ethical principles at work. Where appropriate we will show development in his thinking by comparing his final thoughts in *The Responsible Self* either with earlier comments from the beginning of his reflections on responsibility in his 1952 "Christian Ethics" lectures, or from the time just after his conversion, or from his liberal period prior to his conversion.

We will find that his relational ethics can contribute significantly to liberation thought. Through his existentialist, phenomenological, postcritical, hermeneutical, and transformative approaches, he is able to get beneath the distortions and divisions of modern thought to discover spiritual principles inherent in the tacit relatedness of selves in actual living, which bear the seeds of social transformation: the presence of divine action and the possibility of fitting human response to immanent divinity within the inclusive community of being.

While the logic of responsibility leads into social praxis, Niebuhr's own rethinking of social oppression apparently does not; there is no evidence that transformation within responsibility ethics would have been drawn out to this conclusion. Baffling as this is, we will pick up clues in his engagement with several forms of social oppression that can help make sense of his failure to develop this trajectory of his thought. We will find these clues in elements present in his thinking that contradict the inherent relational commitments of responsibility.

The Fittingness of Justice and Love

Social transformation is towards fittingness in the interactive "matrix" (RS 59) of being. Niebuhr's relational perspective blurs or dissolves--not, to be sure, all distinctions, but--all dichotomies: individual versus social ethics, ideal versus real, friend versus enemy, public versus private, religious versus social or political or economic, and love versus justice. Unlike his brother's distinction in one of his most important books, *Moral Man and Immoral Society*,[71] Niebuhr will not divide individual and social ethics. Rather from his relational perspective, he sees that what is morally justifiable for a person must befit his or her connections to being, and what is justifiable for a society must fit the lives of a multitude of particular individuals. Individual ethical conduct does not issue from adherence to an ideal, whether law or goal, abstracted from and imposed on each situation, nor does social ethics arise from a realistic compromise of ideals, but both emerge from the network of interrelations as individual and society respond to the One Action that is in their midst acting upon them, whether they are open or closed in their response to it.

Love and justice cannot be separated as Reinhold Niebuhr proposes--justice as a realistic possibility but love as an ideal impossible to achieve for society. H. Richard Niebuhr sees both as achievable but never in any final form. Perhaps because his brother wrote so much about love and justice, he uses these terms so infrequently. One rare occasion of their use is at the end of his "Value-Theory and Theology," which offers brief insight into his handling these terms.

Speaking of love and justice as ideals in ordinary human experience, he conceives them in dialectical relation:

> The ideal of love can be validated as the ultimate moral ideal because it stands in a verifiable transcendent relation to all rational idealism. It is both the fulfillment and the abyss of the rational ideal of justice (*Value* 134).

Distinguishing justice as rational from love as imaginative, he says that "[j]ustice is the highest rational moral ideal because reason must seek to deal with human relations and moral conduct in terms of the ascertainable causes and consequences of action." Reason declares in remedial justice that "A good act must be rewarded and an evil one punished." But imagination moved by love--for "[l]ove," according to Santayana, he says, "is justice grown imaginative"--looks beneath the evil act to "the causes which prompted" it, to "the operations of mind and conscience in that secret place where actions are compounded." By doing this it can achieve a "fairer justice" but at the same time will undermine it as love discovers those causes in oneself and society:

> But if it should become so sensitive as to recognize that the evil in the other has its source in the self or the self's society it will destroy every form of remedial justice. "Let him who is without sin cast the first stone." Thus love is both the fulfillment and the denial of remedial and punitive justice.

Similarly, in distributive justice imaginative love moves beyond equity of equal protection of interests to a concern for the needs of the neighbor, disregarding one's own, in "actions of generosity":

> The neighbor's interests are avowed rather than my own and no effort
> is made to protect myself against the neighbor ("resist not evil"). Thus
> morality is fed by a realm of transcendent possibilities in which the
> canons of the good, established in ordinary experience, are both fulfilled
> and negated (*Value* 134-35).

Niebuhr does not often speak of justice and love because he sees
these terms used in ways that abstract from a person's relational context.
In applying a standard of equality to acts, justice disregards the systemic
nature of evil and consequent historical inequities for which a society, and
not merely the doer of the evil act, is responsible. In performing acts of
generosity beyond one's just deserts, love disregards a society's
inequalities and their insidiously powerful debilitating effects.

In Niebuhr's brief discussion there is no dividing of love and justice
in terms of individual and society, ideal and real; rather both can be at
work in the world--justice demanding equality, love searching out "the
secret place where actions are compounded" by individual and society,
and both interacting as love continually fulfills and undermines justice.
Refusal to separate justice and love will become in the language of
responsibility the refusal to separate ethical action from interpretation of
what is going on. Both will be subsumed under the category of fitting
acts, for each is a response that affirms being. As such, love is present
in the commitments that motivate the establishment of justice, whether
understood as fairness, equitable distribution of goods, or harmony of
functions. To work for justice is to affirm the being of others, even
though it does not go on to enhance and to rejoice in the being of the
other, nor onto gratitude for, reverence of, and loyalty to the other in the
way love does. We can say, then, that love is a response with a greater
degree of fittingness than justice to the fullness of being and the divine
intention, but both are at work together in the world. To probe the secret
place and source of justice and injustice is an act of loving imagination.
As a being-affirming act, to do justice is an incipiently loving response.

A major problem for Niebuhr with discussions of justice is the
desire to judge others. While Barth could assert that the church stood
above both capitalism and communism and could judge both as sinners,
and Reinhold Niebuhr could insist that one can and must judge between
powers because there was an inequality of guilt, H. Richard Niebuhr's
ethics refused to judge others but only one's own faithfulness: "you don't
have to judge relative good or bad but only whether you are true to your
own covenants." He goes on:

I'm caught in my own guilt. I ask to be obedient to my own covenants. Is the sin of Russia that it isn't capitalist, and of America that it is not communist? The sin of America is that it isn't democratic; it doesn't live up to its covenants; it doesn't accept the covenant of America that deals with all as equals. The Founding Fathers took an oath way beyond; they saw men as citizens of a larger community than America, that is of nature. The sin of communism is that it violates its covenant of the classless society. Hitler violated the covenants which Germany had previously made. He sailed under the flag of national socialism. We're being judged by our own standards. The thief must be helped and have society protected against him; it is not a question of the policeman's goodness. This is the same as the biblical ethic: judge not that ye be not judged (*Sin* October 24, 1961).

Not judging others, Niebuhr refuses to begin with a concept of justice to apply to every situation. What one definition of justice reveals in a given situation might not be adequate to the full complexity of actual injustice. Action issues from interpretation of the situation, emerging from the well of images in our being in the world, rather than from conception holding aloft a single ideal; it seeks fittingness rather than conformity.

While nonjudgment of others and criticism of self are biblically admirable and exhibit Niebuhr's relativism that wisely denies that any perspective, which is unavoidably partial, could be of the whole, they, nevertheless, disenfranchise the oppressed from judging their oppression and thus obstruct work to rectify injustice. Refusal to judge is a first clue of Niebuhr's unconscious resistance to praxis, for it contradicts responsibility thinking's affirmation of situational interpretation--which while conceptually larger than judgment nevertheless includes it--and of determining which actions are fitting and unfitting.

A Community of Action:
Responding to Social Domination

Interpreting what is going on is always shaped by a community of reflection and embedded in a community of action, for response not only carries interpretation with it but is action in relation to society and nature. Committed to social transformation and the fittingness of justice and love, Niebuhr's Christian ethics discerns, and seeks to be responsive to, several forms of social domination in what is going on. We will explore three that he does not consciously attend to but for which his ethics of responsibility are rich with significance--sexism, environmentalism, and anti-Judaism. Then we will investigate three he does focus on--war and racism in this chapter, and classism in the next.

i. Sexism and the Feminism of Responsibility

We have already embarked upon a discussion of feminism and Niebuhr at the end of Chapter Three, and now move from feminists' critique of his conception of divine sovereignty to a consideration of the feminist potential in his thought. While his talk of radical monotheism has unfortunately signalled the very patriarchal conception he intends to transcend, and while he lacks feminism's gendered inclusive language and reflection upon women's experience, he does share themes with contemporary feminist theologians and ethicists: affirmation of an experiential basis for theology and ethics, opposition to social domination, endorsement of sexual equality,[72] belief in the connectedness of self and world, critique of dualism and hierarchy, conception of divine immanence, and development of a postpatriarchal language of dialogue--as he roots his thought in the shared ground of the relationality of personal being.

The metaphor of response expresses Niebuhr's commitment, similar to feminism's, to experience as the basis for reflection and decision. Through historical relativism he affirms the particularity of each knower's spatial and temporal perspective within society, even though not specifying his social location in terms of sex, race, and class (see RS 112-13).

Feminists not only affirm experience as the basis for theology and ethics; they oppose the various forms of social domination which they also find in their experience. The metaphor of response is inherently nondominating. It stresses that our initial state in every moment is not aggressive nor even initiating but receptive. We are acted upon and then we react to that action. The reaction should be neither to control the other nor to defend oneself but to fit the divine intention and whatever else is happening in the situation. Action-reaction is not dominating but relational. The metaphor of dialogue, of question and answer, to express this relation is an alternative to, and implicit criticism of, patriarchal hegemony. So also is the emergent character of thought and action: they arise from what is happening beneath consciousness and its control, as more or less fitting interpretative patterns rather than as dualistic impositions by conscious reason or will.

Equality is inherent in responsibility. Each person is acted upon by the multiple levels of the world and by the divine agency, and has the opportunity, capacity, and unavoidable necessity to respond from his or her own perspective, and the possibility to respond well. Niebuhr sought to create and maintain such a space for all people, as is evident in his relativism (i.e. "relationism," see *Ref* 73) in which he would not assert power over others nor exclude them and their points of view but recognizes their right to be. He conceived of God correlatively as One who cares for all humans and all creatures in the community of being and not simply or especially for one group.

Mutuality is similarly inherent in responsibility. The self is relational and unique. It is not an isolated atom but interrelated to all of being, existing in each moment as a unique configuration of response-relations on many levels and in the duration of time as a constancy of responding in those relations. He stresses selves relating to each other in the concrete particularities of their lives, which cannot be fully measured by the standard of equality. The idea of fittingness carries a sense of respect for the integrity of the other and of an appropriate give and take between them.

This is evident in his view of marriage. In his often interrogatory mode of lecturing in his "Christian Ethics," he questions the rightness of a patriarchal family: "Is the patriarchal relationship in the family right?" (*CE[RMK]* April 28, 1961). A few years earlier he distinguishes three types, a marriage of common interests, common minds, and responsible selves. The third is

> characterized by mutual respect for each other as responsible selves, independent of each other yet bound to each other in trust and responsibility. . . . Responsibility to each other and for each other as selves, concern for each other's good even when it is not obviously a common good, in short, *faithfulness* or *fidelity* constitutes the bond in such a marriage (FE 56; his italics).

He speaks of the possibility of a "patriarchal family, in which intense living together promotes similarity of manners, customs and ideas" developing into "an egalitarian family, in which there is less common life but more responsibility, independence, respect and fidelity among the members" (FE 56-57). And he recognizes the possibility of immature marriage maturing into a union of responsible selves

> when persons who enter into marriage immaturely, without responsibility as selves and without understanding of the partner's selfhood, grow into maturity, surrender their possessiveness and egocentrism and substitute

honor, respect, trust and fidelity to the other for self-interestedness (FE 56).

While he does not speak of it, this description of a responsible union can obviously be extended to same-sex unions and other unconventional intimate connections in which mutuality can similarly be achieved in respect for the partner's otherness and one's own identity, in trust in and fidelity to the other, and in strength of integrities interacting in fitting ways.

Fundamental to feminism and Niebuhr's view of modernity is a critique of dualism. The dichotomies of subject and object, mind and body, spirit and nature have shaped patriarchal culture. Wherever such divisions occur they invariably are turned into hierarchy of dominance and subordination. The metaphor of responsibility is the culminating effort in Niebuhr's life to transcend western dualism. While his language is not gender inclusive, his perspective is. He does not seek masculine control through disintegrative analysis or authoritarian proclamation, but develops a dialogical idiom in which there is interaction, give and take, question and answer, action and reaction, anticipated and remembered response; in which there is sharing, recognizing we are all parts of a larger whole expressed through symbol and myth.

And fundamental to both as well is the rejection of divine power as dominating. For Niebuhr, divine power is not dominating but evocative. It elicits--drawing us down into the depths to become aware of the constant divine action upon us. It expands--broadening our context out to the community of being. It transforms--changing our consciousness to a relational perspective that sees the immanent Action and our interwovenness with all being. It integrates--bringing about unity in the self as the self relates to the whole of being. It liberates--freeing us from dualistic exclusivity and denigration of parts of being and freeing us for creative dwelling in the world to nurture fittingness throughout being. It meets our needs--empowering us to contribute toward the fulfillment of physical, social, and spiritual needs.

Nevertheless, while all of the above is part of responsibility thinking, it is likely that Niebuhr would have resisted certain aspects of feminist thought. His insistence on nonjudgment of others would have conflicted with feminists' judgment of male privilege and sexual oppression. And despite his affirmation, at the end of his life, of the bodily being and feelings of the self, he probably would not have followed these insights out to a feminist inclusion of the positive (indeed sacred) passion of unboundaried, intimate connection-making eros.

ii. Environmental Exploitation

While showing no consciousness of the environmental crisis, dying only a few years after the publication of Rachel Carson's *Silent Spring* and before it began to work its way into the social and political fabric of our time, Niebuhr exhibits--since his conversion from idealism's spirit/nature dualism--an inveterate concern both for nature as a fundamental ingredient in what it is to be human and for how we should relate to it.

Christian action from the perspective of responsibility is situated within the entire community of organic and inorganic being. As responsive action it seeks a relation to the environment which is not dominating but fitting. Fitting relations to nature are contextual, tacit, dialogical, and mythic. Niebuhr's interest in nature as context is evident in his discussion of triadic relatedness. The first triad is the self in relation to society and nature. He defines nature as "that large world of events and agencies that we regard as impersonal, as purely objective or thing-like in character, energies that we know but that we do not interpret as knowing us or knowing themselves" (RS 79). While this is a physical, rather than biological, definition of nature, he elsewhere acknowledges organic forms, such as sparrows and flowers (RS 165-66). In an earlier writing he regrets that "[o]nly in occasional instances are the values relative to animal life included in the system of human values" (*Value* 109). While the above definition is "critical," inasmuch as it considers all phenomena as objective and thing-like--and is, therefore, another clue to understanding Niebuhr's resistance to praxis--his affirmation of triadic relatedness involves nature not only as object consciously focused on but as context unconsciously indwelt. As I focus on nature, I am responding to society; and as I focus on society, I am responding to nature.

> When I respond to natural events I do so as a social being; on the other hand, when I respond to my companions I do so as one who is in response-relations to nature. I do not exist as responsive self in two separate spheres or in two distinct encounters. . . . I engage rather in a continuous dialogue in which there are at least these three partners--the self, the social companion, and natural events (RS 80).

These unfocused upon responses cannot be explicit; they must rather be tacit. They are present in my constant unconscious relating to nature and in the "medium of language" through which I encounter nature (RS 80). The triadic logic that moves towards increasingly inclusive contexts situates us finally within the totality of the natural world as context we relate to and dwell within tacitly. Nature is not then merely an object known, not even in science: "Biology and sociology as well as psychology have taught us to regard ourselves as beings in the midst of a field of natural and social forces, acted upon and reacting, attracted and repelling" (RS 56). Nature is a field of interaction, a habitation for our lives; all our recent "pattern of thought now is interactional" (RS 57).

Niebuhr thinks in dialogical terms of this interaction with natural events. What "is implicit in the idea of responsibility" is the self "engaged in dialogue, man acting in response to action upon him." Using a "synecdochic analogy" he says: "In trying to understand ourselves in our wholeness we use the image of a part of our activity; only now we think of all our actions as having the pattern of what we do when we answer another who addresses us" (RS 56). He goes on:

> An agent's action is like a statement in a dialogue. Such a statement not only seeks to meet, as it were, or to fit into, the previous statement to which it is an answer, but is made in anticipation of reply. It looks forward as well as backward; it anticipates objections, confirmations, and corrections. It is made as part of a total conversation that leads forward and is to have meaning as a whole (RS 64).

Natural phenomena and ourselves are thus inextricably bound up with each other inasmuch as we are companions in dialogue and the meaning of the dialogue is not merely what we say and do but the whole interaction.

Finally, nature is mythic. It is not merely congeries of energies but a whole we orient ourselves within as bearing ultimate meaning for our being: as death-dealing or life-giving, as inimical or trustworthy, as something to be defended against or as something to embrace as good in its very being. We image it as "the story of recurring cycles" of birth and death, of "infinite progress," of "everlasting winter lying on the frozen wastes of existence," or of "all-destroying fire raging before and after the brief interval of its life" (RS 106).

Within the responsibility myth Niebuhr affirms the immanent presence of God acting within the cosmic whole upon all beings. This means for him that apart from their utility to humanity, each creature has a meaning and importance transcending our desires. In Jesus as responsible self Niebuhr sees natural phenomena affirmed within the mythic orientation of nature as the field of divine grace:

> Will of God is present for Jesus in every event from the death of sparrows, the shining of sun and descent of rain. . . . [H]ere are signs

of cosmic generosity. The response to the weather so interpreted leads then also to a response to criminals and outcasts, who have not been cast out by the infinite Lord. So it is also with carefree birds who deserve no pay for useful work, and with flowers that have done no heroic deeds to merit their colorful ribbons and brilliant medals. . . . [T]hey [are] to be understood as signs of the presence of an overflowing creativity, of an infinite artistry, that rejoices in its creations, that rejects, because it is all grace, the censorships of human laws (RS 164-66).

Niebuhr stands in an American ecological tradition that goes back through the romantics to Jonathan Edwards (see Perry Miller, "From Edwards to Emerson"), and founds his view in Jesus's own affirming the integrity of nature. He in fact appropriates the term "environmental or ecological" in 1961 for ethical "diagnosis of the moral malaise of our day" advocating an "ecological analysis rather than . . . the foreign agent theory of our illness" (*EthCrisis* 46-47). The affirmation of the inherent interrelatedness of existence and infinite value of each being within this web because of God's creating, sustaining, and acting upon each creature is an incipient ecological theology whose potential he did not realize.[73] We are not encapsulated selves free to exploit nature however we wish but exist in inherent relatedness to it as tacit context, dialogical companion, and mythic framework. The fitting response to the divine action in each new moment fits as well not only our social embeddedness but the natural environs of all being.

iii. The Christian Imperialism of Anti-Judaism

While Niebuhr was unaware of the term "anti-Judaism"--the denigration of Judaism by defining the Christian as comparably superior and as superseding the Hebraic covenant[74]--he, nevertheless, explicitly opposed a theological imperialism asserting Christian superiority, was sensitive to the integrity of Judaism, and was openly grateful to Jewish thinkers for what he received from them. Arguing in 1946 against the Christian assertion "that our Christian faith can enable all men to enjoy a fullness of life which not only equals but surpasses that which any other faith can accomplish," he says: "The Jewish people [are] more faithful than any similar group in the keeping of the moral laws they share with the Christians, more assiduous in the practice of repentance, [and] more diligent in forgiveness" (*Utilit* 3-4). Before the recent recognition of the subordinating character of Christian talk about the Old Testament, he chose often to speak rather of the "Hebrew Scriptures." In the face of the typical Protestant assertion that the New Testament fulfills the Old

Testament, he says that fulfillment is not just one way. Speaking of Christians' use of the Hebrew Scriptures, he says: "One may even say that the Old Testament fulfills the New for them in practice, and not only the New the Old." The reason is that while for Christians the Hebrew Scriptures "point beyond themselves to Christ," they also "give concreteness and filling to the ethos exemplified in Jesus" (RS 168).

About the Christian attitude towards law in Judaism he says: "There may be some sense but there is also evidently much nonsense in what many Christians have said about the legalistic character of Hebrew and Jewish ethics." Looking from his perspective of Christian responsibility, he attempts to trace "the logic of Hebrew ethics as that ethics runs through all the pages of Hebrew Scriptures and through the tragic, yet wonderful story of this people of God." While acknowledging the centrality of law (although not recognizing the inadequacies of translating Torah as "law"), he sees this logic as essentially that of universal responsibility:

> It is an ethos of laws, to be sure, but an ethos which centers even more in responsiveness to omnificence, to the all-doer. There is no evil in the city but the Lord has done it. No nation exists that he has not called into being. It is he that besets man behind and before and lays his hand upon him; from him no flight is possible though one makes one's home in Sheol. To discern the ways of God not in supernatural but in all natural and historic events, to respond to his intention present in and beyond and through all finite intentions, that is the way of responsibility to God. It is a way of universal responsibility because there is no action in the whole extent of actuality in which the universal intention, the meaning of the One beyond the many, is not present (RS 169-70).

Interpreting Joseph and Isaiah in this light, he acknowledges, "Of course this is a Christian's interpretation of Israelite ethos." Nevertheless, he goes on to express gratitude for what he has received from Jews: "But it is that of a Christian who is indebted to the Jew, because his Christ was a Jew; who must understand his Christ with the aid of the Hebrew Scriptures" (RS 169-70). While he does not elucidate the non-imperialistic implications of the Christian speaking of "his" or her Christ rather than "the" Christ, he ends the Earl Lectures affirming both the central significance of Christ for Christians and the possibility that reconciliation with God occurs for non-Christians through other symbols: "And for all this we are indebted to Jesus Christ. . . . Could it have so happened otherwise; could the same results have been achieved through other means? Are they being produced elsewhere through other means? That seems possible; nevertheless this one is our physician" (RS 178).

His gratitude to and dependence upon Jews is perhaps most forcefully manifest in his address celebrating Martin Buber's eightieth birthday at a party in New York City with him present. Expressing highest esteem, he said:

> More than any other person in the modern world--more even than Sören Kierkegaard--Professor Buber has been for me and for many of my companions, the prophet of the soul and the witness to that truth which is required of the soul, not as solitary but as companionable being. . . . For me and those for whom I can speak he has been a Socrates who has . . . helped us to recognize and acknowledge a knowledge of ourselves and one another as selves (*Buber* 2).

Finally of all the Jews he says they are for Christians, regardless of their own intentions, both a sign of universal responsibility and saviors of Christians from polytheism: "They are given to us for a sign; they point us to universal responsibility. They are, whatever their own intentions may be, our saviors from a polytheism into which we Gentile nations are forever tempted to fall" (RS 170). Through his relational perspective he both owns his own commitments and symbolic tradition and affirms the being and integrity of other people and other traditions upon whom, he believes, God is acting to lead them through their perspectives into a deepening fittingness with God and the community of being.

iv. War and Pacifism

Turning now from implicit significance in Niebuhr's responsibility ethics for responding to certain forms of social domination, we take up the subject of war and pacifism about which he wrote extensively from 1932 to 1943, and which he continues to comment on, albeit in the midst of other things, on into his last lectures on Christian Ethics. Throughout his postconversion years Niebuhr consistently sets up an opposition of attitudes towards war between pacifism and coercionism, and criticizes both sides from the perspective of a third alternative which attends to God. Neither rejecting war outright nor categorically rejecting pacifism, he focuses on what God is doing in the whole of actual history and (what he comes to call) our response to it. While each person must respond in his or her own way, he generally advocates--as we have seen in his attitude toward justice--the nonjudgment of others and the confession of sinful self-interest.

He thus comes into direct conflict with his brother, who came to side with the coercionist against the pacifist and to insist on making moral judgments about others in order to discriminate in any military conflict the relatively just from the relatively unjust sides, and then to intervene on the side of the relatively just. The underlying difference is that his brother believes that God is outside the world upholding a standard by which the justness of conflicting sides can be measured. Once measured, one can work through inevitable compromise to achieve more rather than less justice, regardless of how far it falls short of the ideal. H. Richard Niebuhr believes, on the other hand, that God is an active presence in history demanding our response and undercutting the absolute moral stands of both coercionism and pacifism. He thus enjoins an attentive waiting upon what God is doing while recognizing the self-conceived nature of all ideals and the self-serving character of all human efforts to achieve an ideal. While this would appear to his brother to be inaction, H. Richard Niebuhr does not advocate passivity, but rather refocuses attention from human to divine action--and the human response to it. Something is being done about justice in every situation, but it is not simply by humans, as with his brother, but by God and by authentic human responses to God.

Niebuhr's major thinking on war occurred before he became methodologically clear about responsibility. What he is reaching for in speaking of a third alternative becomes his ethics of responsibility. While there is no evidence late in his life that he considered rethinking his position on war, there is, nevertheless, a potential in the language of responsibility to construct the principles and appropriate actions of this third position more specifically than he has. At the same time there is a further clue here to Niebuhr's resistance to praxis in his lack of specificity about his third option, which is tied up with his refusal to judge others and with a fundamental indictment of all self-assertion.

Niebuhr's first discussion of war is in a public debate with his brother in 1932 over United States intervention in the Sino-Japanese War. Against his brother's emphatic assertion of the moral right of aggressive involvement in this conflict siding with the more just cause, he counsels self-reflection that confesses one's own sins and waits, refusing to judge which is the better side. Setting up the first form of his opposition between coercionist and pacifist, he distinguishes between the "conservative," who believes "greater good will result" from "the clash of national . . . self-interests," and the "pacifist," who has "renounced all violent methods of settling conflicts" (*Grace* 217). He rejects both, the former because the conservative's opportunism leads him to "rush to the protection of his own interests" which "encourages the self-asserters" and at the same time "fills them with fear of . . . the new competition," and the latter because the pacifist's "mounting anger" over the situation he has refused to enter violently will result in either "forcible interference" or "apoplexy" (*Grace* 217-18).

The third option, represented both by "radical Christianity" (*Grace* 220) and Communism, affirms an "inactivity" that while recognizing there is "nothing constructive to be done in the present situation," sees the situation as "preliminary to a radical change" (*Grace* 218), and recognizes "the actual processes of history will inevitably and really bring a different kind of world with lasting peace" (*Grace* 219)--but not without "a revolutionary change which will involve considerable destruction" (*Grace* 220). Unlike Communism, however, radical Christianity believes that it is God at work in actual history as a "total divine process." While this process includes "human thoughts and prayers," it does

> not rely on human aspirations after ideals to accomplish this end, but on forces which may often seem very impersonal--as impersonal as those which eliminated slavery in spite of abolitionists. The forces may be as impersonal and as actual as machine production, rapid transportation, the physical mixtures of the races, etc., but as parts of the real world they are as much a part of the total divine process as are human thoughts and prayers (*Grace* 219).

While he neither rejects war nor endorses pacifism in this essay, he does reject U.S. military engagement in this instance and advocates radical Christianity's nonviolent "inactivity" which is "far more effective than direct interference, for it is able to create the conditions under which a real reconstruction of habits is possible" (*Grace* 221), such as by "build[ing] cells of those within each nation who, divorcing themselves from the program of nationalism and of capitalism, unite in a higher loyalty which transcends national and class lines of division and prepare for the future" (*Grace* 220).

Concluding this initial response to his brother, he explains how war is a result, at the same time, of the clash of self-interest and of the divine will: "That structure of the universe, that will of God, does bring war and depression upon us when we bring it upon ourselves, for we live in the kind of world which visits our iniquities upon us and our children, no matter how much we pray and desire that it be otherwise" (*Commun* 229). War is God's judgment, but it is also that through which God is working for redemption. "History is not a perennial tragedy but a road to fulfilment"; this does not imply, however, a "faith in progress, for evil grows as well as good, and every self-assertion must be eliminated somewhere and somehow--by innocence suffering for guilt, it seems" (*Commun* 229-30).

Two years later he considers the same opposition in reflections on the split within the Fellowship of Reconciliation led by his brother who, while a pacifist, chaired it, then in 1934 broke from it. Never a member, H. Richard Niebuhr criticizes the idealism of both the pacifists who stay with the F.O.R. and those who withdraw from it. Idealism is self-assertive, the aggressive pursuit of one's own goals, and thus "utilitarian"--what he will later call "teleological"--because it seeks its self-conceived idealistic purpose through whatever means it can. Those who remain with the F.O.R. employ a "pacifism of non-violent aggression" whose essence is "an aggressive effort to realize the goal" (*Incon* 43), except that they stop short of direct violence. The mind/body dichotomy in idealism allows them to be "self-deceived," to deny the implicit violence in verbal and economic aggression and the inevitability that once "the process of aggression" has begun, it will lead to physical violence.

Those coercionists who have split off from the F.O.R. recognize their desire to establish "the ideal end" and the inherent logic that leads to using whatever means are necessary to achieve it, including violence. As idealists they are, however, "realistic utilitarians" since they recognize the need to coerce others to achieve their ideals and acknowledge the inevitable sacrifice of "our own purity" as well as "the lives of certain individuals" in the pursuit of "national or human welfare" (*Incon* 44).

He concludes his brief essay by expressing sympathy for the pacifist majority who remain with the F.O.R. because their pacifist commitment includes the genuine Christian "pacifism of non-resistance" (*Incon* 43), even though their idealism contradicts it. Jesus for Niebuhr was such a pacifist. His non-resistance rejected idealism and affirmed the realism of dependence upon God at work in the world, upon a "divine teleology"--what he will later name the "One intention and action":

> A Christian pacifism, or, better, a Christian non-resistance, which we may define historically as the type of attitude we see in Jesus, rejects the dominant position of the present Fellowship--the idealistic principle of aggressive fighting for our ideals, whether by tongue and boycott or by sword. It rejects the whole humanistic faith upon which this idealism is built. It is as deterministic as communism is. But it knows that there is a divine teleology, and that the aggressiveness of the righteous runs counter to it as often as does the aggressiveness of the unrighteous. It sees that the characteristic deed of Jesus was not enacted in the temple but on Golgotha . . . (*Incon* 44).

The way of this genuine pacifism is the way of the cross, the non-aggressive suffering of the innocent, for which "there can be no exemption for pacifists" (*Incon* 44). Rejecting both coercionism and pacifism because of their idealism, Niebuhr declares "the necessity of [developing] a consistent pacifist position" (*Incon* 43) and points to the possibility of overcoming the inconsistencies in F.O.R. pacifism by eliminating its idealism and articulating a "Christian pacifism," like Jesus's, of "Christian non-resistance" (*Incon* 44).

In his next consideration of war in 1941 he backs away from developing a Christian pacifism of non-resistance as the third alternative and subsumes it under the pacifism that is in opposition to coercionism. Rejecting both pacifism and coercionism, when they are narrowly focused on regard for the self, he explores a third alternative of a universal perspective: while coercionist or pacifist can be "self-regarding," either can and should be "under the discipline of a universal cause":

> Non-resistance may be an act in the context of fear for the self, physical, or moral; it may be an act in a context of love for the neighbor. . . . There is a coercionism which is self-regarding and one which puts itself under the discipline of a universal cause. The coercionism of a highwayman differs as radically from that of a soldier as the non-resistance of a coward differs from that of a Quaker. So the real issue for any individual is not that of non-resistance or of coercionism but of the context.

The conflict between pacifists and military interventionists is misplaced because they both idealistically pursue their own self-serving limited goals. Each should shift their commitment to violence or nonviolence from a narrow to universal perspective, "to make each particular word and deed part of a continuous action which is redemptive rather than defensive" (*CCh* 16). Hence making war or refusing to make war is morally acceptable if the manner is redemptive within a universal context of love. Thus while he has backed away from developing a certain kind of Christian pacifism as his own, he, nevertheless, creates a space for it-- and as well for war--to flourish within.

During World War II Niebuhr wrote three essays that developed his universal contextualist God-centered ethics further as an alternative to the self-regarding perspectives of either coercionist or pacifist. In the first, "War as the Judgment of God," he speaks of war as divine judgment and defines the justice of God at work in the war-torn world as redemptive rather than vengeful, vicarious in which "suffering of innocence is used for the remaking of the guilty" (*WarJudg* 631), absolute in which we can see our own failings and not justify our relative goodness over against our enemy, and unified in which all of political and economic life as well as spiritual life is encompassed.   He recognizes that both pacifist and coercionist can see war in this universal context, as divine judgment, and can abandon judgment on others and their own self-centered defensiveness and aggrandizement.   Fighting or refusing to fight can each be fitting responses to divine judgment, but "only if it be part of a total action in which concern for others has been given preeminence over concern for self and its values" (*WarJudg* 632).   But he will not dictate to others what God's intention is for them: "These are but general reflections which do not presume to say to anyone what his particular duty in response to God's judgment must be" (*WarJudg* 633; cf. *WarCruc* 515).

In his second war-time essay, "Is God in the War?," he develops this universal contextual perspective in terms of the vicarious suffering of God at work in the world of war.   He rejects the "dualism" of "subjectivists" who look for "God's action within, and will judge the world *with* him rather than be placed under the judgment of objective reality."   This locates God's activity solely within the human spirit and says "there is an actuality in which God is not, and there are therefore situations and events in life which do not allow a rational, meaningful response on the part of men."   Rather, he insists that "God must be objective before he can be subjective," for "[t]o deny that God is in war is for the monotheist equivalent to the denial of God's universality and unity--to the denial that God is God" (*IsGod* 954; his italics).   The choice this time is represented as between the universal perspective that affirms the objectivity of God and his vicarious suffering or a limited perspective that makes God subjective and rejects vicariousness.   Pacifists and coercionists alike either "can get along without the concept of vicarious suffering" or "rest under the common conviction of their personal and social sin inspired by the view of the contemporary cross" and bring "forth the fruits of repentance" (*IsGod* 955).

In his third essay, "War as Crucifixion," he explores his third alternative over against what he calls the "power realists" and the "just war" theory.   Both are inadequate.   While the "amoral" realist theory is right that humans are self-interested, it fails to recognize that a person "is always interested in values beyond the self and desires not only power but also the enjoyment of the good. . . . Power cannot be abstracted from human rationality and morality."   Nor can the behavior of individuals and nations be separated:

It may be said that while individuals do this [i.e. make great sacrifices for distant values] in war, nations always act amorally. But this again is to deal with unreal, wholly abstract beings, since nations and their governments are human, so that the mixture of motives which is discernible in individuals is always present in groups also.

The just war perspective, on the other hand, is inadequate because of "the impossibility of applying the whole scheme of moral judgment and retributive justice to social relations." In the long view it is extremely difficult to indict one side and not another for war-guilt. Retributive justice cannot in fact be put into practice because you cannot exclude one nation from the society of nations, and because suffering and death in war are inflicted upon the "just" as well as, and more than, on the "unjust" (*WarCruc* 513).[75]

Rejecting both alternatives, he focuses his third perspective on interpreting war through the metaphor of the cross, which reveals a new understanding:

that the order of the universe is not one of retribution in which goodness is rewarded and evil punished, but rather an order of graciousness wherein, as Jesus had observed, the sun is made to shine on evil and on good and the rain to descend on the just and the unjust (*WarCruc* 514).

Shifting significantly from his earlier essay that saw divine judgment in war, he now says that divine graciousness, not divine judgment, is in the war: the "cross does not so much reveal that God judges by other standards than men do, but that he does not judge." God's justice is not separate from grace: "God's righteousness is his graciousness and his grace is not an addition to his justice." "Man's rightness," similarly, "does not lie in a new order of judging justice, but in the acceptance of grace," not of a "standard of graciousness--but of an act of graciousness to which they respond graciously." That war is a

hidden demonstration of divine graciousness is hard for us to understand. The cross in ancient history is acceptable to us; the cross in "religious" history, in the history of man's relation to a purely spiritual God, is also acceptable; but the cross in our present history is a stumbling block and a folly which illustrates human sinfulness, but not divine graciousness.

But when war is seen as crucifixion,

[t]hen our attention is directed to the death of the guiltless, the gracious, and the suffering of the innocent becomes a call to repentance, to a total revolution of our minds and hearts. And such a call to repentance--not

to sorrow but to spiritual revolution--is an act of grace, a great recall
from the road to death which we all travel together, the just and the
unjust, the victors and the vanquished (*WarCruc* 515).

The third alternative, once again, does not delineate appropriate actions
but urges a reorientation of mind and heart that will understand war
within the universal context of God's gracious action.

Although he does not write again of war, he speaks of it in his
"Christian Ethics" lectures. Now within the language of responsibility,
he sets up another opposition over war, between withdrawal and exertion
of our own will. As before, he rejects both as he articulates a third
alternative as the basic principle of response to divine agency: "We need
to respond to God so as to say not my will but thine be done. We should
say this when others are acting upon me and when I am acting on others"
(*CE[RMK]* May 17, 1961). He goes on: we are "not responsive to God's
will if we withdraw from a pressure system so as to maintain our peace
and purity." On the other hand, he rejects the possibility that "we can
barge into a situation and exert our will instead of withdrawing"
(*CE[RMK]* May 17, 1961). Both the purist and the happy warrior are
irresponsible.[76]

Niebuhr from 1932 to 1961 consistently criticizes both coercionism
and pacifism from a third perspective that seeks to reorient the self to the
universal context within which God is acting redemptively, with love and
grace. At first he presents this universal perspective as a third option to
the other two, then he shifts to represent it as a different context and way
of using or refusing to use violence. In either case, he never concretely
imagines what acts would issue from such a universal perspective. It may
be that the acts are not different, only the attitude with which they are
performed is different. In his lack of specificity, we have another clue
to Niebuhr's resistance to social praxis, for it contradicts the stress
responsibility ethics places on God acting on us in the particularities of
a given situation. In the language of responsibility what he lacks is a
description of responsible work within a situation of oppression.

Why is this missing? We find another clue within these writings on
war in his attitude toward aggressive acts. He lacks specificity because
he believes that all aggressive or assertive acts are self-serving and
therefore sinful. This is evident in his condemnation of F.O.R. pacifists
because of their "aggressive effort to realize the goal" (*Incon* 43) and in
his implicit rejection of Abolitionists' work to eliminate slavery by setting
in opposition the "human aspirations after ideals to accomplish this end"
and the impersonal forces that "eliminated slavery *in spite of* abolitionists"

(*Grace* 219; my italics). This "in spite of" suggests that all work is tainted. The idealism he rejects here would appear to be not only a focus on abstract ideas rather than persons and a preoccupation with goals rather than interpreting the situation, as he defines it within responsibility, but any work to accomplish anything. As we have seen him say: "the aggressiveness of the righteous runs counter to it [a divine teleology] *as often as* does the aggressiveness of the unrighteous" (*Incon* 44; my italics). He is certainly right to warn us against self-righteousness and thus to enjoin us to "remember that sinners are restraining sinners. The society restraining criminals is itself criminal. Our justice is shot through with injustice" (*CE[RMK]* May 17, 1961). Nevertheless, to balance the aggressiveness of the righteous and unrighteous with the phrase italicized above, "as often as," suggests that aggressiveness itself is the problem. Hence the aggressive work to rectify oppressive situations is presumably as bad as the oppressive acts themselves. The choice is, therefore, not between coercionism and pacifism, for either action is self-assertive, but between this "humanistic faith" (*Incon* 44)--presumably humans attempting to accomplish something--and attending to what God is doing in the world.

But this contradicts responsibility thinking that affirms the interaction of divine action and human response. There is nothing inherently nonaggressive about response. The point of responsible action is not the level of human energy but the attention to and fittingness with the divine action upon us. There is, then, in the responsibility perspective the potential for developing a conception of responsible work to overcome oppression, whether physical violence or other forms of injustice, and, I would argue, for developing a Christian pacifism--not idealistic pacifism, which he rightly criticized, but a relational pacifism.

He in fact says things in his lectures on "Christian Ethics" that points in this direction. In 1952 he says categorically: "I as a churchman must say: War is wrong. I cannot condone it; I can't go into it and not have a guilty conscience" (*CE[YCE]* 180). In 1961 he speaks affirmatively of aggressive acts, of "positively acting and exercising pressure on others." He says: while it is "responsible to use the power we have," it is "irresponsible to will the destruction of another. That is why capital punishment and genocide are irresponsible." But then he rationalizes war by an appeal to desire--a move that contradicts his endorsement of need over against wishes--in going on to say: "In war the desire is to restrain but not to destroy the individual, although the individual is destroyed" (*CE[RMK]* May 17, 1961).[77] Ambivalence remains, yet he can speak of a pacifism that is a third alternative to his opposition between withdrawal and self-exertion: "Christian pacifists I know are more interested in reconciliation and peace-making than withdrawing" (*CE[RMK]* May 17, 1961). We have already seen Niebuhr in 1934 begin to sketch out a third position of "Christian pacifism" (*Incon* 44) on the basis of Jesus's non-resistance but draw back from it in 1941 as he repositions pacifism in opposition to coercionism and seeks a third option in a refocused universal context. But it may be that what he glimpses in 1934 and points to in 1952 and 1961 can in fact be realized by carrying out the logic of responsibility beyond Niebuhr's own contradictory lack of specificity and his indictment of self-engaged-action, for its principles lead to a Christian relational pacifism.

His first principle, responsiveness to the divine action and intention, negates all ego assertion because a response is not a self-serving assertion but an answer to divine action. To make war is unavoidably to engage in ego assertion--regardless of the desire to restrain the other--by being committed to impose one's own will on another by destroying him. Moreover, killing another terminates the possibility for the other to discover God's action on him and respond appropriately.

His second principle, fittingness, is the antithesis to war's destruction. Fittingness is a harmonizing of the elements in a situation, whereas war removes elements from the pattern, negating part of the community of being. The relational self, presupposed in the principle of fittingness, is also incompatible with war; since our being in its isness is connected to the being of others, we cannot kill others without killing a part of ourself. The moral justification of war assumes a separability between self and other which Niebuhr consistently denies. It also assumes a dichotomy between moral reason and feeling, which in his last years he denied. Reasoning is only moral if it is feeling, arising from and sensitive to our relational interactions. To make war requires detachment from fellow-feeling and stirring up dehumanizing feelings. Such distortion of feelings leaves deep psychic scars.

While Niebuhr does legitimate forceful restraint (e.g. by a police force) as responsible, he does not carry out his logic to admit that modern war makes restraint impossible in its devastation of civilian populations and threat of nuclear annihilation. The inherently self-destructive character of war-making becomes unavoidably clear (although many still seek to avoid it) in the ultimate weapon of nuclear bombs.

Finally, Niebuhr is committed to a process of mythic transformation, from our mythology of death to the myth of life and resurrection. This cannot be advanced by perpetuating the mythology of death through war's destructiveness. While he is emphatic that defensiveness against some aspect of the community of being and thus against some realm in which God is acting on me is sin, the ethical conclusion should be that war is a social manifestation of such defensiveness.

Niebuhr never develops the "consistent pacifist position" (*Incon* 43) he called for in 1934. Yet the potential for this within responsibility can be developed once the elements of abstractness and negative assessment of assertive acts are seen as contradictory to the concreteness and energy of response to God's immanent action within the relational matrix of being.[78]

v. Rethinking Racism:
From Liberalism to Responsibility

While Niebuhr sees racism as a major religious and social problem, his thoughts about it in his 1952 "Christian Ethics" lectures on responsibility are liberal and unreconstructed. Enlightenment liberalism began in part as a solution to the fratricidal religious wars in Europe of the sixteenth and seventeenth centuries by reaching beyond differences to a universal conception of humanity. But in doing so it embedded a disregard for particularities, engendering a hegemonic imposition of this definition of the human on all colonized peoples whose differences did not need to be heeded because of the reliability of this apparently universal conception (see Charles Long's illuminating discussion in *Significations* 3-4, 8, 54-58, 79-94, 196-97). Niebuhr moves as a liberal to the universal human, intentionally disregarding both racial particularities and their historical significance, and the material consequences of and remedies for racial oppression. While this is an important improvement over denying African-Americans their common humanity, it, nevertheless, moves--as in his discussion of war--into abstraction and away from the concreteness of our bodily being in the world, of how others treat our being there and what we do, what responsible work we do, to transform the world.

Because Niebuhr does not believe that racial particularities lay any claim upon our response to God, he provides no special section on race in his 1952 lectures: "There is no place for such a section, despite the fact that it is for us an acute problem; that is, there is no place, insofar as we are seeking to develop an ethics of response to the fundamental will of God" (*CE[YCE]* 147). Nevertheless, he discusses it at length. In 1961, however, he offers no discussion as he deletes his traditional section, "Christian Responsibility in Common Life," from his "Christian

Ethics" lectures, anticipating reworking it before giving his last set of lectures in 1963 prior to retirement.

There are, however, comments on racism in *The Responsible Self*. Between 1952 and the early 1960s, we can discern a movement in Niebuhr's thinking about racism from abstract liberalism into the language of responsibility. He recognizes the need to rethink racism beyond deontological law and teleological ideal. Yet he does not embark on this, but only points to the need to reinterpret the national past, that is within us still, by probing the historical and mythic structures of white consciousness's guilt, tragedy, and defensive fear of destruction and death, in order to reconstruct our future as new patterns of interaction between the races within the history and myth of resurrected life.

In 1952 he identifies "the race problem" of "segregation and discrimination" (*CE[YCE]* 149) as "the perversion of all order" and as "sin": "it is not of God, but of sin. It is the outward expression of a deeper sin, a deeper lovelessness, a deeper hopelessness. It is individual and social sin" (*CE[YCE]* 147). The solution is *metanoia* or repentance, restitution, and common work.

> Repentance requires recognition of sin, sympathy for the consequences for the victims; it requires that we call attention to the feelings of the oppressed. . . . But we must also come to see the conflict in the soul of the oppressors. It requires a technique of preaching the gospel in concrete terms, to create the feeling of vicarious suffering (*CE[YCE]* 149).

Restitution is called for, and "not just equalization" but, like Albert Schweitzer going to Africa, "to make amends for the evil done." The "common, objective work" is "a task having nothing to do with race" so that "members of various races can best lose their self-consciousness." The liberal aim is color-blindness: "The solution may finally come when color or race is ignored in doing a common task together" (*CE[YCE]* 149).

His acknowledgment of sin, suffering, and need for repentance is vintage Niebuhr. His concern for feelings and concreteness is expressive of his last stage of thought. His recommendation of restitution anticipates the African-American demands for compensation in the 1960s. And his call for a commonality to be found in work intends reconciliation which he will name as the cause of Jesus Christ (RS 43). He wants to affirm our basic common humanity--"all are one race" (*CE[YCE]* 147)--yet does so in a way that denies racial particularity. Here is the heart of his unreconstructed liberalism: he reaches for a common humanity by ignoring the particulars of racial difference.

He calls racial particularity a "convention." Using the language of Emil Brunner, he says that race is not an "order of creation" and therefore "[t]he problems of race are not merely the perversion of an order, but the perversion of all order" (*CE[YCE]* 147). What he means by denying that race is an order of creation is that there is no particular responsibility a person has because of his skin color:

> How can I be responsible to the action of God as a white man or as a Negro? We must love our neighbor as ourselves; but we have no distinct responsibility as Negro or as white man that we can define. There is no moral action I can carry on because of the color of my skin; it is not under my control; skin color is a physical characteristic; it can't be used as an instrument (*CE[YCE]* 147).

In his disregard for particularity, contrary to responsibility's affirmation of it, we find a further clue to Niebuhr's resistance to social praxis. He disregards physical characteristics in favor of the idea of commonality, and denies the historical meaning of such physical characteristics: "I feel no special moral responsibility from the point of view of a white man. There is no community of the white man as there are communities of family, nation, property" (*CE[YCE]* 147). Interpreting race, his sense of historicity evaporates, leaving the alternative of a metaphysical order or mere convention. Confronted with such alternatives, it seems one would logically say that property and nation (and perhaps family too) are similarly convention. Contradictorily he will speak of the ethical significance of sexual characteristics: "Sexual characteristics bring responsibilities. . . . The self is somehow connected with sex; we are challenged to self-control and a discharge of responsibility to others . . ." (*CE[YCE]* 147). Here are two physical characteristics, but one is seen as having ethical significance because it leads to social grouping, that is a family. Yet communities result from race, and in advocating repentance and restitution he implicitly acknowledges this. Nevertheless, Niebuhr does not speak of such communities of the racially oppressed and the racial oppressors with historical memories which from the point of view of responsibility do have special moral responsibilities given in their life situations.

In his reflections on racism in 1952 Niebuhr exhibits Enlightenment liberalism that moves, in the name of our common humanity, to the abstract universal. Yet he does begin to recognize some significance of historical particularity--affirming the inherent connection between the universal and particular characteristics of responsibility--when he speaks of equality.   While useful, he says, equality is a democratic not a Christian concept. Self-denial is the Christian ideal:

> Equality, however, is a principle of democracy; it is not a Biblical concept or a Christian ideal. Pragmatically, it is a good concept; it is a rough and ready measure of justice. But the Christian ideal is: Let each man consider the other better than himself. Jesus did not teach equality. It is rather, as Augustine put it, that God treats us all as if we were one and treats each of us as if he were all. Equality is not an adequate Christian principle, but we can make use of it, and then go beyond it (*CE[YCE]* 148; for explicit discussion of "Christian self-denial" see *CE[RMK]* May 15, 1961).

Distinguishing democratic equality and Christian self-denial suggests a critical stance towards classic liberalism, but he does not in 1952 introduce the category of fittingness as a way of embracing and transcending equality. Rather he uses equality and goes beyond it--and here is the recognition of historical particularity--as he looks at the African-American's situation in wider scope of the history of oppression and denial of opportunities, rather than treating each as equal because free to compete in the present moment:

> We have defrauded the Negro. We have to begin by giving better educational opportunities to him. Yale Divinity School has consciously tried to avoid prejudice; Negroes and white folks of equal qualifications have always had an equal chance of acceptance. Their number has been proportionately low, because they haven't had the opportunities previously which raise them to the standard of qualification. We must do more because they have been denied the opportunity (*CE[YCE]* 149).

Nevertheless, we should be alert to yet another clue in Niebuhr's uncharacteristically affirmative talk of a "Christian ideal." The ideal of self-denial abstracts one from the particularities and interactions of a situation by taking a dogmatic stance of inferiority towards it, focuses attention on one's own isolated self rather than the interaction, and inscribes each situation with the idea of inferiority and superiority rather than mutual engagement. Self-control, mentioned above in relation to sexuality, similarly assumes an isolated self abstracted from interactions and focused on oneself who relates to itself through domination.

While the handling of racism in 1952 is liberal--except for recognizing the particular historical circumstances of African-Americans having been denied opportunities--by 1960 Niebuhr has begun to speak of racism in the language of responsibility. In *The Responsible Self* he says that the issue of desegregation is not adequately handled by either deontological or teleological approaches but needs to be rethought in a way that will catch more of the complexity involved:

> Practical debate on the achievement of desegregation, for example, moves between the insistence that the law of the country must be obeyed and the young Negroes' demand that the ideal state of affairs be realized. What these debates suggest to us is that helpful as the fundamental images are which we employ in understanding and directing ourselves they remain images and hypotheses, not truthful copies of reality, and that something of the real lies beyond the borders of the image; something more and something different needs to be thought and done in our quest for the truth about ourselves and in our quest for true existence (RS 55-56).

While he is here pointing to the need for going beyond the alternatives of law and ideal, he has once again identified social and political aggressiveness as idealistic and cannot see that the labors of Martin Luther King, Jr. (whom he does not even mention) and other civil rights workers are not idealistic--attempting to achieve an "ideal state of affairs"--but responsive to racial oppression and the divine action towards transformation of the social and material conditions in the situation.

One aspect of reality that traditional approaches do not catch and that the perspective of responsibility can is the defensive posture of whites borne of guilt and the fear of death:

> But we have many illustrations in contemporary history of defensive social ethics. In the destructive interactions of castes or racial groups in the United States and in South Africa and elsewhere in the world we must take into account that beyond all loyalty to law and beyond all idealism there is operative in the minds of the defensive group a deep fear of coming destruction. The future holds for it no promise, no great opportunities, but only loss and descent, if not into the grave then *ad inferos*. Its actions are those that seem to it to be fitting, i.e., to fit into a situation and into a history whose past is full of guilt, acknowledged or not, and whose future is full of death in one of its forms (RS 99).

What is needed is a reinterpretation of our past to come to a new understanding that will move us toward freedom, freshness, and fittingness--toward social and individual transformation. While we reinterpret the Civil War in each new generation, we usually do so in ways that leave unchanged our ongoing interactions:

> In America we re-examine, generation after generation, our great
> national tragedy, the Civil War. Our ever-renewed attention to it has
> been in part, of course, simply an effort to maintain established patterns
> of interpretation so that in the present North and South, Negroes and
> whites, industrialists and agrarians, may encounter and respond to each
> other as they have always done (RS 103).

But this past is not a "no-longer" but is still within us; any new
understanding that does come can affect our behavior:

> But to a large extent our study of that history has been a reconstruction
> of a past which is still in us, in conscious and unconscious ideas, and in
> complex associations of emotions with those ideas. Insofar as the
> reinterpretation of our past had led us to some new understanding and
> acceptance of the past actions of and upon our groups, our present
> encounters with each other as North and South, Negro and white, have
> been guided by somewhat new ideas (RS 103).

Without articulating the content of such new understanding, he,
nevertheless, knows that it can transform us into free, fresh, and fitting
forms of new interaction:

> Every nation with similar social recollections of past animosities, with
> a similar inherited complex of emotional and personal attitudes of group
> to group, seeks, I believe, to move toward freedom, toward freshness
> and fittingness in present interaction by similar reconstructions of its past
> (RS 103).

Such transformative thinking would be mythic. Taking, for
instance, the Civil war in its historicity as symbolic, we can grasp the
structure of our racial existence now in America and catch the tragedy
and guilt, the courage and grandeur in our struggle:

> we observe in America today how in America the story of the Civil War
> functions among us symbolically without ceasing to be historic; with its
> aid we apprehend the structures of our national, historical existence, as
> North and South, as black and white, as agrarian and industrial; we also
> discern the tragedy of the judgment that lies on us in past and present
> and the grandeur of sacrifice and courage that appears in the midst of
> this guilty existence. But this is not the place to explore the relations of
> history and myth . . . (RS 156-57).

To speak of this history as myth, although Niebuhr does not develop it
here, suggests that this structure of national racial existence connects with

the "ultimate context" in which we either defend ourselves against death by wielding destructiveness upon the other or embrace the other as we open ourselves to the "power of being" in "the conviction that we are surrounded in history by life and not by death" (RS 106-07).

Conclusion

Thus we find in Niebuhr's theo-ethics of responsibility a potential for development of liberation concerns for the social oppression of sexism, environmentalism, and anti-Judaism; an engagement with war and racism that leads into talk about, but not development of, them in the language of responsibility; and clues about Niebuhr's own unconscious resistance to following out the logic of responsibility to social praxis. The clues we have so far gathered at points where Niebuhr's thinking contradicts his responsibility perspective are: nonjudgment of others in his discussion of justice and war--which contradicts interpretation and discrimination of fitting from unfitting actions; a "critical" definition of nature as thing-like in our consideration of his potential dealing with environmentalism--which contradicts nature as contextual; an abstractness in his discussion of war and racism--which contradicts affirmation of the particularities of a situation within which God acts on us; the indictment of assertive action in his consideration of war and racism--which contradicts the energy and transformative characteristics of response; a disregard of bodily differences and material conditions in movement to the universal in his remarks on racism--which contradicts the embodiedness of self and inclusiveness of all aspects of life in the category of the fitting; and affirmation of the Christian ideal of self-denial and self-control in his reflections on racism--which contradict the relational realism of selves involved with each other beyond the dualistic categories of superior and inferior and self-domination. What sense we can make of all these clues awaits our exploration, in the next chapter, of the final form of social oppression Niebuhr engages--the oppression of classism and capitalistic exploitation.

CHAPTER EIGHT

CHRISTIAN LIFE AS ACTION:
II. LIBERATION FROM CLASSISM
AND PRINCIPLES FOR THEO-SOCIAL ANALYSIS

Although Niebuhr does not provide a section on racism in his "Christian Ethics Lectures" of 1952, he does discuss it; with classism, however, he provides a section titled "Responsibility in the Economic Community," but does not discuss it. In 1961, he neither discusses it nor announces a section on it. This is remarkable because of his radical critique (i.e. the socioeconomic questioning of the material base) of capitalism during his liberal stage. We will see, as noted in the Introduction, that this central socioeconomic critique later becomes peripheral criticism and is altogether absent from his consideration of religion and culture in *Radical Monotheism*, the last book he lived to see published. How is this change to be explained?

Changes in Niebuhr's Socioeconomic Critique

While it is possible that the fiery critique of his youth guttered in his mature social location as a white, male, professor chaired at an elite university, there is throughout much of his later writings ongoing criticism, even if no longer central, of economic and other forms of social oppression.

Beverly Wildung Harrison speculates on why he stopped short of doing "the sort of social-ethical analysis which he aspired to in light of his deep desire to transmute the individualism of past interpretations of Christian faith." She records a flip response: "Several of H. Richard Niebuhr's students have reported that when pressed to address the questions of political power or international power dynamics, H. Richard

Niebuhr replied that he would 'leave that to Reinie'." While his filial connection to another outstanding American theological ethicist may indeed have been a restraining complexity in his life, she gets closer to it, I think, when she comments about his growing awareness of the problem of language and symbol: "No doubt his profound sense of the crisis in language and symbol, signalled by the 'twilight of the gods,' identified at the end of his lifetime, dissuaded him from pursuing his course" (Harrison 301, n. 1, & 312).

Harrison's view fits with what Niebuhr himself says about the changes in his thinking. In his autobiographical essay of 1960, he recalls how in the 1930s he "saw the sovereignty of God usurped by the spirit of capitalism and of nationalism" (*Ref* 75) and conceived for the church "the problem of separating itself . . . from the idolatries and henotheisms of the world" (*Ref* 77). His ongoing "[r]eflections on the sovereignty of God" led him in later years, however, to realize that the problem of the church was more deeply one of separating itself "from its own idolatries and henotheisms" (*Ref* 77):

> If my Protestantism ["{a}s a convinced Protestant (not an anti-Catholic)" (*Ref* 75)] led me in the past to protest against the spirit of capitalism and of nationalism, of Communism and technological civilization, it now leads me to protest against the deification of Scriptures and of the church. . . . The immediate reformation of the church that I pray for, look for, and want to work for in the time that may remain to me is its reformation not now by separation from the world but by a new entrance into it without conformity to it. I believe our separation has gone far enough and that now we must find new ways of doing what we were created to do (*Ref* 77 & 78).

He then goes on to speak of the current situation both of the "world" as representing those "deeply disillusioned about themselves" and "their idols--the nations, the spirit of technological civilization," and of the church as those who have been through a recent "religious revival" but not so much "of faith in God and of the hope of glory" but "of desire for faith and of a hope for hope." Exemplifying Harrison's view, he continues, "in the West the most sensitive . . . are living in a great religious void; their half-gods have gone and the gods have not arrived," and concludes "I look for a resymbolization of the message and the life of faith in the One God" (*Ref* 79) so that "the human spirit is revived within itself" (*Ref* 80).

Harrison is right that later in his life Niebuhr was increasingly preoccupied with the crisis in modernity of a spiritual void and the need to resymbolize and to revivify our existence in the world with God. In his later years he dove deeper into the nature of the self, its relational being and inherent linguisticality (which I have explored in *Recovering the Personal*). Obvious from his own remarks, this deepening involved a confessional probing of his own communal idolatries within the church rather than continuing a direct attack on capitalism. I would not say, however, that these deepening reflections on the self "dissuaded him from pursuing his course" (Harrison 312), but only delayed it; this indispensable probing of the roots of modernity was prerequisite to the socioeconomic critique he did not live to accomplish. Had he lived, it is evident, he would have rethought the economic dimensions of this relational, metaphor-making and -using self from within the perspective of responsibility. Nevertheless, there is no evidence that this intended rethinking would have led to social praxis. Here, as in the previous chapter, we shall gather up clues as to why at the points in his thinking that contradict the relationality of responsibility.

Toward a Radical Critique within Responsibility

In this chapter we will explore the nature of Niebuhr's radical critique of capitalism within theological liberalism, show how it is sustained through his conversion but fundamentally altered in its meaning within the radical theological context of his relational thinking emerging from his new commitment to divine immanent action. And we shall trace how, after his conversion, the economic critique shifts from center to periphery. Through the six principles we have discerned in his new theo-ethical framework of responsibility, we can attempt to imagine how this radical critique could be wielded within his mature relational ethics by applying these ethical principles to the issue of economic justice between employer and worker. Imagining Niebuhr's comprehensive response to economic injustice will show how analysis of the societal structures of domination might emerge from his theo-ethics of responsibility. Thus we hope to show in such a method of analysis one way in which "his social phenomenology" can be developed, as Harrison rightly remarks it was not, to connect with "the actual social *praxis* of human communities and movements" (Harrison 304). Then in the Conclusion, we shall reflect on the clues we have gathered and try to make sense of these elements, in Niebuhr's thinking, that resist the development of social praxis inherent in responsibility.

A Radical Socioeconomic Critique
within Liberal Theology

In three incisive essays in the 1920s Niebuhr raises from within his liberal theology a radical critique of economic oppression, engaging in analysis of class conflict, attacking excessive individualism, and advocating solidarity. In "Christianity and the Social Problem" (1922) he says: "Economic freedom is at least as important as political freedom" (*CSP* 288). In "The Alliance between Labor and Religion" (1921) and "Christianity and the Industrial Classes" (1929) he makes it clear that the church, when faithful to Christ, "feels its kinship with the poor" (*ALR* 203; cf.*CIC* 13). He argues that the labor movement is religious; even though its loyalty is to humanity rather than to Christ, it has real affinities with the church. But the church all too often fails to recognize this because of its support of the leisure class and the status quo:

> So akin by nature, so closely connected in history, Christianity and the labor movement might have been allies and seed-plots for each other's truth. That this has not been the case is the tragedy of both labor and the church. . . . The church has lost not only the social enthusiasm and the energy of the labor class movement, but has failed also to appropriate for itself the spiritual qualities which labor could give to it; on the other hand it received from its connection with the leisure class qualities which stand often enough in direct contrast with spiritual realities: worldliness and satisfaction with the things that are; customs, habits of thought, conventions of every kind, that obscure the real things in life; a practical belief in the class-division of mankind into upper and lower groups and a spirit of narrow nationalism and racial prejudice (*ALR* 201-02).

In alliance with the upper class the church preaches "peace and law and order and condoning of sin that the sinner and his system might not be harmed." When labor resorts to force, the church preaches peace, not "justified as it surely is by the ethics of Christ," but on the basis of "interest in the material possessions of the Church and in the mere stability of a worldly society, wherein the Church had made itself at home." It preaches "the bearing of the cross," not as that which "the injustice of society lays upon the man who fights that injustice," but "as the lot assigned to one by social condition." And it preaches forgiveness, not to the upper class "enemy against whose sin relentless warfare is to continue that he may be saved along with his victims," but as a "condoning of the sin of the social order and resignation to its unalterable power" (*ALR* 202).

In his affirmation of the solidarity of person with person and Christ with humanity--indeed, in his definition of Christianity in these terms: "faith in that solidarity and loyalty to its embodiment in Christ is the Christian religion" (*ALR* 201)--Niebuhr criticizes the excessive individualism of mainstream Protestantism and modern industrial culture. The gospel is unequivocally social:

> The social gospel is no new gospel. It is the *Sermon on the Mount* and the *message* about the *Kingdom of God*. . . . The viewpoint of Protestant thought, especially of Lutheran thought, has been individualistic. It has said: Man's chief concern should be the salvation of his soul . . . [and] [o]riginal sin has been passed down from father to son. The social interpretation does not deny this, but it emphasizes . . . : [t]he sin from which men must be redeemed is not so much passed down from one individual to another, as it is ingrained in social institutions, and perpetuated in false social standards. . . . The social gospel is the gospel which proclaims that between man and his society there is the closest possible relation; that Christ sought to save individuals for the sake of the Kingdom; that He proclaimed the Kingdom for the sake of individuals; that none of us liveth to himself and none dieth to himself, that members of the human family must by the law of life suffer, sin and be saved together, that we are members of one another and that just this relationship between men is the point where the saving work of Christ begins and ends. . . . [T]he content of the social gospel [is] . . . the *value of the individual*, the *kingdom of God*, the *principle of service* (*CSP* 278-79; his italics).

Modern culture dominates the lives of individuals because "institutions . . . find their ends in themselves rather than in the individuals whom originally they were meant to serve." But in its very "suppression of individuality" it fosters excessive individualism. Modern domination is "the suppression of individual by individual," the weak and poor by the strong and wealthy, through the spread of the socioeconomic systems of: competition--which "results in the *control of the weak by the strong* and the ethics of the jungle"; the acquisition of wealth--which is "the retirement of ethical human values in favor of economic values"; private property--which is enthroned "above the human beings whom property was meant to serve"; industrial production--which is exalted "above the interests of men for whom that production was to be made"; violence--which issues from "the unusual degree of the separateness of . . . personalities" who have thus become "extremely sensitive to the violation of the sanctity of their personality" who thus "assert themselves much more violently . . . against any infringement of their personal values" (*CSP* 286-87; his italics); "the growth of cities"--which brings together "the most various groups with widely varying standards of conduct and morals" leading to "the mutual breakdown of the morals which guided the conduct of each group" (CSP 287 & 283); rapid communication--which brings to bear on any situation the "public opinion of the moment, rather than group morals" (*CSP* 287); the machine--which separates the individual from "the family [as] the former unit of production" so that "the individual became the economic unit of production" (*CSP* 283); and "the creation of class consciousness"--which is "an individualistic principle, tho[ugh] it be the consciousness of a group" (*CSP* 283).

Niebuhr's liberal solution to his radical critique of the problems of class oppression and excessive individualism is the "method of aggressive suffering" (*ALR* 202) and ideal reassertion of "solidarity" and "kinship with the poor" (*ALR* 201 & 203). The church must "strive" towards "the establishment of justice" by leading "the way to the goal of the cross" (*ALR* 203). The cross's "method of *self-sacrifice* for its ideals and convictions" is "not for the sake of present peace," but "for the sake of the attainment of the kingdom of God" (*CSP* 291; his italics).

From the perspective of responsibility we can say that the structure of Niebuhr's radical critique is teleological idealism. It seeks to clarify goal and means. The goal is to establish the ideal kingdom of God--the society of peace and justice and solidarity with the poor. The means to achieve it is only through the self doing something, the way of the cross-- aggressive suffering and self-sacrifice. Responsibility asks not What is the ideal end and how should it be achieved?, but rather What is going on and how should it be responded to fittingly? To understand what is going on involves understanding self, situation, and divine action.

While radical in criticizing capitalism's excesses of individualism and in affirming solidarity with the poor, the framework is liberal as Niebuhr affirms the self as an isolated rather than a relational self. As a separate individual the self is able to "identify with" others. "For is not the foundation of religion to be sought just in this capacity of man to identify himself with another and with humanity, to lose his life within the larger life" (*ALR* 201). It is a self-contained individual in possession of itself, of its boundaries, that can "identify itself with" "humanity" (*ALR* 201), or with the "poor" (*ALR* 203), or with "the world of sin" (*CSP* 280 & 281). Because an individual possesses itself in its separateness and is not inherently related to others or God and cannot therefore realize this relatedness of its existence, it can (and should) choose to enter into solidarity with humanity and lose itself in the larger life of the kingdom.

Niebuhr develops his radical criticism of individualism and class conflict and affirmation of solidarity as a liberal. He judges from the outside, comparing the situation with an external ideal rather than trying to understand the situation within which he exists in its full temporal and spatial interrelatedness, and rather than seeking for the particular divine action in that situation.

Recontextualizing the Radical Critique within Relational Theology

Niebuhr's radical socioeconomic critique continues from his liberal days into the 1930s but is significantly altered when he pursues it from a radical theological basis. Encountering divine sovereignty as God's pervasive presence in the world, his shift in approach to capitalism is from an external to internal perspective. He no longer sees it as merely a cultural form to be measured against an external ideal but as a spiritual condition, a way of response to divine immanence within the world. As a spiritual condition or a "faith," as he calls it, it is part of a larger whole; it is an orientation within a context, a pattern of relations in a world. It is therefore connected with everything. The institutional form of capitalism and the damage it does is part of the encompassing context of the world and not a separate reality that can be criticized from outside, for we participate in both the capitalist system and the larger world.

From an inclusive perspective, rooted to be sure in our particular historical location, we can see our own destructive involvement in systems of social oppression and repent of it (undergo a *metanoia*, a change of mind), and can recognize that the problem is not so much the "what" as the "way," not the cultural form as the way it is being lived. The measure is not an ideal (a clear and distinct concept) to which to conform but reality (an experienced web of interrelationships). With these relationships we should live in harmony, but the present capitalist system and ourselves are instead unfitting. To see the systems of oppression within an inclusive view enables not only criticism but creativity that can imagine fresh solutions and draw upon spiritual resources beyond the opposition of "me" against "them." From the divine action and human responses to it, change may occur in possibly unsuspected ways.

This social shift is apparent in Niebuhr's first writing after his conversion essay. Advocating a synthesis of American social gospel with German theocentric Protestantism, he speaks in 1930 of an "anchorage in an inclusive faith" (*Can* 914) which recognizes "that conflicting values do not necessarily exclude each other forever, that somehow the disparate experiences and the apparently exclusive loyalties, which now require decisive choice, yet form part of one whole" (*Can* 915). Two years later, in obvious agreement, he describes Tillich as criticizing "[c]apitalist society" as "not a scheme of economic organization only" but "a culture with a definitely religious character" which is "based upon faith in the self-sufficiency of the human and finite world" whose "purpose is the establishment of human control over the world of nature and mind." Everywhere this faith seeks "domination over"--"over things in which there is no respect for the given and no true appreciation of human or any other kind of individuality" (*Trans* 10).

In 1930 he says the impact of this dominating faith is to transform people from agricultural to "economic man" (*Irrelig* 1307), to remake persons as "workers"--with "greater wants," willingness to learn "more profitable methods of manufacture," and an ability to "be fitted into the nervous, clock-like, mechanical rhythm of industry"; and as "consumers"--with "interest in novelties" and "immense quantities" "produced by the new methods" (*Irrelig* 1306). By shaping selves to "a dominant interest in the consumption of goods" and "in profit," the resulting spiritual condition "is the most discontented of all cultures because it must depend for its vitality upon the increase of discontent" (*Irrelig* 1307). In this negative transformation of self and society, all is reduced, Niebuhr says in 1935, to economic values:

> The capitalist faith . . . fashions society into an economic organization in which production for profit becomes the central enterprise, in which the economic relations of men are regarded as their fundamental relations, in which economic privileges are most highly prized, and in which the resultant classes of men are set to struggle with one another for the economic goods (CAW 602).

As a faith it is not the system of private property ownership that is the underlying issue in capitalism but the way in which that ownership functions. While "[n]o antithesis could be greater than that which obtains between the gospel and capitalist faith," the system of private property in its early stages of development in the modern world had not yet nor inevitably had to become perverted as it would come to be:

> It is not our intention to deny many elements in the Marxian analysis: the reality of the class struggle, the destructive self-contradiction in modern capitalism, the effect of capitalism upon government, law, the established religion. Neither are we intent upon defending the principle of private property as an adequate basis for the modern economic structure. But

we are implying that modern capitalism does not represent the inevitable product of the private property system in which early democracy and Puritanism were interested, that it has corrupted and perverted that system, making of it something which it was never intended to be nor was bound to be (CAW 602-03).

From his new perspective, in 1941, it is the context within which property is held that manifests either an "inclusive" (*Can* 914) or "dominati[ng]" (*Trans* 10) faith:

> the real issue of our time in matters of property does not lie in the act of social or private ownership but in the context of such ownership[.] From one point of view it appears that the question of social ownership is no longer really debatable. Whatever theories are held regarding property the whole drift is toward ownership of the means of production by social groups. And the great question is whether such ownership shall stand in the context of egoistic, or of nationalistic, or of what we now like to call democratic, but which I think we ought to call, universalistic socialism . . . [which involves] respect for the rights of men as members of a universal society (*CCh* 14).

The sharpness of his earlier critique of capitalism borne by his self-confident application of an external standard is now complicated by the claim that the real problem is the context or spiritual orientation, with which we are implicated, rather than the cultural form that expresses it, from which (we think) we are separate. This contextual approach involves a different way of thinking. The character of criticism is altered by recognizing that inclusive faith replaces the teleological thinking of liberalism with the relational thinking of what he will come to call responsibility. In "Utilitarian Christianity" (1946) he criticizes the "utilitarian spirit . . . in which religion is used as a means for gaining social order and prosperity" (3). Rather than imposing our desires on the world, seeking to organize it according to our own ends, however enlightened by Christianity, we should seek to be in harmony with reality "which calls for a complete change of mind not because repentance is socially effective, or individually effective for that matter, but because the mind is out of harmony with reality" (*Utilit* 5).

To achieve this harmony he advocates a "disinterestedness," a concept which epitomizes the shift from liberal to relational socioeconomic critique. Within this inclusive perspective he speaks of gaining distance on political and economic problems: "such radical repentance . . . may lead to that sort of disinterestedness which is able to deal with the questions of politics and economics objectively and helpfully just because it does not take them too seriously, just because it has gained a certain distance from them" (*Utilit* 5). His intention is to dislodge people from a passion for fulfilling their own well-intentioned desires and to liberate them to be "able to think the new thoughts which the crisis of the times requires and which they cannot think so long as they remain bound by the passion of this--worldliness" (*Utilit* 5).

This disinterestedness does not lead, however, to the negation of assertive action which he expresses earlier in his war essays of the early 1940s or later in his discussion of racism in his "Christian Ethics" lectures of 1952, for he speaks here of "work in society." A non-utilitarian Christianity "still has social relevance because its imperatives direct it to work in society" (*Utilit* 5), and yet not to impose its own desires: "this relevance must stem from its own imperative and not from the wishes and desires we entertain" (*Utilit* 4). He then names the categories of such work, and their urgency, in a non-teleological manner:

> It is imperative for such a Christian faith to remember and to realize the dignity of every man as an eternal being, in his political and economic relations as well as everywhere else. . . . It does direct its followers to seek by means of all the intelligence they can muster to find out what to do to alleviate distress, to heal physical and mental disease, to order the vocations and to distribute justly the goods men produce (*Utilit* 5).

While not yet able to articulate this alternative in other than deontological terms of commands and principles, he is reaching for a way to express the immediacy of the divine and the integrity of our relatedness, and, in one of the few places, in the terms of love and justice:

> Imperative Christianity does not ask whether the love of neighbor will bring forth a society in which all men will love their neighbors; it acts in hope, to be sure, but love and justice are its immediate commands and not its far-off goals. It does not condemn that abuse of atomic power because we have thereby imperilled our future but because we violated our own principles (*Utilit* 5).

Disinterestedness is not then the opposite of interest, the denial of passion for social change, but of circumscribed interest. The criticism of injustice and advocacy of social transformation is no longer for the sake of achieving our best goals but to bring us into harmony with reality, into a universal interestedness that seeks a fittingness, as he will later call it, with the total context of being.

While there is a wisdom in transcending a situation in order to think creatively about it, there is a clue in disinterestedness to Niebuhr's resistance to social praxis, a clue we have already seen in Chapter Seven in his handling of war and racism, namely, a move to abstractness. His talk of not taking these problems "too seriously" and of dealing with them "objectively" suggests a detachment from the particulars of a social situation characteristic of the privileged class. While more concrete, through the discussion of work and naming its material conditions, than in his consideration of war and racism, his thinking, nevertheless, remains abstract. He focuses on the self's orientation, as utilitarian or imperative Christianity, and thus does not direct our attention to the socioeconomic system of power and how it obstructs the alleviating of distress, the healing of disease, the ordering of vocations, the just distribution of goods, and the making of peace in an atomic age--and thus does not attend concretely to ways to bring the social order into greater harmony with reality. In the Conclusion we will seek to understand this abstractness, as it contradicts the economic relatedness inherent in responsibility, along with the other clues we have picked up in the previous chapter.

From Center to Periphery:
Gestating a Relational Reordering

While a radical socioeconomic critique has been of central concern in his liberal and early postconversion days, it shifts to the periphery after "Utilitarian Christianity" of 1946. While still radical within essays focused elsewhere, it becomes either a momentary sharp criticism of socioeconomic injustice or an illustration for some ethical point.[79] The last book he published, *Radical Monotheism*, carries none of this criticism; however, in the Robertson Lectures, given the same year as the book's publication (1960), he presents illustrative criticism (RS 59, 62, 76, 100, 116, 120-21, & 139), and in "The Ethical Crisis" (1961), he maintains sharp criticism.

As socioeconomic criticism moves from center to periphery, it becomes peripheral to an exploration of the context and orientation, the underlying way of being, that issues in such forms of oppression. He comes to realize that criticizing the effects of capitalism, however important in raising consciousness, will not finally engender a major change in the system, because the problem is not rooted in the what but the way of it. He seeks to go to the roots not merely of capitalism but of modernity, its generative context, to effect a transformation of an entire way of being. Drawing our attention away from the systems of oppression maintained by capitalism, he seeks a transformation of consciousness that will carry us beyond modernity.

While in his autobiographical essay he distinguishes himself, as always focused upon "the reformation of the church," from his brother, who was concerned with "the reform of culture" (*Ref* 74-75), he, nevertheless, sees "human religion . . . as one part of our human culture which like other parts is subject to a constant process of reformation and deformation, of *metanoia* (repentance) and fall" (*Ref* 77) so that reforming the church contributes to reforming society. In the 1930s he saw the spirit of capitalism, "the deification of national or economic principles" (*Ref* 77), subjugating the sovereignty of God so that he pursued reform by working towards the church's "separation from the world." In the latter part of his life in deepening realization that religion and the church are part of the whole of being, he advocates "a new entrance into it [the world] without conformity to it" (*Ref* 78). Reforming the church by entering anew into the world is in order to "find new ways of doing what we were created to do" (*Ref* 78). The overcoming of all forms of social oppression is rooted in the transformation of the spiritual condition, most accessible to Niebuhr within the church, which can issue in "doing creation": meeting the needs of those within and without the church many of whom "have become deeply disillusioned about themselves and . . . their idols--the nations, the spirit of technological civilization, and so on" (*Ref* 79). Doing this by "a resymbolization of the message and the life of faith in the One God" (*Ref* 79) to the end that "the human spirit is revived within itself" (*Ref* 80) will transform the societal structures, for "the reformation of religion is the fundamental reformation of society" (*Ref* 80).

Although he spent his career after his conversion articulating aspects of his new theological foundation, it was only just at the end of his life that he was achieving emergence of his whole postcritical perspective into clarity, breaking explicitly free from the critical dualism he had earlier pressed to its limits, especially through inner and outer history. He did not have the time to rethink the social implications of this phenomenology of responsibility before his sudden death--especially the implications for war, racism, and economic justice which he had worked hard on earlier in his writing and lecturing.

That his thinking was changing rapidly in his last few years, especially 1960-62, is evident in comparing his unpublished "Christian Ethics" lectures on responsibility of 1952 with *The Responsible Self*, containing the Robertson Lectures from 1960 and portions of the Earl

Lectures from 1962. In the latter book, the nature of responsibility has been clarified and dualism transcended in the deepening phenomenological, postcritical understanding of the self in its relational and linguistic being. In what turned out to be his last lecturing on "Christian Ethics" in the spring semester of 1961, he deleted the usual final part on "Christian Responsibility in the Common Life" because of apparent dissatisfaction with his usual handling of marriage and family, economics, politics, race, war, and international relations. Word passed among ethics students that he hoped to rework this section prior to delivering his final lectures before retirement in 1963, which he did not live to enjoy.

We have looked in these last two chapters at what, in fact, he did say about the issues of social oppression of war, racism, and classism, and at a potential in his thought for addressing other forms of social oppression--sexism, environmentalism, and anti-Judaism--he did not consider. We have shown his taking up social issues within the language of responsibility and his recognition of a need to develop them within this perspective. By asking why there is no evidence that responsibility, while inclined logically toward it, would have been developed by Niebuhr into social praxis, we have gathered clues in the contradictory elements resisting his relational thinking that we will endeavor to make sense of in the Conclusion. As his theological methodology was emerging into full consciousness at the very end of his life, its implications for his social ethics were gestating at the periphery of attention. There is evidence in his late thoughts of the workings of a tacit integrative process that was assimilating and organizing his ethical commitments into a pattern that could have informed a new socioeconomic analysis. But this integrative process, while begun, was cut off by premature death.

Imagining Responsible Theo-Social Analysis

Inherent within Niebuhr's ethics of responsibility is capacity to reshape the radical critique of his liberal period by his mature commitments to context and divine immanence, and the other four principles of his relational ethics, into a method of full-blown social analysis that can elucidate forms of social domination. While it will not have the self-assured singular intensity of the critique of his liberal period, borne of an assumed separate self wielding external ideals to judge a situation of which it is not intrinsically a part, it will be more thoroughly radical in its comprehension of the full complexity of relatedness we actually dwell within. Imagining what Niebuhr did not live to develop by applying his principles and weaving together economic concerns expressed in his late writings, I will suggest how such theo-social analysis might work with a specific example of economic injustice between employer and worker.

Social analysis within his ethics of responsibility begins with a creative--we could even say, "meditative"--engagement with the situation to understand what is going on. We begin with the particular problem in the here and now and move toward understanding the comprehensive context in space and time, and the nature of self and divine action within it. Take as our example the problem of employer and worker both wanting more income. Niebuhr draws our attention not to their ideas, their goals or laws, but to their ways of response:

> When we think of the relations of managers and employees we do not simply ask about the ends each group is consciously pursuing nor about the self-legislated laws they are obeying but about the way they are responding to each other's actions in accordance with their interpretations. Thus actions of labor unions may be understood better when we inquire less about what ends they are seeking and more about what ends they believe the managers to be seeking in all managerial actions. One must not deny the element of purposiveness in labor and in management, yet in their reactions to each other it is the interpretation each side has of the other's goals that may be more important than its definition of its own ends (RS 62).

Spatially, in the narrowest scope each interprets the other as seeking to acquire, maintain, and maximize an economic base for adequate living. While there is a difference--the worker seeks income to make a living whereas the employer seeks it not only to make a living but a profit--each affirms the other's desire for increased income as positive: increased income will enable workers to make a better living by extending their consumer activity and managers to vitalize the economy by extended profits which can be reinvested. In fact, however, when workers demand higher wages, management resists to protect profits but will negotiate if pressed and seek the least increase acceptable to labor. Within this narrow scope there can be no recognition of oppression. The issue is only seen as how much management will give and labor get.

But "I respond to this action not as isolated event but as action in a context, as part of a larger pattern" (RS 77). As the sphere of understanding is expanded to the nation, Niebuhr moves from interpreting individual to social identities. Yet society is not understood as represented by an "impartial spectator" or a "generalized other" in Adam Smith's or G. H. Mead's words, which by its abstractness would divert attention from the diverse particularities in the situation which do not fit the generality, but is understood as the constancies of actual interaction: "I do not abstract some vague general figure from all the particular individuals who together constitute my society, but I refer to the constancies in the responses of individuals" (RS 78). Then various elements, not before noticed, become visible: the unemployed who serve as a resource for cheap labor when management periodically needs them but who can be laid off when profit-making demands it; those who are not normally conceived of as potential labor (houseworkers, elderly, handicapped, children); general conditions of workers resulting from the means of production throughout the country; government controls enabling profit-making and/or protecting rights of citizens; access to and ability to pay for medical treatment; distribution of wealth either widely among the population or concentrated among a few; proportion of population able to engage in consumer activity. For those looking from within this larger sphere it becomes possible to see the unfairness and destructiveness to many people of the concentration of economic power among a few.

Niebuhr's radical critique during his liberal period engaged economic oppression from within such a national context, but without recognizing, because of its presumed separateness, that the analysis is situated in this sphere and that there are still more comprehensive contexts encompassing it. Moving in the logic of responsibility to the global sphere of the international economic system, other aspects become visible: international businesses can elude the welfare achievements of the past century by moving plants to countries with lower wages and no unions and then can move again if workers organize to demand fair wages and healthy conditions. "Fair trade" agreements can be made, designed to overcome national welfare or environmental restraints on business. While able to wield considerable power for peace by soothing conflicts between nations in the interests of stability for conducting business, international corporations can seek to re-establish a global laissez faire economy in which profits are unrestricted while workers' rights are unprotected. What might have appeared to be a livable situation for the working class and middle management seen from within the sphere of a national economy can now be seen from within a global perspective as sustained by the oppression of many around the world whose livelihood is marginal. What had appeared from the narrowest view as simply the workers' desire for higher wages can now be seen, through social analysis that moves to the total economic system of the world, as one small ingredient in a system of unjust domination.

While modern dualism conceives the economic system as separate from other cultural spheres, responsible analysis discerns their interrelatedness. When separated, the political effects of economic power are overlooked. When the situation is expanded to include the political, then ways in which economic power is used politically to maintain conditions conducive to profit-making regardless of people's well-being become visible--such as government cuts in aid to inner cities while expanding contracts to corporations, increases in taxes on blue collar workers and the poor while creating more loopholes for the rich, or lowering standards for a clean environment while giving tax incentives for polluting companies to increase production. Within the global context, economic power effects political decisions to maintain dictators or invade small countries in order to maintain stability for the sake of business investments. While a political system seen as isolated may appear to sustain considerable freedom for its citizens, when recognized as interconnected with the economic system, it can become evident how ostensibly free political choices are being shaped by economic factors, presenting us with only certain kinds of options while denying basic human freedoms to others to insure our options.

Another aspect with which the economic is interrelated, the cultural, enables awareness that there is more to life than economic activity, whether profit-making or laboring and consuming. The values of being human are expressed in and nourished by the arts, gardening, convivial associations, and a host of other activities not directed toward economic achievement. The cultural identity of a nation is the pattern of these activities interwoven with the economic and political, but also the geographical and biological, and the dreams, stories, myths--the way of interacting with every aspect of being. Within a global perspective a particular nation's cultural identity is relativized as one among many other nations, just as a national identity is recognized as made up of a diversity of ethnic sub-cultures.

The logic of Niebuhr's dynamic moving from narrower to larger spheres is finally to reach to the cosmos. We exist in triadic relations, as part not only of society, but of nature. A particular economic problem is situated within the environment of living and inorganic reality, each of which has its own right to be, its own integrity. His social analysis takes into account the meaning of the particular issue for the cosmic as well as the economic, political, and cultural contexts.

Thus, the narrowest sphere that only considers the particular economic problem of a demand for a wage increase is inattentive to political decisions, cultural identities, or environmental effects. Attending to the comprehensive sphere of being enables seeing not only that there are other aspects and that they are interrelated, but ways in which political possibilities and decisions are determined by economic power, and ways in which certain cultural identities are elevated to social paradigms both domestically and internationally while others are denigrated, ignored, or destroyed. It shows ways in which elements of the environment are abstracted from the total web and exploited for economic purposes without recognition of the deleterious effects upon our own earthhome. It illuminates shifting meanings of freedom: to make a living, to consume, to make a profit, to vote, to exercise economic power for one's own political and economic advantage, to exercise one's own creativity, to be oneself as an individual and group, to honor what is most important in life, to dwell in an environment supportive of life and well-being. And it illuminates shifting definitions of self from a unit of measurable economic power to a self of transcendent depth dwelling in the community of being.

The social analysis implied in Niebuhr's ethics of responsibility is attentive not only to the full spatial breadth of any particular economic problem but, as well, to the full sweep of time. Interpretation changes as the temporal context broadens back into the past and further into the future. Within the present moment of the demand for a wage increase management and labor both remember the previous raise and anticipate giving as little or getting as much as possible to resolve the current problem. As time lengthens, managers may remember their own inheritance of wealth or struggle from poverty to their present position and anticipate maintaining and increasing present wealth, while laborers may remember the difficulties of getting a job, unmanageable medical payments, inflation, earlier ease or inability to purchase various goods, the poverty or wealth of their parents, and anticipate improving their lot. Niebuhr suggests--although with an optimism unwarranted by recent evidence from either the corporate or political worlds--that when

> [t]he industrialist who has been guiding his activities with a view to
> predicted events in the interactions of his enterprise with society becomes
> a government official, . . . the future lengthens at the same time that the
> society broadens, and he begins to think responsively and responsibly in
> terms of generations rather than of a decade or at best two and in terms
> also of the interaction of his larger society with other nations (RS 105).

Within a still larger temporal scope, the workers can see that they have advanced beyond serfdom, and corporate executives beyond shopkeepers. Each can remember their immigrant origins in America--

struggling for riches in pioneer or industrial worlds, or suffering oppression as English religiously persecuted, Africans enslaved, women disenfranchised, or indigenous peoples invaded. They can anticipate ongoing oppression and efforts to overcome it or the continued march of progress toward greater wealth.

Politically, the larger time can be remembered as the slow development of protection for workers or increasing governmental controls over business. War is remembered as a past moment of glory or horror in a presently drab or dramatic existence, as an economic disaster or impetus to economic growth. The right to vote can be remembered as the natural evolution of the English tradition or as the struggle to overcome disenfranchisement of African Americans, other people of color, women, and Native Americans.

The logic of Niebuhr's analysis is to interpret the present moment of demand for wage increase within the longer time of the national moment but to move beyond that to the beginnings of western civilization, to humanity itself, indeed to the origins and end of the entire cosmos, which drives the self deeper into its inherent timefullness and the ultimate meaning of its existence. Present in the full timefullness of the given issue of the moment is a defensiveness borne of a "history whose past is full of guilt, acknowledged or not, and whose future is full of death in one of its forms" (RS 99). Niebuhr goes on:

> As for defensiveness in personal ethos, common observation as well as psychological analysis bring to our attention how much our actions are those of men who try to do what they think is fitting, in order that they may maintain status in a society which they believe threatens them with isolated existence, with a kind of social death; or who must gather wealth or prestige or righteousness in order that they may be remembered, be not relegated to the realm of those who might as well not have been or otherwise end in nothingness (RS 100).

Employer and worker, though in different ways, fear loss of control and lack of knowing by which to control their destinies. They fear loss of ego-identity and thus seek to shore it up with economic success. They fear transformation, the changes that come from beyond knowing and control. They fear integration, embracing parts of oneself and parts of being that have been rejected, suppressed within and projected without upon an inferior other. They fear isolation, death, and nothingness. Hence they respond not out of their full humanity but as a diminished self, as one who loses himself in a mass and responds not as a self but as a part of a machine, or of a field of forces, or of a system of ideas. It responds in all its action not to the act by which it is a self but to the action by which the group of bodies or of minds or of emotions exists (RS 116).

And so it understands itself as an element in the economic system, as beneficiary or victim of economic power. It seeks to lose itself in "systems of society," such as "feudalism, industrialism, capitalism, communism, nationalism" (RS 139), which may be called "with Walter Rauschenbusch, superpersonal forces of evil."

They are not all evil powers. . . . But they are powers not identifiable with the willed influences of human groups or individuals. And they exercise dominion over us at least in this sense that we adjust our actions to them, do what fits into their action (RS 139).

Reduced to an economic measure, we lose the sense of our "hidden self . . . with a small seed of integrity, a haunting sense of unity and of universal responsibility" (RS 139), and we lose awareness of our connectedness to the "radical action" (RS 110) by which we come into existence and are sustained as a self.

The social analysis, potential in Niebuhr's ethics, understands what is going on by interpreting every particular issue within the universal context of full spatial breadth and temporal stretch. From such an inclusive perspective, grounded, to be sure, in one's own specific location, each particular is seen as having its true meaning as part of a whole, and any particular can be recognized as oppressive whenever it presents itself as the whole, wherever it denies meanings to parts other than in relationship to itself and according to its own imposed definitions.

But such complexity exceeds the capacity of anyone to figure out the appropriate response to all of it. Our figuring must then be shaped by response to yet another action in each situation upon us. Dealing with the particular demand for a wage increase in the midst of this timefull cosmic context, both capitalist and worker are enjoined to look for the immanent divinity intending transformation and fittingness as it acts on us amidst the multiple actions of the situation. To respond thus to the divinely intended redemptive whole of this given moment will bring a fitting response to this particular demand.[80]

Conclusion

While Niebuhr's considerations of social domination are incipient and fragmentary, there is inherent in the principles of responsibility ethics the basis for restructuring the radical critique of his liberal days into a much more comprehensively radical analysis of social oppression in its many forms. While he recognized the need to rethink his ethics in response to oppressive social forms, he did not live to develop a comprehensive statement. What he has achieved and can contribute to the current discussion is the conception of social transformation as spiritual.

His relational principles, which we have focused and organized, have potential fruitfulness for social analysis and praxis. To deal adequately with social injustice it must be approached relationally because the meaning of any social problem is contextual and theological (in the sense that we are in relationship to mystery which acts on us in every moment). Within this spiritual, relational approach, what is distinctive is his hermeneutical method that interprets a social issue through multiple languages and perspectives as a part of an encompassing spatial and temporal whole. In this whole, God as a universally pervasive presence acts on each self and the entire community of being, eliciting fitting response. While no solution within this framework is as simple or as certain as the teleological or deontological approaches that decide by imposing the abstract structures of a clear goal or law, it will work more adequately with goal and law by incorporating them as responses within its larger whole.

Responsibility ethics nurtures greater sensitivity to all the needs involved as it seeks to understand from multiple perspectives, greater inclusiveness as it naturally transcends all boundaries to the totality of being, greater flexibility as it reacts afresh in every new moment to the ever changing pattern of relatedness, greater humility as it recognizes our responses to these patterns emerge out of mysterious depths acting on us beyond our knowing and control, and greater engendering of life and social well-being as it mends through attention to the relational weave the fabric of being.

CHAPTER NINE

THE CHURCH AS CHRISTOMORPHIC COMMUNITY

What then is the nature of the community of Christian life from the theo-ethical perspective of responsibility? How does the church, illuminated by this metaphor, bear within itself seeds for transformation both of social and individual forms of oppression and of resistance to fittingness and divine immanence? The communal identity of a life of Christian action is self-consciously shaped by the symbolic form of Jesus Christ. It is a community of response to self, world, and God, and therefore a community simultaneously of reflection and action. It thinks about and manifests its relatedness to self, world, and God in its own distinctive style of action. Although Niebuhr wrote a classic statement about the nature of the church in 1956, he did not gather together his many subsequent insights from his culminating perspective into a comprehensive rethinking of the nature of the church and its interconnectedness with--not separateness from nor superiority to--the world.

We seek in this last chapter, as in other aspects of his ethics of responsibility, to discern the larger pattern and direction in the various particulars of his thinking. We will gather into a whole his insights about the church within the metaphor of responsibility, incorporating both his incipient and our imagined reworkings of a responsible approach to social domination from the previous two chapters. We will explore the nature of the church in its communal identity as transformative action as it lives in and relates to the world.

A Phenomenology of the Christian Life

While his preconversion work with diverse social thinkers began his thinking about the self in its social relatedness, Niebuhr's conversion reconfigured his whole theo-ethical orientation in relational terms based on the immanent sovereignty of God and the interconnectedness of self and world in reciprocal interaction.   Throughout much of his postconversion thought, however, he developed this relational perspective within a historicized dualism (e.g. "inner" and "outer history"). Even though sensing its restrictiveness, it was not until his last few years that he explicitly transcended this dualism (see MR 65-66 & 81-83, and RS 82-83).

Thus, when we look at his most complete statement on the nature of the church, *The Purpose of the Church and Its Ministry*, we find him using in 1956 the dualistic categories of subject and object in order to define the church as "the subjective pole of the objective rule of God" (PCM 19). This dualistic approach assumes separateness between church and God:

> The Church . . . is always distinct from its Object. It is integral to the self-consciousness of such a subject that it distinguishes itself from its Object. . . . Definition of subject and object are correlative. What the Church is as subject cannot be stated without some description of the Object toward which it is directed. Though an object is independent of a subject, yet it is inaccessible as it is in itself. What is accessible and knowable is so only from a certain point of view and in a certain relation (PCM 19-20).

In defining the nature of the church explicitly, he is thinking in "critical" categories of the subject-church separate from the object-God, who is independent and inaccessible in his own being, yet knowable from a certain historical (that is, relational) point of view.

The ensuing discussion in *Purpose of the Church* of church, world, and God, nevertheless, affirms the inherent interrelatedness of being as Niebuhr treats the church as a community of selves interconnected with each other and the world, and its purpose as the increase among persons of the inclusive love of God and neighbor. This tension between the conceptual sharp dichotomizing and the actual relating of God, church, and world is overcome in the later ethics of responsibility: there he consistently affirms the inherent relationality of all being; defines the church in triadic rather than dualistic terms, connecting it inextricably with the world; and conceives God as acting in every moment upon us in our churchly, worldly, and individual existence.

Niebuhr's culminating thought on the church is a phenomenology of the Christian life that transcends dualistic separateness (whether subject/object, mind/body, or spirit/matter) and its oppressive hierarchical organization of superior and inferior. This phenomenology seeks a fittingness, beyond all injustice and alienation, of action and re-action between church, world, and God.

Toward a Definition of the Church

Within the perspective of responsibility the church is that part of the total community of being that recognizes and accepts this interrelatedness as shaped by the symbolic form of Jesus Christ. In his Prologue to *The Responsible Self*, he defines a Christian as "a follower of Jesus Christ" (RS 43). Regardless of how Jesus Christ is defined--as sacrificial atonement, incarnate Logos, moral exemplar, or spiritual presence--and regardless of the person's moral quality and spiritual proximity to Jesus, a Christian is one who has been shaped by the presence and cause of Jesus Christ in history, and who accepts that presence and identifies with that cause.

The purpose of the Christian, the cause of Jesus Christ, is "the reconciliation of man to God," which is "the establishment of friendship between God and man--between the power by which all things are and this human race of ours" (RS 43-44). Speaking in the first person, Niebuhr says:

> Jesus Christ is for me, as for many of my fellow Christians, the one who lived and died and rose again for this cause of bringing God to men and men to God and so also of reconciling men to each other and to their world. The establishment of this friendship is to me the key problem in human existence. Because through Jesus Christ--his fate--as well as by him--that is, his ministry--this has become evident to me; because in him I see the prospect of my own reconciliation; because I have been challenged to make this cause my own--therefore I call myself a Christian. (RS 44).

The church is therefore the body of persons who are followers of Jesus Christ as reconciler, establisher of friendship between divinity and humanity and between persons. This does not assume superiority--moral, intellectual, spiritual--to non-Christians but an intentional involvement with Jesus Christ. The followers are not ideal but actual, not a disembodied spiritual society but real people living in the world, in fellowship with certain other followers through institutional forms of the church and in connection, as well, with those who are not followers. They are caught up in life as the action of establishing friendship which has within it the potential of overcoming all forms of domination through establishing friendship among persons, between persons and the world, and with God.

In his Earl Lectures Niebuhr articulates this in symbolic terms. The church is the community shaped by the symbolic form of Jesus Christ, through which it apprehends other selves: "With the use of the symbolic form of Jesus Christ, the Christian--consciously or unconsciously--apprehends, interprets, and evaluates his fellow man." Through this form it apprehends God as well:

> As with the apprehension, understanding, and evaluation of the fellow man so it is with the apprehension or the understanding of God, . . . Jesus Christ is the symbolic figure without which the Christian can no longer imagine, or know, or believe in the Determiner of Destiny, or the final end, or the ultimate source, or the last environment to which he is related in all his relations (RS 155).

This is an unconscious as well as conscious shaping. In fact, "[w]hen it is least conscious it may, indeed, be most effective. It seems even true that the symbol is highly effective among many men who are not consciously Christian at all." While "[s]ymbol and reality participate in each other," the Christian "stops short of identifying symbol and actuality." The symbolic form is formative; it informs the Christian's and church's life. Hence Niebuhr speaks of the Christian viewing the self as a "Christo-morphic being": "The needy companion is not wholly other than Christ, though he is not Christ himself. He is a Christo-morphic being, apprehended as in the form of Christ, something like Christ, though another" (RS 155). Applying this to the entire body of followers of Jesus Christ, we can speak of the church as the Christomorphic community, the community knowingly and willingly--however inadequately, and also unconsciously--formed and transformed by the symbol of Jesus Christ.

Christ forms this community towards the increase of love, as Niebuhr said in the mid-1950s, but also towards the acknowledgement and deepening of faith and hope. The Christ-formed community is, therefore, shaped by the theological virtues. But as we have seen at the end of Chapter Six, the so-called theological and natural virtues are not separate from each other but are all "true activity of a personal capacity for response" (*FHL* 153) to God's action. We can say then that the church is a Christomorphic fabric of virtues, of relational responsiveness--in fact and aspiration. Its purpose of friendship or reconciliation weaves together theological and natural virtues--not in a way more virtuous necessarily than other communities--as a Christomorphic tapestry. Committed to reconciliation, it carries within itself, often buried deep, the commitment to transform self and world: to actualize in fullness the "small seed of integrity, a haunting sense of unity and of universal responsibility" (RS 139); to transcend "our closed societies" and "our passionate devotion to limited causes that [have] involved us in conflict with others equally passionate in their restricted loyalties" (RS 142); to be freed from the "dominion over us" of the "ways of thinking" of capitalism and nationalism, "the manias that possess whole peoples for long periods," the "superpersonal forces of evil" (RS 139); to respond fittingly--to be meet, consentaneous, and becoming--within "the universal society of being" (RS 107).

The church is defined neither in terms of proclamation of the Word nor administration of the sacraments, although word, sacrament, and institutional structuring are intrinsic to its community. Rather, it is defined by dialogue which through word and ritual shares experience of Word and world with others: not words of dogmatic theological speech from a single perspective but multiple languages from variegated perspectives, not of conceptual talk alone but of story-telling and of poetic symbols and images as well; and not sacraments as institutional rites merely but as ritually evoked experience of the real presence of God. Niebuhr does not talk about the church as mediator, repository, or witness of the plan of salvation or the mighty acts of God; responsibility eschews the hegemonic and heroic in the everydayness and intimacy of its relationality.

A Community of Responsibility

Transforming defensiveness and domination, living into the fullness of fittingness, the church is a community of responsibility. While Niebuhr does not make the explicit connection, it is evident that the church manifests the four characteristics of responsibility (RS 61-65). It is, first of all, a community of response. It exists in relations: interconnected with self, others, the social and natural worlds, organic and inanimate, God, and the full sweep of time, personal, social, natural, and divine. Within this matrix of relations the church is active, re-acting to actions upon it from within and from without, changing in response to actions upon it.

Secondly, the church is a community of interpretation. Consciously, but also deep in buried memories, feelings, and intuitions, the church is aware of realities as events acting on it, relating them in patterns so as to grasp their meaning, understanding them as parts of wholes, symbolic of larger meanings. The church, thirdly, is a community in time, anticipating actions upon it in reaction to its own reactive actions, accountable to past and future interpreted events, participating in ongoing dialogue with itself, world, and immanent divinity. Finally, the church is a community of solidarity, maintaining a continuity of identity in its diversity of actions and interpretations, a constancy of relating to the community of agents acting upon and within it over time, yet transformable in response to new, or newly understood, divine action.

The Christian Ethos

The six principles we have discerned in Niebuhr's ethics and in the symbolic form of Jesus Christ are embodied in the common life of the church as the Christian ethos. The church is attentive, to one degree or another, to divine intentional agency. While he speaks in *Purpose of the Church* of this as "the objective rule of God," he speaks in the ethics of responsibility of God as the One Action acting upon us in every moment in the midst of the world's multifarious actions upon us. To this immanent One Action the church responds, interpreting it as Creator, Orderer, and Redeemer, expressing its own experience of a faithfulness in things.

The church lives within a larger context. Finding God at work, in one way or another, in relation to it, the church relates itself to divinity and to the world as God's world in a way that intends to fit the divine intention. For all of its exclusivism and dualistic rejection and domination of parts of God's creation, the church aspires to actualize an inclusive commonwealth of justice and love, the kingdom of God, the community of being.

While diversely defined and haltingly enacted, liberation is ingredient in the Christian commonweal. Not merely a "freedom from" but a "freedom for," liberation is most fundamentally a "freedom of" being, not only of the individual but of the corporate fellowship, with a universal intent toward a freeing up of the whole world, toward establishing friendship where there has been domination and alienation. Such freedom is always limited by God, neighbor, and relational matrix of the world, yet in relation to these limits there is always the possibility of--indeed, demand for--transformation. The church is a community of *metanoia*. All members know they are different for participating in the body of the church. For all of its recalcitrance and endorsement of the status quo, it knows itself to be under the pressure of divine presence (whether understood as near and immediate or distant and mediated) to respond to the mysterious depths of divinity and to be changed.

The church is a community of people on the way to being integrated. It would not exist institutionally without some degree of integrity. It knows its own identity as shaped by its relation to God. It knows the fragments of itself are brought into coherence through divine action and human response, and that its coherences are unwoven, shredded, in the reweavings of divine agency that engender hope amidst pain.

Finally, the church lives with the intention of responding to the One Action by meeting the needs of its fellow creatures. As Niebuhr says in *Purpose of the Church*: the church's goal is "the increase among men of the love of God and neighbor" (PCM 31). But as we have seen, love is bound up with faith and hope, and these three are intertwined with the so-called four classical natural virtues of courage, temperance, justice, and prudence, as well as others such as patience, endurance, and humility (*FHL* 152), so that the common life of Christians is a rich weave of virtue, distinctive in its style but in no way inherently superior to the warp and woof of other religious communities. Love, faith, and hope are embodied in these six principles of the Christian ethos seen through responsibility; thus his earlier perspectives culminate in a vision of the church as a common life of faith, hope, and love (see PCM 31-33 & 39), manifest to some degree, aspiring to greater freshness and fullness.

A Bible-Informed Community

At the end of his Prologue to *The Responsible Self*, he says "my approach is not Bible-centered, though I think it is Bible-informed." While there are those who would define the church as Bible-centered and exclude those who disagree, we can, using this clue, define it more broadly as a community given form and being formed by the Bible. To be so informed is to affirm the historicity of the Bible and of the people who use it. As he says: "I find myself . . . ill at ease with theologians who deal with the Scriptures as a nonhistorical book and undertake to explain it as though they were nonhistorical men" (RS 46).

In his Earl Lectures he elucidates what he means by the historicity of the Bible. While it certainly means that the Bible was constructed by various people influenced by their times and places, and that this writing of the past influences our present, it also means concreteness. This is evident as Christians "turn to the Hebrew Scriptures, especially to the prophets and the Psalms, not only as writings which point beyond themselves to Christ but as books that give concreteness and filling to the ethos exemplified in Jesus." While many Christians look at the Hebrew Bible in such a way as to see it foreshadowing the coming of Christ, he suggests a very different function: to draw us into the actual texture of everyday existence in which we experience God acting upon us. Opposed to the typological method, in which the Hebrew text is emptied of its historical density of human existence in order to point to Christ, he says: "One may even say the Old Testament fulfills the New for them [Christians] in practice, and not only the New the Old" (RS 168).

The Hebrew Scriptures fulfill the Christian because the Hebraic embodies "an ethos of universal responsibility" in a great variety of specific life-situations. Niebuhr shows this in the stories of Joseph in relation to his brothers and Isaiah in relation to Assyria where in the concreteness of the accounts the difference yet interconnectedness is evident "between the particular intentions that guide a finite action and the divine intention that uses or lies behind such actions." He concludes: "the logic of Hebrew ethics . . . is a way of universal responsibility because there is no action in the whole extent of actuality in which the universal intention, the meaning of the One beyond the many, is not present" (RS 168-70).

While Christians, contrary to belief in incarnation, all too often etherealize Christ, transcending his concreteness to focus on the doctrinal and metaphysical truths about him, Niebuhr sees scripture informing the church by drawing us back into the concreteness of our existence, because that is where God is to be found acting on us. Scripture, in presenting the historical actuality of people's lives simultaneously, functions symbolically: "For history may function as myth or as symbol. . . . When we grasp our present, not so much as a product of our past, but more as essentially revealed in that past, then the historical account is necessarily symbolic; it is not merely descriptive of what was once the case" (RS 156). Thinking causally, the particulars of the past are what produced our present; thinking symbolically, the particulars of the past disclose the structures and significance of our present existence.

Scripture as revelatory concreteness is a deep well of imagery: "It is impossible to describe with any adequacy the variety and richness of the imagery derived by Christians from the story of Jesus and employed by them not only in their descriptive language but in their apprehensions, evaluations, and decisions." While the story of Jesus for Christians is "a fundamental, indispensable metaphor," it is one among other symbolic forms in scripture. Niebuhr rejects Karl Barth's Christocentric exclusiveness since "he cannot interpret the meaning of Jesus Christ without the aid of other metaphors and symbols such as Word of God, Son of God, Servant, Lord, covenant, humiliation, exaltation, reconciliation, salvation" (RS 156-58).

To speak of being Bible-informed suggests the need to indwell this richness of symbolic concreteness in story and figure in order to be able to interpret what God is doing in our present lives. Using a distinction from his earlier work, we can say Niebuhr's approach looks *with*, rather than *at*, the Bible (MR 73). The Bible-centered approach draws out a fixed notion from the density of the text and sets it up as an object to be conformed to. The Bible-informed approach indwells that density and through unconscious creativity draws from it to interpret consciously what is going on. While the Bible-centered view attends to an idea and seeks to conform to it, the Bible-informed method attends to divine action and seeks creatively to make sense of it. Consistent with his conversion, the Bible-informed approach only makes sense if you believe that God is at work in the concreteness of the here and now, and that our task is fitting response. If God is not present, then we can only be grateful for a God-given idea to which to conform. But God's presence is the basis of Niebuhr's ethics of response, so the scripture is a deep well of metaphor and symbol in historical narrative; with it, he looks at what is happening now and learns how to respond to God within all of being.

Church and World in Triadic Perspective

Niebuhr in his preconversion liberal days saw the church's relation to the world as compromise of Christian ideals. After his conversion, he saw the church as prophetically standing against the world (such as in *The Church Against the World*) seeking to bring it into accord with divine sovereignty. Finally, he came increasingly to realize the implications of his conversion affirmation of being as prior to ideals; the church exists in relation to the world as its context.

In the 1940s and 1950s he articulates this relationship in the language of the "both/and" of transformation. The church is necessarily both community and institution; both protestant, protesting the confusion of symbol with symbolized, self with God, and catholic, affirming the catholic "principle of incarnation," that "the Infinite is represented in finite form" (PCM 25); and both church and part of the world. Transformation seeks to maintain the balance in these polarities. Church and world interact and both are being transformed by God.

To this both/and approach the metaphor of responsibility adds a third element. No longer a polar reality set alongside the church, the world becomes context for our existing as individuals, social beings, and members of the church. The church, like other social groups, exists in response relations within the entire world. God is present, not only within the church, as in Niebuhr's liberal thought, but within the world acting on individual and society, seeking to elicit response to the One particular yet universal Action in each moment.

In place of two discrete entities, church and world, relating to each other, the church exists in triadic relations. The church, like the Christian, and every person, exists simultaneously in relation to nature and society, encountering each in the context of the other; it exists in relation to God and nature, and to God and society; within society it exists in relation to its own companions and their cause, which, as the divine center of the world, takes them beyond the church's boundaries to the community of being:

> as I respond in the church I respond to my companions, that is, to the fellowship of the members of the church. They have taught me the language, the words, the logic of religious discourse. But the discourse is not about them, it is about a third. To these fellow members I am challenged to be faithful, but not otherwise than in faithfulness to the common cause. That common cause is represented to me by the prophets and apostles. Yet they point beyond themselves. And even when I find that I can be responsible in the church only as I respond to Jesus Christ, I discover in him one who points beyond himself to the cause to which he is faithful and in faithfulness to which he is faithful to his companions--not the companions encountered in the church, but in the world to which the Creator is faithful, which the Creator has made his cause.
>
> To the monotheistic believer for whom all responses to his companions are interrelated with his responses to God as the ultimate person, the ultimate cause, the center of universal community, there seem to be indications in the whole of the responsive, accountable life of men of a movement of self-judgment and self-guidance which cannot come to rest until it makes its reference to a universal other and a universal community, which that other both represents and makes his cause (RS 86-87).

To exist in a three-way connection means that while the church attends to one reality, it is tacitly relating to the other, and, hence, relating to the one in the context of the other. Since there are several triads in which the church exists simultaneously, there are several tacit connections in which the church exists. Its identity is not as a discrete entity set over against the world but is relational, participating in the natural world, the social world, and its companions' causes, ultimately God, "the center of universal community" (RS 86).

A Community of Reflection:
The Trinity in Worldly Relatedness

The church in its triadic relatedness is a community inseparably of reflection and action. Rejecting the theoretical/practical dichotomy (RS 82-83) of the "critical world," Niebuhr shows how interpretation and action are inextricably intertwined in responsibility. Every action involves interpretation, even if largely tacit; every interpretation is itself a response, and therefore a re-action to action upon us, whether through establishing an attitude or doing a deed. Among many reasons why Niebuhr was both an ethicist and a theologian is that he refuses to separate Christ and culture, spiritual from social concerns, our being in response to God and our being in response to the world. To think about society and divine action--in interaction from the church's own perspective--is the provenance of the church.

Within his ethics of responsibility we have seen the rich panoply of his theological thought--the nature of God, self, sin, Christ, and church. We add now a brief word about the trinity from within his relational perspective of the church in the world. That he has little to say about it is symptomatic of his postcritical ethical perspective that refuses to break loose into speculation divorced from the texture of our actual living. In what he does say, there is a noticeable change at the end of his life as he moves into the matrix of responsibility.

In the 1950s he briefly explores the trinity and comes up with what he calls a "binitarian formula":

> *Spirit*, rather than being a third personal principle in the Deity, is an attribute of the two persons in the Godhead and that which makes it possible for us to be selves with them. We are thus led to a kind of binitarian formula; God is Father and Son in two persons. The Spirit is that which, being of the very nature of God, is given and matured and restored to human persons. It is the principle of community among selves who are united in trust and loyalty to Father and to Son. But

> Spirit on the basis of this analysis is not person in the sense in which
> Father and Son are (FE 105; his italics).

This relegation of the Spirit to secondary status in the trinity may be the result of residual dualism in his thinking: Father and Son are Subject and Object, both discrete entities. Between subject and object in a "critical" framework there is no third option, so the Spirit is an attribute of either or both. On the other hand, he conceives the Spirit as "interpersonal reality," "consubstantial with Father and Son. What we cannot say for ourselves is that the Spirit is not the Father, that he is not the Son, and that he is equal to Father and Son--as a power or a person like them but distinct from them" (FE 108). Possibly here Niebuhr conceives a third reality, not objective but relational, even though subordinated to the objective.

In any case, he comments that "[t]rinitarian belief may indeed seem speculative" if it is "founded on analyses we have not ourselves made." He has expressed what his experience has been but recognizes

> the doctrine of the Holy Spirit appears on all the pages of the New
> Testament which testify to the experience of spiritual power quite
> different from that with which we are familiar. Moreover all the
> Christian mystics in all times speak to us of an experience of the Holy
> Spirit which again is not the normal experience of a great number of
> Christians (FE 106-07).

Because others have experienced the Holy Spirit, he is "not in a position to deny that the classic formulation is true" but asserts its truth, not out of trust in God, but loyalty to the church, as an expression of "our secondary but real loyalty to the community of faith" (FE 108).

From the perspective of responsibility at the very end of his life, however, where he has explicitly rejected dualism, he begins to talk of the Spirit in different terms as equal to the Father and Son, although he does not discuss it at the length he does in *Faith on Earth*. As he develops much more the reality of the relational and tacit, he distinguishes Christ and the whole-making spirit moving in the depths. For a Christian:

> Jesus Christ, too, is the symbolic figure with which he understands or
> apprehends the ultimate spirit that moves in the depths of his life and of
> all creation. He tests the spirits to see if among all the forces that move
> within him, his societies, the human mind itself, there be a uniting, a
> healing, a knowing, a whole-making spirit, a Holy Spirit. And he can

do so only with the aid of the image, the symbol of Christ. "Is there a Christ-like spirit there?" (RS 155).

Here the Spirit is the ultimate depths in self and world that is reconciling and knowing being.

From this perspective it would be possible to go on to speak of a full trinitarian reality as Action acting upon us and all being, the Symbolic Form of Jesus Christ, and Whole-Making Depth--or as Agent, Form, and Mystery. Recognizing the problematic nature of "person-talk" and all substantialistic categories, and avoiding by its ungenderedness the problem of exclusive masculine language for God, this incipient trinitarian conception is appropriate to his development of responsibility in its transcendence of dualism and its affirmation of relational reality.

Niebuhr's trinity is relational, not because he would ever engage in speculation about the inter-trinitarian dynamic within the Godhead, but because he experiences the inherent interconnectedness of divine presence and the world in multiple aspects from the perspective of the Christomorphic community. Immanent divinity is encountered as Action impacting on each of us and as Mysterious Depth engendering wholeness. Through the shaping power of the symbolic form of Jesus Christ we understand that Action and Depth weave us together not only with fellow Christians in the church but with all other people and all creatures in God's community of being, and that we are called to ongoing transformation of ourselves and society toward fittingness of being to being in general. The trinity emerges then in reflections within the church on our experiences in the world--experiences of divine action, of the symbolic gestalt of Jesus Christ, and of transforming integration. We can experience within the Christian ethos ourselves being acted upon by the One, interpreting this action under the shaping by the symbolic form of Jesus Christ, and knowing ourselves being gathered toward wholeness and unity in and by the ultimate depths.

The Church as Christomorphic Community

The relational communities of Niebuhr's postcritical ethics display the social implications of his conversion to divine sovereignty. God is present acting on me, other selves, and other creatures within the world to transform us from unfittingness and irresponsibility into responsive fittingness within human society and the entire community of being. The world is the full extent of space and time as context for God's restructuring action, eliciting our connectedness and fitting integration with all being. The church, shaped by the symbolic form of Jesus Christ, is the community which dwells wittingly within the matrix of being, seeking to respond in every moment to the divine action upon it in the world so as to manifest consciously, and unconsciously, fittingness in all its relations to God and world.

Grasped, shaped, pervaded, transformed by the gestalt of grace and the glory of being (RS 175-76), the church is Christomorphic community. Sharing in God's cause, understood through the symbolic form of Christ as reconciliation and the establishment of friendship between all humans and God and God's world, Christians are "empowered to become sons of God." They are

> not as those who are saved out of a perishing world but as those who know that the world is being saved. That its being saved from destruction involves the burning up of an infinite amount of tawdry human works, that it involves the healing of a miasmic ocean of disease, the resurrection of the dead, the forgiveness of sins, the making good of an infinite number of irresponsibilities (RS 177).

Salvation means, not the guarantee of an otherworldly reality, but the transformation of our present existence, the healing and making good of all our distorted, divided, defensive responses in our actual individual and social, political, economic lives. Salvation means being at home in the world: "When he feels and knows himself to be a son of God, an heir in the universe, at home in the world, he knows this sonship, this at-homeness, as not only like Jesus Christ's but as actualized by him" (RS 176). To be at home in the world is to apprehend the glory of being. About this glory Niebuhr says earlier:

> there is in the background of existence, whether as memory of childhood, or as Platonic recollection of something heard in another existence, or as the echo of an inner voice, the sense of something glorious, splendid, clean and joyous for which this being and all being is intended. . . . The promise of life is the promise of glory and splendor, not for me, but for existence and for me as a part of this world of being (FE 80).

To be the children of God is to realize this sense of something glorious, to open to the splendor of divinely pervaded being.

But this does not mean that the church displays more Christ-like lives than other communities, that there is in it a superiority of moral life: "Thus Christians understand themselves and their ethos, or somewhat in this fashion. They cannot boast that they have an excellent way of life for they have little to point to when they boast" (RS 177). Neither is it unique. As an

> ethos of universal responsibility . . . [i]t has affinities to other forms of universal ethics. Insistence on the absolute uniqueness of the Christian ethos has never been able to meet either the theoretical or the practical test. In practice, Christians undertaking to act in some fashion in conformity with Christ find themselves doing something like what some others, conforming to other images, are doing. Identity of action there has not been; likeness, however, has often been present. (Christians have had no monopoly on humanitarianism or concern for those suffering deprivation; in reverence for life they have often been excelled by others.) On the theoretic side, when Christians have undertaken to set forth the pattern present in the action of Christ they have found kinship between it and certain patterns of moral conduct set forth by universalist philosophers [such as Platonic, Aristotelian, Kantian, or utilitarian] (RS 167-68).

The church is not even unique in being Christomorphic. Niebuhr uses this term to speak of the needy companion who is not just another Christian, but any and every person seen in the light of Christ: "The needy companion is not wholly other than Christ, though he is not Christ himself. He is a Christo-morphic being, apprehended as in the form of Christ, something like Christ, though another" (RS 155). The church is, then, the community from within which the whole world can be seen as Christomorphic. It is the community of interpretation in which all events are encountered through the symbolic form of Jesus Christ, which means they are "included in universal action," within the universal society of being and time (RS 167); yet this interpretation is not imperialistically imposed upon but dialogically shared with others. To live in the church responsibly is always to be living beyond the church in the community of being. It is to be willingly caught up in God's ongoing transformative action, who through the complex symbolic form of Jesus Christ empowers this community (among others) to trust and hope in and to love that power which is the "whole in which we live and move and have our being" (RS 88; see 44, 140, & 153).

The Christomorphic community of the church is a community of love. To love is to meet the needs of others. To meet the needs of the needy companion is to engage in the transforming of our social, political, and economic structures to make them responsive to those needs, not only the subsistence needs of food, shelter, medical assistance, livelihood, but those needs for dignity and fulfillment as selves in the social, natural, and spiritual matrix of being. Beyond need-meeting and enhancing being, there is that love moving in our depths which is leading us to celebrate and adore, so that we feel ourselves "falling in love, we think, with being itself" (RS 177-78).

The church is also a community of hope for life: "the hope of that life of universal responsibility, of citizenship in the country of being itself, of reaction in all reactions to the God of grace, to the grace which is God" (RS 176). It hopes for transformation of our disintegrating lives from disease, oppression, tawdriness, and the irresponsibilities of defending against certain relations that are part of us. It hopes to achieve a wholeness in ourselves and in the world that will bring all into fitting relations beyond the humanly distorting, sinful structures of our individual and corporate existence. But the hope for transformation is not merely because of our sinful difficulties; being is dynamic, ever changing, so we ongoingly hope to meet the challenge to respond afresh in every new moment to befit what is happening to us in the world and in the divine action ever anew acting upon us. And we hope for glory: "The hope of glory does enter into being" (RS 176); we hope to be opened to the splendor of being in our midst.

Thirdly, the Christomorphic community is a community of trust. Within it we can "confess--we were blind in our distrust of being, now we begin to see" (RS 177). Animosity toward the power by which we are is our usual state: "God is enemy; he destroys our world and ideals, which are ultimately condemned to decay. But now I am being reconciled to the enemy. . . . If the last end is death or the gallows, thrown on the dung heap of the world, then we have most reason to defy God, to become Marcionite. But Jesus Christ was not thrown on the dung heap of the world." Reconciliation for Christians is "in the cross and resurrection." The transition occurs "by action of revelation: we came from untrust and unknowing to confidence and knowing . . . [through] Jesus Christ who is revelation not only of the goodness of power but of power itself" (*CE[RMK]* March 15, 1961). Within it we are part of a "people who participate in some slight way in this attitude to absolute power and sovereignty: . . . to be determined by trust, [to participate in] the transition from God as enemy to God as friend, from anxiety to reliance on ultimate power, . . . the power which tries to bring into fullness of being what it has created" (*CE[RMK]* March 15, 1961).

Seeking to overcome the systems of domination can come from defiance against the apparent meaninglessness and destructiveness of the way of the world, and thus of its God, and from the counter affirmation of the value of all human lives. But Niebuhr calls us deeper to discover the trust in being without which we would not be, and to trust that committing ourselves to live in accord with it will bring us into fitting relations not just with all other humans but with all beings. As long as we are alienated from some realm of being, there will be domination, for we will seek to subjugate that realm in ourselves by projecting it onto others--whether earthiness, mortality, or strangeness. Not only to achieve equity but to establish friendship is to come to "the conviction that we are surrounded in history by life and not by death, by the power of being not by ultimate destructiveness." It is to choose life and life more abundantly for ourselves and for all peoples and to share in "the central work of revising our mythology of death into a history of life . . . redefining . . . what is fitting response in a lifetime and a history surrounded by eternal life, as well as by the universal society of being" (RS 107).

The church is the Christomorphic community of responsive relatedness to all being, formed and transformed by the symbolic form of Jesus Christ: that loves actual and particularized being and desires to love it more fully; that hopes for transformation of self and world beyond all injustice, social domination, and irresponsibility into the fittingness of interrelatedness; and that has faith in the power in which we live and move and have our being, that it is sustaining, transforming, integrating, liberating, and need-meeting--that being itself is trustworthy.

CONCLUSION:

A RELATIONAL ETHICS OF LIBERATING SPIRITUALITY

We have been exploring H. Richard Niebuhr's theological ethics from his early years through his conversion from idealism to realism and onto their culmination in the relational ethics of responsibility. Of the unfinished thoughts of his maturity we have endeavored to show what in fact he has said and to give voice to views that would seem to be the outcome of the trajectory of his thinking. Many questions remain, however. Having addressed the feminist critique of his view of divine sovereignty, and the questions how his ethics are a guide to action, whether they are a genuine alternative to the two traditional Aristotelian and Kantian ethics, the manner in which they are Christian, and what their bearing is towards liberation theology's concern for theo-social analysis of forms of social oppression--still there is more we want to know.

We have drawn out the context, process, and principles of decision-making to show how the ethics of responsibility are a guide to action; yet there remains an abstractness. While Niebuhr rightly preserves each person's responsibility to make decisions in response to the divine action upon them, we want to see examples that would model people making decisions, or even himself making decisions, to help us understand more concretely the meaning of his principles and how God acts on us. His own theme of story-telling, so suggestively developed in *The Meaning of Revelation*, but absent from *The Responsible Self*, could have effectively been combined with the action of responsibility.

We have shown how responsibility ethics as relational is different from the teleological and deontological rationalisms of classical ethics. He has said clearly that response ethics does not exclude goals and laws but incorporates them in the larger interpretive context of our living. Nevertheless, we want to know how they function within responsibility. Again, working with decisions about concrete issues would model how goals and laws are to be used responsibly.

We have seen how Niebuhr's ethics are Christian in an altered context. No longer separating self from God, world, and its own agency and use of language, they are Christian within a relational rather than dualistic framework. As we have seen, the relational is existentialist--as Niebuhr deals with the self in its existing; phenomenological--as he attends to the actual situation that existing selves inhabit; postcritical--as he discovers selves to exist beyond the "critical" framework that separates mind and body, spirit and nature, and to dwell rather within relations to self, society, nature, and an immanent God; and hermeneutical--as he focuses on the meaning and power of language, especially on metaphor and symbol, through which we interpret our being, and what is going on, in the world. Within this relational orientation, Niebuhr's ethics are Christian as they are shaped centrally, but not solely, by the symbolic form of Jesus Christ as both paradigm and evocative agent of responsibility. Through the revelatory power of this multi-facetted metaphor, divine reality is experienced as immanent action and interpreted in its intentions for myself (that is, for each self in the first person) in relation to the whole.

We have discussed Niebuhr's view of justice and love, shown his engagement with the forms of social oppression of war, racism, and classism, and considered the potential fruitfulness of his thinking for sexism, environmentalism, and anti-Judaism. We have traced the shift of his concern about war and economic injustice from the center of attention to the periphery in the mid-1940s, his recognition that he needed to rethink these and other social issues in the light of his responsibility perspective, his beginning to talk of, even though not to develop, them in the language of responsibility, and the potential in responsibility thinking for conceiving a method of transformative theo-social analysis.

Nevertheless, we have found no evidence that had Niebuhr lived he would have developed the social dimension of responsibility into social praxis, the actual changing of the material and social conditions of our lives and the articulation of a way to do this. Toward understanding this resistance in Niebuhr to the trajectory of his own responsibility thinking, we have gathered various clues at points where his ideas contradict his relational thinking. They bear on his relation to the world and the nature of the self. The abstractness, we have just remarked upon, in the absence of examples to show how to make decisions and how to use goals and laws within the framework of responsibility, links with several of these clues. We have seen in war, racism, and classism an abstraction that will not engage the particularities of a situation, the bodily and social differences of racial identities, and the material conditions and system of power of economic existence. And we have seen in environmentalism the abstraction in defining nature as thing-like. These movements toward abstraction are all connected with Niebuhr's commitments to the nonassertive, nonjudging, self-denying, self-controlling self because the nonassertive self is abstracted from all situations; an involved self is assertive. Amidst the particularities of a concrete situation a self is assertive in simply being there, inasmuch as it affects the other elements in the situation by taking up space and time; it is judging in sorting out its way of being in relation to these elements; and in being assertive and discriminating, it is neither denying of itself nor focused for the sake of control upon itself. In fact, a responsive act has just these characteristics as an energetic reaction based on an interpretation of the situation. The move to abstraction from the world and to the denial of the agency of the self severs the relatedness in which the responsible self exists in the world.

What all these clues point to is a still unexpunged presence of mind/body, spirit/nature dualism in which self and world are kept apart so that to be a self, one does not have to engage the concrete particularities of the world and of one's own body but can exist in nonassertive isolation. We have seen Niebuhr, however, overcome the "critical" mind/body dualism both theologically and philosophically. What he did not live to do was to overcome this dualism in his social ethics. The resources are there in his postcritical perspective of responsibility for him to accomplish ethically what he already has embarked upon theologically and philosophically. God is immanent in the world and constantly acting on the self rather than separate from self and world. And the self exists in relatedness, characterized by its elusive mystery, agency, creativity, embodiedness, emotions, and interpretive and symbol-using capacities. From within this context it is logical to extend this way of thinking ethically into an analysis of the socioeconomic aspects of this relatedness and thus into social praxis that seeks to affect the power dynamics from inhibiting to enabling the achievement of fittingness within the community of being.

There is no evidence, as Beverly Harrison put it, that he was "dissuaded . . . from pursuing his course" (Harrison 312), nor is there evidence that he in fact would have pursued it. All we can say is that he felt the need to rethink the social dimension of his ethics; having overcome "critical" dualism theologically (although he needs to develop further the interaction between divine and human) and philosophically through his deepening reflections on the self and language (although he needs to develop further the embodied and linguistic nature of the self), he could have gone on to make the same shift away from these recalcitrant elements in his ethical thinking to actualize the socioeconomic dimension in the relational nature of responsibility.

Nevertheless, amidst all these criticisms, we discern in Niebuhr's ethics of responsibility a fruitfulness now for our further thinking and a power of language evocative of greater religious and ethical awareness. His thinking is irrepressibly relational. He will not separate the theological and ethical, God and world, the making of decisions from the self's cosmic orientation. Persons are of more worth than ideas; ethical thinking is focused on the personal and is primarily interpretive of self and actions within a relational milieu. Its thinking is part-whole, seeing the self as a part of larger wholes, grasping the self in its potential wholeness (as conscious and unconscious, thinking and embodied, creative and receptive, individual and communal), and understanding God as the whole within which we live and move and have our being. Its thinking is not hierarchical, not patriarchal, not dominating of others nor subservient to God, not judgmental (measuring others by our standard, making either/or choices, focusing on boundaries), not perfectionistic (perfecting one capacity or virtue, such as obeying or striving, and subordinating all other capacities to its development).

The ethics of responsibility is aesthetic. In our discussion of fittingness in Chapter Five we have shown the unannounced presence of the aesthetic as central to his moral reflection, which distinguishes him from most western ethicists and allies him with his great American forebearer, Jonathan Edwards. Ethical thinking always goes on within an ethos, whose relatedness extends beyond our conscious knowing. To interpret what is going on requires a sensitivity (of feeling, bodily awareness, tacit knowing) beneath cognition that draws things sensed but not noticed into a gestalt of conscious knowing, that makes sense of the lived context of our choosing and being. This ethical sensing is like the everyday feel for dialogue in which meaning is grasped and expressed in more or less appropriate ways without the hegemony of conscious conceptual control. A decision is not a detached concept to be imposed on a situation but a pattern emergent from and with a network of unnoticed emotional relations to the realities of the moment. Such thinking based on moral sensibility is more caught than taught, shaped in communal relatedness. Like beauty there is a power of intrinsic worth in the pattern of a situation that pulls us on in our search to discover the pattern and what response of ours will fit within it. And like the functioning of beauty in science, the sensing of the fitting makes us feel in touch with the real as we tacitly grasp ingredients in the situation through their patterning. In this postcritical affirmation of non-objectifying thinking there is an important resource for imagining a form of liberation thinking that avoids the combative and dominating character of typical western reasoning.

Niebuhr's is an ethics of spirituality. If spirituality means living and maturing life in immediate contact with God, Niebuhr has made the direct presence of God to the self, articulated through an action model, the foundation of his ethics. The aesthetic sensitivity is focused not only on the feel of what is going on within the largest context but on sensing God's action in it. This then raises the question of spiritual discernment: what are the distinguishing marks (to take a phrase from Edwards) of God's active presence; and how do they correlate with the experience of the self?

Niebuhr has worked explicitly with this question in delineating within the symbolic form of Jesus Christ the characteristics of God's action on Jesus as creating, ordering, and redeeming, and has correlated Jesus's responses--attending to, affirming, and cultivating creation; accepting limiting actions from other beings as divine ordering; and opening in trust and love to all of creation while becoming the means of God's reconciling transformations of others. Yet there are other distinguishing marks implicit within Niebuhr's thinking beyond these three traditional modes of God's functioning that we can identify which will help to recognize the divine action on us.

The experience of divine action on us is fundamentally an encounter with mystery. While Niebuhr does not stress mystery in his action model, he nevertheless affirms it. We are acted on by that "Mystery behind the mystery of human existence" (PCM 36), by that "alien power by which it [the self] existed--the mystery of being" (RS 115; see 112-19), which touches us in the depths of our own hidden self beyond what we know and can control. The self presupposed in such encounter with divine mystery is itself fundamentally mystery. Divine mystery would appear undetectable and unreal from a dualistic perspective which recognizes only two kinds of reality, subjects and objects. The self that encounters (or is encountered by) this mysterious action and is capable of responding to it is a third reality, "mystery" (PCM 36)--what Niebuhr calls "elusive selves" (MR 64) and the "I am, and I am I" (RS 109), which is the uncognizable agency that I am--standing behind yet within everything I do that is knowable (see "Speaking of an Elusive Self" in Keiser, *Recovering* 113-32).

In the search to understand what is going on, the self interprets divine mystery as intending us to realize the universal in the particular, to act with our whole self from our particular place of the moment in a way befitting the one ultimate context of our being, and thus appropriate to all the finite actions upon us. This calls for a sensitivity beneath reason, a trust and humility beyond rational certitude, a hope in as yet unglimpsed possibilities; and calls up energy in its felt sense of engaging sacred reality.

Encountering such mysterious action, we experience inclusiveness drawing us towards fittingness amidst the whole, newness transforming us (letting go of the narrower understanding amidst the complexification of moving toward the inclusive), creativity integrating us (taking up the new into the newly forming pattern of the moment), whole-making engendering a comprehensive reinterpretation of ourselves in the world, and sustenance in meeting our needs. The six ethical principles we have discerned in Niebuhr correlate, then, with the marks of God and the effects of God on us; this is as it should be expected, since these principles emerge as gestalts from our experiencing the One action on us. The principle of God's immanent agency is evoked by experience of the sacred presence of mystery, fittingness by God's inclusiveness, transformation by the power of newness, integration by divinity's creativity, freedom by God's engendering whole-making, and need-meeting by ontological sustenance.

Niebuhr's spirituality-based ethics has significance for liberation both for seeing and changing structures of social oppression. While he did not develop a social power analysis, as we have seen, there is the potential within his thought to interpret what is happening socially within increasingly comprehensive contexts that is sensitive to aspects not noticed by the dominant view set forth by political reason. Responsibility as an ethical metaphor senses an event's or structure's unfittingness with its full relational matrix and grasps a redemptive potential as divinely intended in the particular situation. The scope makes the difference; within a narrow enough sphere the people suffering social oppression are not able to recognize they are part of a class dominated by a social system.

Niebuhr's way of questioning what is going on calls attention to whether the situation understood is encompassing, the self assumed is relational, and the divine looked for is immanently active. And it calls attention to the language being used in a situation. Is the language being used defensive or dialogical, commanding or collaborative, impositional or interactive, exclusive or inclusive, denying or affirming newness, attentive only to surface forms or as well to deep mystery, conforming to an idea of divinity or responding to actual presence? The hermeneutic character of Niebuhr's ethics, focused on interpretation and language within an inclusive context, carries a crucial element for liberation thought, since there is no possibility of changing oppression until it is recognized.

Once it is recognized, the prospects for constructive change depend in part on our understanding of social structures as such. If these are only the expression of human power, then only superior human power can remove them. The effect is, therefore, to shift the subjugating power from one location to another but still to be caught within a system of oppressive power. If, on the other hand, social structures are seen as human creations in response to divine mystery, as well as to other situational elements, then it is possible to loosen people's allegiance to oppressive structures by redirecting their attention to underlying mystery, to open them to different ways of responding to it and of structuring our social existence. If the mystery is understood as active itself, as Niebuhr does, not only is it possible for humans to repattern their ways of living in response to mystery, but the divine action is contributing to this repatterning by intending it and impacting people to bring it about.

Here is where the poetic power in Niebuhr's theo-ethics becomes crucial. The symbolic, metaphoric, dialogical, and mythic are modes of *poiesis* that can awaken us to the social structures of evil we have created and the divine intention and action among them; can shift our allegiance from the human forms to the divine source in relation to which we have created them; can make us aware of, give us hope for, and motivate us to discover new patterns of response to the divine action, which can result in more humane ways of dwelling together on this earth. It is in this sense of an ethics that is relational, aesthetic, spiritually meditative, and hermeneutic (indeed, theopoetic), I believe, that Niebuhr speaks at the end of his 1960 autobiographical essay of transforming society through a resymbolizing reformation of religion. "I look for a resymbolization of the message and the life of faith in the One God" (*Ref* 79), he says, for "we can neither grasp nor communicate the reality of our existence before God . . . unless one has direct relations in the immediacy of personal life to the actualities to which people in another time referred with the aid of such symbols." Agreeing "with both the prophets and, of all men, Karl Marx, that the reformation of religion is the fundamental reformation of society," he does not believe that the "'conquest' of space" or "the cessation of the cold war" will be very important "unless the human spirit is revived within itself" (*Ref* 80). Such spiritual revitalizing occurs for Niebuhr by turning, through the evocative, discerning, and symbolically formative power of religious language, to the divine mystery in the world acting on each person in every moment. Teaching us to respond fittingly in both individual and social patterns within the context of the entire community of being, the immanent divinity of mysterious action works towards human liberation from domination and is the roots of Niebuhr's relational ethics.

ABBREVIATIONS OF CITED WRITINGS BY NIEBUHR

ALR   "The Alliance Between Labor and Religion." *Theological Magazine of the Evangelical Synod of North America* 49 (1921): 197-203.

Aspect   "An Aspect of the Idea of God in Recent Thought." *Theological Magazine of the Evangelical Synod of North America* 48 (1920): 39-44.

Attack   "The Attack Upon the Social Gospel." *Religion in Life* 5 (1936): 176-81.

Attempt   "An Attempt at a Theological Analysis of Missionary Motivation." Paper presented April 1951. *Occasional Bulletin from the Missionary Research Library* 14.1 (January 1963): 1-6.

Back   "Back to Benedict?" *Christian Century* 42 (July 2, 1925): 860-61.

Buber   "Address on Dr. Martin Buber's 80th Birthday." Unpublished lecture, typed transcript, delivered at New York City (April 17, 1958): 1-10. Niebuhr Box 1, file 7.

Can   "Can German and American Christians Understand Each Other?" *Christian Century* 47 (July 23, 1930): 914-16.

CAW   *The Church Against the World.* H. Richard Niebuhr, Wilhelm Pauck, and F. P. Miller. Chicago, New York: Willet, Clark & Co., 1935. H. Richard Niebuhr, "The Question of the Church" and "Toward the Independence of the Church." 1-13 & 123-56. *Theology in America: The Major Protestant Voices from Puritanism to Neo-Orthodoxy.* Ed. Sydney E. Ahlstrom. Indianapolis and New York: Bobbs-Merrill Company, 1967. 590-618.

CC   *Christ and Culture.* New York: Harper & Brothers, 1951. Harper Torchbooks. New York: Harper & Brothers, 1956.

CCh   "The Christian Church in the World's Crisis." *Christianity and Society* 6 (1941): 11-17.

CE(EBK)   "Christian Ethics." Student lecture notes, handwritten by Elizabeth Bassett Keiser, delivered at Yale Divinity School, spring semester, 1961. 1-113.

CE(RMK)   "Christian Ethics." Student lecture notes, handwritten by R. Melvin Keiser, delivered at Yale Divinity School, spring semester, 1961. 1-58.

CE(YCE)   "Christian Ethics." Student lecture notes, transcribed by Robert Yetter, Gene Canestrari, and Ed Elliott, delivered at Yale Divinity School, spring semester, 1952. 1-182.

CEL   "Christian Ethics Lectures." Niebuhr's lecture notes, handwritten for class in "Christian Ethics" at Yale Divinity School, [contains layers from previous years mixed with most recent] spring semester, 1961. Niebuhr Box 1, file 10. 1-239.

CES   *Christian Ethics: Sources of the Living Tradition.* Ed. with Introductions by Waldo Beach and H. Richard Niebuhr. New York: The Ronald Press Company, 1955.

CEvangel   "The Christian Evangel and Social Culture." *Religion in Life* 8.1 (Winter 1939): 44-48.

Churches   "Churches That Might Unite." *Christian Century* 46 (February 21, 1929): 259-61.

CIC   "Christianity and the Industrial Classes." *Theological Magazine of the Evangelical Synod of North America* 57 (January 1929): 12-18.

Commun   "A Communication: The Only Way into the Kingdom of God." *Christian Century* 49 (April 6, 1932): 447. *The Christian Century Reader.* Ed. Harold E. Fey and Margaret Frakes. New York: Association Press, 1962. 228-31.

CSP   "Christianity and the Social Problem." *Theological Magazine of the Evangelical Synod of North America* 50 (1922): 278-91.

CV   "The Center of Value." *Moral Principles of Action: Man's Ethical Imperative.* Ed. Ruth Nanda Anshen. New York: Harper & Brothers, 1952. 162-75. *Radical Monotheism and Western Culture, with Supplementary Essays.* New York: Harper & Brothers, 1960. 100-13.

Dehmel   "The Problem of the Individual in Richard Dehmel." Unpublished M.A. thesis. Department of Germanics, Washington University, St. Louis (June 1917). 1-50.

Disorder   "The Disorder of Man in the Church of God." *Man's Disorder and God's Design.* Vol. 1: *The Universal Church in God's Design.* New York: Harper & Brothers, 1949. 78-88.

Earl   "Christian Responsibility." The Earl Lectures delivered at Pacific School of Religion, 1962. Consists of three lectures (written and on cassette tapes): I. "The Root Metaphors of Morality" (delivered February 27, 1962), II. "The Idea of Responsibility" (February 28, 1962), and III. "Responsibility to God" (March 1, 1962). Niebuhr Box 2, file 1.

Ego   "The Ego-Alter Dialectic and the Conscience." *Journal of Philosophy* 42 (1945): 352-59.

Emotions   "The Religious Emotions." Student seminar notes, handwritten by R. Melvin Keiser, taught at Yale Divinity School, spring semester, 1962. 1-26.

EthCrisis   "The Ethical Crisis." Delivered at Wayne State University, November 1961. *Universitas: A Journal of Religion and the University* 2.2 (Spring 1964): 41-50.

EthicsC   "Ethics, Christian." *Encyclopedia of Religion.* Ed. Vergilius Ferm. New York: The Philosophical Library, 1945. 259.

ETPR   "Ernst Troeltsch's Philosophy of Religion." Unpublished Ph.D. dissertation. Yale University, 1924. 1-270.

Faith   "Faith in Gods and in God." Originally published as "The Nature and Existence of God: A Protestant's View." *Motive* 4 (December 1943): 13-15 & 43-46. Revised in *Radical Monotheism and Western Culture, with Supplementary Essays*. New York: Harper & Brothers, 1960. 114-26.

FaithNat   "On the Nature of Faith." *Religious Experience and Truth: A Symposium*. Ed. Sidney Hook. New York: New York University Press, 1961. 93-102.

FaithWork "Faith, Works, and Social Salvation." *Religion in Life* 1.3 (Summer 1932): 426-30.

FE   *Faith on Earth: An Inquiry into the Structure of Human Faith.* [1958.] Ed. Richard R. Niebuhr. New Haven & London: Yale University Press, 1989.

Feeling   "Toward the Recovery of Feeling." "Next Steps in Theology." Lecture III. Unpublished Cole Lectures, transcribed from tape recordings, delivered at Vanderbilt University, April 10-12, 1961. 1-30. Niebuhr Box 2, file 5.

FHL   "Reflections on Faith, Hope and Love." [1953.] *Journal of Religious Ethics* 2 (Spring 1974): 151-56.

Future   "Toward the Future." "Next Steps in Theology." Lecture I. Unpublished Cole Lectures, transcribed from tape recordings, delivered at Vanderbilt University, April 10-12, 1961. 1-21. Niebuhr Box 2, file 5.

Gospel   "The Gospel for a Time of Fears." *The Washington Federation of Churches and the School of Religion, Howard University*. Washington, D.C.: Henderson Services, 1950. 1-22. Three Lectures: I. Our Eschatological Time, II. The Eternal Now, III. The Gospel of the Last Time. Delivered Howard University, Washington, D.C., April 18, 1950.

Grace   "The Grace of Doing Nothing." *Christian Century* 49 (March 23, 1932): 378-80. *The Christian Century Reader*. Ed. Harold E. Fey and Margaret Frakes. New York: Association Press, 1962. 216-21.

Hidden   "The Hidden Church and the Churches in Sight." *Religion in Life* 15 (1945-46): 106-16.

Hope   "The Hope of Glory." Student notes, handwritten by R. Melvin Keiser, delivered at Yale Divinity School Chapel, December 12, 1961. Niebuhr Box 1, file 11.

Illusions "The Illusions of Power." *The Pulpit* 33 (April 1962): 4(100)-7(103).

Incon   "Inconsistency of the Majority." *The World Tomorrow* 17 (January 18, 1934): 43-44.

Intro   "Introduction to Theological Study." Student lecture notes, handwritten by R. Melvin Keiser, delivered at Yale Divinity School, fall semester, 1960. 1-16.

Irrelig   "The Irreligion of Communist and Capitalist." *Christian Century* 47 (October 29, 1930): 1306-07.

IsGod   "Is God in the War?" *Christian Century* 49 (August 1942): 953-55.

JCI   "Jesus Christ Intercessor." *International Journal of Religious Education* 3 (1927): 6-8.

KGA   *The Kingdom of God in America.* Chicago and New York: Willett, Clark and Company, 1937. Harper Torchbooks. New York: Harper & Brothers, 1959.

Life   "Life Is Worth Living." *Intercollegian and Far Horizons* 57 (October 1939): 3-4, 22.

Man   "Man the Sinner." *Journal of Religion* 15 (1935): 272-80.

MR   *The Meaning of Revelation.* New York: The Macmillan Company, 1941.

Moral   "Moral Relativism and the Christian Ethic." *Theological Education and the World Mission of Christianity: Preliminary Papers for the Conference on Theological Education.* New

York: International Missionary Council, 1929. 1-11. Paper given at a Conference of Theological Seminaries, meeting at Drew Theological Seminary, Madison, New Jersey, November 29-December 1, 1929.

Next   "Next Steps in Theology." Four Lectures: I. Toward the Future, II. Toward New Symbols, III. Toward the Recovery of Feeling, IV. Toward the Service of Christendom. Unpublished Cole Lectures, transcribed from tape recording, delivered at Vanderbilt University, April 10-12, 1961. 1-114. Niebuhr Box 2, file 5.

PCM   *The Purpose of the Church and Its Ministry: Reflections on the Aims of Theological Education.* H. Richard Niebuhr, in collaboration with Daniel Day Williams and James M. Gustafson. New York: Harper & Brothers, 1956.

Prot   "Protestant Theology Since Schleiermacher." Student lecture notes, handwritten by Joe E. Elmore, Yale Divinity School, Fall 1951.

ProtDem   "The Protestant Movement and Democracy in the United States." *Religion in American Life.* Vol. 1: *The Shaping of American Religion.* Eds. James Ward Smith & A. Leland Jamison. Princeton: Princeton University Press, 1961. 20-71.

Realism   "Religious Realism in the Twentieth Century." *Religious Realism.* Ed. D. C. Macintosh. New York: The Macmillan Company, 1931. 413-28.

Ref   "Reformation: Continuing Imperative." *Christian Century* 77 (1960): 248-51. *How My Mind Has Changed.* Ed. with an Introduction by Harold E. Fey. Meridian Books. New York: World Publishing Company, 1961. 69-80.

RelEth   "Religion and Ethics." *World Tomorrow* 13 (November 1930): 443-46.

Religion   "From the Religion of Humanity to the Religion of God."
             *Theological Magazine of the Evangelical Synod of North
             America* 57.6 (November 1929): 401-09.

RespCS   "The Responsibility of the Church for Society." *The Gospel,
             the Church, & the World.* Ed. Kenneth Scott Latourette.
             New York: Harper & Brothers, 1946. 111-33.

RMWC   *Radical Monotheism and Western Culture, with Supplementary
             Essays.* New York: Harper & Brothers, 1960.

RS   *The Responsible Self: An Essay in Christian Moral
             Philosophy.* [1960, 1962.] Preface by Richard R. Niebuhr.
             Introduction by James M. Gustafson. New York, Evanston,
             and London: Harper and Row, 1963.

RSMS   "'The Responsible Self' Manuscript." Drafts of two chapters
             for projected book. I. "Metaphors and Morals," 41 pp.
             (typewritten); II. "The Meaning of Responsibility," 34 pp. +
             numerous addenda (typewritten). (Found on Niebuhr's desk
             at time of his death [Preface, RS 3; Grant 168].) Niebuhr
             Box 2, file 6.

Sin   "The Christian Theory of Sin." Student Seminar notes,
             handwritten by R. Melvin Keiser, taught at Yale Divinity
             School, fall semester, 1961. 1-34.

SocGosp   "The Social Gospel and the Mind of Jesus." Originally
             delivered to the American Theological Society, April 21,
             1933. *The Journal of Religious Ethics* 16.1 (Spring 1988):
             115-27.

SSD   *The Social Sources of Denominationalism.* New York: Henry
             Holt and Company, [October] 1929. Living Age Books.
             New York: Meridian Books, 1957.

TheoDis   "Theology in a Time of Disillusionment." Unpublished
             lecture, handwritten, delivered as Alumni Lecture, Yale
             Divinity School, 1931. 1-22. Niebuhr Box 1, file 7.

TheoPsy   "Theology & Psychology: A Sterile Union." *Christian Century* 44 (January 13, 1927): 47-48.

Towards   "Towards a New Other-Worldliness." *Theology Today* 1 (1944): 78-87.

Trans   "Translator's Preface." *The Religious Situation*. By Paul Tillich. New York: Henry Holt & Co, 1932. vii-xxii. Living Age Books. New York: Meridian Books, 1956. 9-24.

Utilit   "Utilitarian Christianity." *Christianity and Crisis* 6 (1946): 3-5.

Value   "Value-Theory and Theology." *The Nature of Religious Experience: Essays in Honor of Douglas Clyde Macintosh*. Ed. J. S. Bixler, R. L. Calhoun, H. R. Niebuhr. New York: Harper & Brothers, 1937. 93-116.

WarCruc   "War as Crucifixion." *Christian Century* 60 (April 1943): 513-15.

WarJudg   "War as the Judgment of God." *Christian Century* 49 (May 1942): 630-33.

What   "What then Must We Do?" *Christian Century Pulpit* 5 (1934): 145-47.

WhatSay   "What Has a Christian To Say in the Cold War?" Student notes, handwritten by R. Melvin Keiser, Common Room Conversation, Yale Divinity School (December 6, 1961).

Who   "Who are the Unbelievers and What Do They Believe?" Report submitted to Secretariat for Evangelism, World Council of Churches, Second Assembly. *The Christian Hope and the Task of the Church*. New York: Harper, & Brothers, 1954. 35-37.

Notes

1. William R. Hutchison in *The Modernist Impulse in American Protestantism* has provided a useful and succinct characterization of both liberalism and neo-orthodoxy. The heart of theological liberalism, what he calls the "modernist impulse" within liberalism, involves three beliefs: the "adaptation of religious ideas to modern culture," "that God is immanent in human cultural development and revealed through it," and "that human society is moving toward realization (even though it may never attain the reality) of the Kingdom of God" (2). Neo-orthodoxy is defined by: "Biblical faith; the necessity of choice; transcendence; certitude; openness to 'the most disheartening facts' [especially 'human sinfulness']" (295).

2. See Michael Polanyi, *Personal Knowledge: Towards a Post-Critical Philosophy* and *The Tacit Dimension*.

3. Paul Tillich is an exception here in that he saw the subject/object split as problematic and sought ways to transcend it. Nevertheless, he retains this "critical" dualism as definitive of the human condition rather than as a human construct of modern philosophy and, with his fellow neo-orthodox, shifts emphasis within it from subject to object, from human to divine agency. For a "critical" reading of Tillich's theology see my "Phenomenology and Spiritual Maturity in the Tillichian *Magisterium*."

4. For an incisive and succinct feminist depiction of Aristotelian substance see Catherine Keller, *From a Broken Web: Separation, Sexism, and Self* 49, 68, & 172-74.

5. Niebuhr expressed it this way late in his life; see *Ref* 71-72.

6. Niebuhr, *Ref* 73. Reinhold Niebuhr similarly acknowledges this in his contribution to Harold Fey's *How My Mind Has Changed* (117) and Paul Tillich embraces elements of earlier liberalism in his *Systematic Theology*, v. I (97). Cf. also Hutchison's recognition of similarities between liberalism and neo-orthodoxy in *Modernist Impulse* 309-10.

7. Harrison 312, 304, & 301; her italics. I am grateful to Katie Cannon, then of Episcopal Divinity School, for calling my attention to Harrison's dissertation.

8. H.R.N., "Winter Peace," *The Keryx*, 2, No. 5 (December 1912), 1, as listed in William Chrystal's bibliography of Niebuhr's writings in the Archives of Eden Theological Seminary (231).

9. This opposition of spirit and nature is evident throughout Niebuhr's writings of this first period. See *Back* 860-61; *TheoPsy* 48; *CIC* 14-15; & SSD 4.

10. SSD 5; insert is from SSD 284. For "penetrate" see SSD 5, 8, & 278.

11. Niebuhr illustrates the essential points of liberal Christianity as delineated by Kenneth Cauthen. Speaking of one of liberalism's leading exponents, William Adams Brown, Cauthen says of him: "He discovers the essence of Christianity in the teachings and in the person of the historical Jesus. In him there is to be found . . . [t]he fatherhood of God, the brotherhood of man, the worth of the individual soul, greatness through service, salvation through sacrifice, the kingdom of God as the goal of humanity . . ." (43). Brown's stress on the finality of Christianity is not, however, an element of Niebuhr's thinking.

12. For earlier and later references to Schleiermacher during this idealistic period see Niebuhr, *Aspect*, 39, *ETPR* 266, and *TheoPsy* 48. For employment of Macintosh's

views see Niebuhr, *TheoPsy* 48; and of Kantian dualism see *ETPR* 111, 216-17, & 266, and *Back* 860-61.

13. See especially Niebuhr's three essays in the 1920s: *ALR* (1921), *CSP* (1922), and *CIP* (1929), which we will discuss in Chapter Eight.

14. *Dehmel* 48-50; quotation as cited by Niebuhr is from George Santayana on Hegel in *Egotism in German Philosophy*.

15. *ETPR* 214; quotation as cited by Niebuhr is from Ernst Troeltsch, "Konservativ und Liberal," *Die Christliche Welt*, XXX, vol. 661 (1916); "Kontingenz," *Ges. Schr.* II, p. 771.

16. *EPTR* 4-5; quotation as cited by Niebuhr is from Adolf Harnack, "Rede Am Sarge Ernst Troeltschs," *Die Christliche Welt*, vol. XXXVII, No. 7-8 (February 22, 1923). Sydney Ahlstrom has insightfully remarked of these words in an eloquent conclusion to his memorial essay for Niebuhr: "These words could have been spoken equally of H. Richard Niebuhr--and now, four decades later, they in some small measure assuage our loss" (217).

17. *ETPR* 266. For Troeltsch's opposition to mysticism see *ETPR* 113-14 & 148; for his embracing it see *ETPR* 112 & 148; and for Niebuhr's explanation of the apparent contradiction see *ETPR* 149-50.

18. Under the influence of the empirical realism of his Yale mentor, D.C. Macintosh, Niebuhr speaks of revelation as providing an object for study in attacking the nineteenth century's psychologizing of religion: "If theology would resolutely turn its back on all psychologism, if it would devote itself with the wholeheartedness which characterizes the natural sciences to the observation and intense study of its object as it is revealed in history and in the ethical and spiritual life, then it might eventually be found worthy of the name of science" (*TheoPsy* 48). He speaks, secondly, of it as a stimulus to religious movements in quoting Troeltsch: "'Really creative, church-forming movements,' writes Troeltsch, more truly than felicitously, 'are the work of the lower strata. Here only can one find that union of unfettered imagination, emotional simplicity, unreflective thought, spontaneous energy and the vehement force of need out of which unconditioned faith in a divine revelation, the naiveté of complete surrender and intransigent certitude can rise'" (*CIC* 13). And finally, as we have already seen, revelation proffers an ideal: "Its purpose is the revelation to men of their potential childhood to the Father and their possible brotherhood with each other" (SSD 278).

19. *ETPR* 267; quotation as cited by Niebuhr is from Ernst Troeltsch, *Der Historismus und Seine Probleme. Erstes Buch: Das Logische Problem der Geschichte und Philosophie. Gesammelte Schriften* 3ter Band (Tuebingen 1922), 675f.

20. For Niebuhr on bodily "animal knowing" see MR 79; on language as constitutive of reality see MR 13, 22, 96-97, & 141; on theology as stating the grammar of religious language see MR 18; and on that grammar being first personal see MR 60-62, RMWC 45, & RS 110-17. Niebuhr represents Troeltsch's negative view of the body in speaking of monads: "Its identity with the Infinite can be only a limited one. This is apparent in the dependence of all intuition upon real contact with the environment of our body--which limits the knowledge of other selves to those with whom we may [have] some such contact--in the connection of all knowledge and of all standards with the sense organs and the conditions of the corporeal ego, in the limited ability of human logic to overcome contradictions, and, finally, in the

character of human thought which always leads to antinomies or circles in reasoning" (*ETPR* 268-69).

21. The time of Niebuhr's conversion can be located fairly specifically. James Fowler places publication of *Social Sources* in the month of October (35; cf. 49). In November, 1929, Niebuhr publishes "From the Religion of Humanity to the Religion of God." While speaking of the theological shift from nineteenth-century preoccupation with the subject to twentieth-century focus on the object, a theme already struck in 1927 (see *TheoPsy*), and while using words such as "faith," "revelation," and "realism," it does not present any hint within its objectivism of the relational pattern of being and goodness which elicits his personal commitment of trust in "Moral Relativism and the Christian Ethic." Since there is always some delay between the writing of an essay and its publication, we can assume that "From the Religion of Humanity to the Religion of God" was written prior to November. Since Niebuhr presents "Moral Relativism" at a conference at the very end of November, it would appear that November is the time of his transformation.

22. Delivered April 21, 1933; see especially *SocGosp* 10-11 & 15-16.

23. From the beginning of his writing, even before his work on Troeltsch, Niebuhr accepts historical relativism; see *Dehmel* 13,20,36, 38, & 41, and *Aspect* 39.

24. See *Man* 278-79, where Niebuhr draws implicitly but obviously upon Edwards's *Doctrine of Original Sin Defended* and quotes from *Freedom of Will*.

25. See Niebuhr's reference to the world against the transcendent God in *Back* 860, and his criticism of theological subjectivism in *TheoPsy* 48.

26. While on sabbatical leave in Germany, spring and summer, 1930, Niebuhr discovered Tillich's writings (see Fowler 4 & 59, n.11), and may even have heard him lecture (see Chrystal 235).

27. For two interesting considerations of this 1932 dialogue from different angles that bear on the distinction I am making between Niebuhr's realism of an immanent divinity and Reinhold Niebuhr's of a transcendent divinity, focused on two types of spirituality or two conceptions of tragedy, see Stanley Hauerwas, *The Peaceable Kingdom* 135-51, and John D. Barbour, "Niebuhr Versus Niebuhr: On Tragedy in History" 1096-99, respectively.

28. For Niebuhr's use of "trust" see *Dehmel* 35 and *JCI* 7; for "loyalty" see *Alliance* 201, *JCI* 7, and SSD 279. While Niebuhr does not directly connect the notion of loyalty with Royce he first refers to him, for whom loyalty is a central category, in 1920; see *Aspect* 42. For Niebuhr's use of "faith" see *Dehmel* 38 & 49; *Aspect* 42-44; *Alliance* 198; *ETPR* 254-55; *CIC* 14-15; and SSD 5, 268, 275, 278-79, & 284.

29. There is one place earlier where trust and loyalty appear together, but loyalty is Jesus's, rather than the self's, toward humanity. See *JCI* 7.

30. While trust and loyalty occur fleetingly together in *Man* 276-77, and his contributions to CAW 614-16, they are systematically developed in CC 253 and RMWC 16.

31. For references to "trust" see *TheoDis* 3, *Man* 277, CAW 614, *Value* 106, and *CEvangel* 44; to "loyalty" see *Can* 915, *Grace* 220, *Man* 276-77, CAW 609 & 614-16, KGA 101, and *Ego* 359; to "confidence" see *Value* 108; to "faith" see *Can* 914-15, *RelEth* 445, *Realism* 423, *Trans* 9 & 13-15, *Grace* 219, *What* 147, CAW 600 & 613, *Value* 103 & 105, *Life* 3-4 & 22, *CCh* 11, *IsGod* 954, and *Faith* 118.

32. For Niebuhr's discussion of faith in Tillich see *Realism* 422-23 and *Trans* 9 & 13-15; for Reinhold Niebuhr's discussion of faith in dialogue with his brother see "Must We" 228, and for H. Richard Niebuhr's reply see *Commun* 229; for Edwards's development of "consent, propensity and union of heart to being in general" in terms of the virtuous life, although not specifically denominated "faith," see Edwards, *The Nature of True Virtue* 3-4.

33. For Niebuhr's handling of feeling in Dehmel see *Dehmel* 36, 44, & 47-50; in Troeltsch see *ETPR* 254-55; and in his idealistic liberalism where feeling is an impetus toward life see *Aspect* 43 and *Alliance* 197, stimulus to follow the ideal see *Aspect* 44 and *CIC* 16-17, a contributor to church revitalization through religious enthusiasm see *CIC* 13-14, and love defining the ideal community see *Aspect* 44, *Alliance* 203, and *JCI* 7-8. It is interesting that his rejection in 1927 of the "subjectivism" of Schleiermacher in favor of the "empirical theology" of D. C. Macintosh does not include an indictment of feeling, although he criticizes implicitly Freud's handling of feeling; see *TheoPsy* 47-48.

34. For Niebuhr's beginning to deal explicitly with this theme see his criticism of idealistic liberal theology for its failure to speak to the religious imagination and human heart, in *TheoDis* 14 and KGA 90-91, 101, 105-06, 111-16, & 127; for his late development of the theme of feeling see *Feeling*, *CEL* (especially March 15, 1961), *Intro*, and *Emotions*.

35. KGA 106; see also 90-91, 111-16, 128, & 136-37. For Niebuhr's later exploration of the religious affections in Edwards see *Feeling* 22-23 and *Emotions* February 13 & 20, 1962.

36. For his nondistinctive use of "responsibility" within his idealistic period see *Dehmel* 17, *Aspect* 43 & 44, *Alliance* 200 & 201, *CSP* 280, *CIC* 13 & 16, and SSD 274-75 & 279.

37. For the use of "responsible self" see CAW 593; for the quiet gradual reflections on responsibility see MR: regarding use of the word (145-46), use of the "fitting" (114), and questioning "What is going on?" (123); for discussion of "responsibility," "respond," "answer," "accountable" see *RespCS* 114-20; and for use of "responsibility" and the "fitting" see "Outline and Bibliography for Niebuhr's Lecture Course in Christian Ethics, Winter and Spring Terms, 1952-53," "Appendix" in Fowler 271-75.

38. See *Dehmel* 27, 37, & 44-45; *Aspect* 41; *Alliance* 198-99; *ETPR* 161-62; *Back* 861; and SSD 274-75 (note the possible intimation of future developments in joining, although still in an idealistic context, both words "responsibility" and "integrity").

39. For later uses of "integrity" see *Can* 915; *Man* 278 & 279; KGA 7-8 & 137-38; MR 77-78, 109-10, 117, & 184-85; RMWC 47; and RS 121-26 & 137-42.

40. For Niebuhr's later use of this notion explicitly acknowledged as from Royce, see RS 83; for its similarity to Edwards see *The Nature of True Virtue* 3-4; for Niebuhr's explicit acceptance of Edwards's concept of consent see *CV* 105, n. 1; for Niebuhr's use of Mead and Bergson within the context of responsibility see RS 71-72, 76-77, & 99.

41. For Niebuhr's recognition of the linguistic, metaphoric nature of responsibility see RS 48, 56, 149, 151-54, & 159-60.

42. For Niebuhr's awareness of his method as metaphoric comparison see RS 48, 148, & 151-54; for his discussion of metaphor and symbol see RS 48, 56, 151-54, &

159-60; of myth see RS 106-07; of dialogue see RS 56-65, 77-80, 93-97, & 151-52; and for his development of a theory of religious meaning see RS 55-56, 79-81, 118-23, & 152.

43. According to James Fowler, Niebuhr studied at the University of Chicago in the summer of 1921 where he first encountered the thought of G.H. Mead (Fowler 3). For references to Royce, James, Perry, and H.G. Wells see Niebuhr, *Aspect* 40-44; to Santayana see *Dehmel* 12; to Durkheim, Lévy-Brühl, and Freud see *TheoPsy* 47; to Troeltsch, Weber, Marx, Lenin see *CIC* 13 & 17; to Comte see *Churches* 259; and to the theology of the social gospel see *CSP* 278ff. For references to Kant and Schleiermacher see *TheoPsy* 47; and to Harnack see *CIC* 13. For reference to Whitehead see *Religion* 409.

44. Sydney Ahlstrom put it in this fashion, in a remark made both in conversation and in a seminar on Jonathan Edwards at Yale Divinity School in the spring of 1963, that "Niebuhr's entire theological enterprise was to bring Jonathan Edwards through the historicism of the nineteenth century into our own time."

45. After Niebuhr's conversion, "sovereignty" first appears in CAW 597; cf. KGA 17, 52, 101, 164, & 194.

46. Edwards, "Personal Narrative" 58-59 & 63; see 62, and Faust and Johnson cxvi & 419-20 on the time of Edwards's conversion.

47. KGA 111; see also MR 65, CC 241-43, PCM 130, and RMWC 45.

48. *Commun* 229-31; my italics. See also Niebuhr, *Can* 915-16, *FaithWork* 426-27 & 430, *SocGosp*, *What*, CAW 590-91 & 615, *Man* 272 & 278-79, *CCh* 15, KGA ix-xvii, 1, 10-14, and 111. For examples in books from 1941 on consider MR 48-54 & 59-62, CC 234, PCM 32, RMWC 23, and RS 94.

49. *ETPR* 261; quotation as cited by Niebuhr is from Ernst Troeltsch, *Christian Thought* 26; my italics.

50. This brings Niebuhr close, as he recognizes at the end of his life, to the universalistic ethics of Spinoza, who "sees the human problem as one of enslavement by those fuzzy, inadequate, and self-centered ideas which lead man to interpret whatever happens to him in terms of its apparent beneficence or maleficence toward his personal private self and so to react with emotion. Deliverance comes through a universalized interpretation of what is happening" (RS 171. Cf. the passage on Spinoza from *CE(YCE)* April 9, 1952, in Fowler 193; cf. also MR 104).

51. David L. Miller raised similar concerns about Niebuhr's view of divine sovereignty in the mid-1970s (in *The New Polytheism: Rebirth of the Gods and Goddesses*). The feminist theological critique, unaware of his criticisms, has drawn my attention because of its programmatic relational and experiential commitments. I am grateful to Welch and these other feminist critics of Niebuhr (as well as to Miller) who have provoked my further clarifications of why Niebuhr has something to contribute to our present theological setting as well as of the limitations inherent in his language wherever it carries residual dualism.

52. For an exploration of Niebuhr's development of feeling in these unpublished materials see the second half of "V. Heuristic Metaphors: Faith and Feeling" in my *Recovering the Personal: Religious Language and the Post-Critical Quest of H. Richard Niebuhr* (98-107).

53. I would view Holler's critique of Niebuhr's dualism in the same light of his developing thought. I am in thorough agreement with her criticism of dualism in

Niebuhr's conception of external history. She contrasts this with the more relational view of his value theory (see Holler 90 & 94-95). Rather than drawing these into conflict as contradictory, I see them developmentally: while both are based in his conversion, his value thinking is developed after his historical epistemology and is a means towards further realization of the relational roots of his point of view. In responsibility he explicitly leaves behind his earlier Cartesian dualism (RS 82-83). Although Holler reads this passage merely as an expression of Niebuhr's concern about the theoretical/practical dualism, I see Niebuhr in his typically irenic way-- refusing to make sharp separations or heroic declarations of a major shift in his perspective--indicating his use of responsibility to get beyond this and other modern dualisms, even though with characteristic humility, he is unsure it will solve the problem of the self's unity. Later he criticizes the Cartesian epistemology that begins in doubt (RS 101-02). In *The Responsible Self* he embraces his relational commitments developed earlier especially as inner history, although then within the dualism of historicized Kantianism, and reworks his epistemology beyond dualism but no longer in the mode of history but rather through a postcritical theology of language.

54. Like Keller, David Miller, in *The New Polytheism* 36-50, concerned to embrace diversity of experience beyond any restrictive conceptual mode, similarly mistakes Niebuhr's radical monotheism as "abstract, formal, logical, and speculative" (47), "one-dimensional" (63), and asserting a "principle of being behind the diversity and richness of what appears on the face of all life" (47-48). Niebuhr is, I believe, however, much closer to what Miller, as he is to what Keller, wants to affirm--the rich particularity of our experience and the divine presence within it.

55. See "III. A Postcritical Ambience" in my *Recovering the Personal*, especially the section on postcritical philosophers as dialogical companions of Niebuhr's last years.

56. While the phrase "radical monotheism" is not integral to responsibility, it does not go without mention; see RS 129 & 132. See also his use of "the monotheistic believer" (RS 86).

57. We do not know what Niebuhr would have titled his magnum opus on responsibility. He lectured for the last ten years or so of his life on it simply under the title of "Christian Ethics." As the simplest effort toward accuracy, we refer to it as A Christian Ethics of Responsibility. Sources for investigation of "responsibility" in Niebuhr are as follows. While the words "responsible" and "to respond" occur in his early liberal writings (see *Dehmel* 17, *Aspect* 43 & 44, *Alliance* 200 & 201, *CSP* 280, *CIC* 13 & 16, and SSD 274-75 & 279), the earliest development of the relational theme of responsibility is in "The Social Gospel and the Mind of Jesus," a lecture to the American Theological Society in 1933. The earliest actual use of the word, "responsible," indeed as "responsible self," is in *The Church Against the World* (593) in 1935. In subsequent years word and theme occur repeatedly (see *Attack* 178; *CCh* 12, 13, 15, & 16; *WarJudg* 630 & 632; *IsGod* 954; *WarCruc* 515; *Towards* 78 & 87; *Ego* 353 & 356; and *EthicsC* 259). After the initial effort to distinguish the ethics of responsibility from the classical teleological and deontological, without clarity of terms, in "The Social Gospel and the Mind of Jesus," they are distinguished with categorial clarity in the *Encyclopedia of Religion* article, "Ethics, Christian" of 1945. In the following year the first essay devoted to developing the theme of responsibility appears, "The Responsibility of the Church for Society."

The only piece of his mature thought on responsibility to be published is the posthumous *The Responsible Self* of 1963, a combination of the Robertson Lectures delivered at the University of Glasgow in the spring of 1960 and part of the Earl Lectures (much of Lecture I. and all of Lecture III.) delivered at Pacific School of Religion in the spring of 1962. The Earl Lectures are entitled "Christian Responsibility" and consist of three lectures (written and on cassette tapes): I. "The Root Metaphors of Morality" (delivered February 27, 1962), II. "The Idea of Responsibility" (February 28, 1962), and III. "Responsibility to God" (March 1, 1962). The author's son, Richard R. Niebuhr, in combining these two series of lectures as *The Responsible Self*, drew Appendix A. "Metaphors and Morals" from Lecture I and Appendix B. "Responsibility and Christ" from Lecture III.

The unpublished literary remains on responsibility consist of the following. The earliest is "Christian Ethics" (student lecture notes, transcribed by Robert Yetter, Gene Canestrari, and Ed Elliott, delivered at Yale Divinity School, spring semester, 1952). While this is a full stenographic record of Niebuhr's Christian Ethics lectures in 1952, his thought on responsibility developed significantly during his last ten years, especially during 1960-1962. An indication that his thinking was only slowly emerging is evident in the absence of any reference to the ethics of responsibility as a third alterative to the two classical views in his source book, *Christian Ethics*, which he and Waldo Beach published in 1955. Even though he distinguished them clearly in "Ethics, Christian" in 1945, this later work speaks only of two types of ethics, teleological and deontological, subsuming biblical ethics under the latter.

In the 1960s there are the "Christian Ethics Lectures" (Niebuhr's lecture notes, handwritten, for class in "Christian Ethics" at Yale Divinity School, spring semester 1961, Niebuhr Box 1, file 10). While these are the notes from which he gave his last Yale Divinity lectures in spring 1961, they are laminated with older strata of notes. There are student lecture notes no doubt still extant among Niebuhr's students who attended these lectures over the last ten years. Among these are my own and my wife's student notes from his last "Christian Ethics" delivered at Yale Divinity School, spring semester, 1961.

The last lecture course unfortunately deleted what James Gustafson says Niebuhr called "Christian Responsibility in Common Life," which earlier had dealt with "interpretation of marriage and the family, politics and economics, war and international relations in the light of the idea of responsibility" (RS 9). There was word at Yale Divinity School at the time that this was because he was not satisfied with it and anticipated being able to work on it before offering his final set of lectures before retirement.

Unpublished as well from the 1960s--according to Richard R. Niebuhr's Preface to *The Responsible Self*, his list provided researchers ("H. R. Niebuhr: Unpublished Materials" [n.d.]), and C. David Grant's Bibliography for *God The Center of Value*--are "The Responsible Self Manuscript," found on Niebuhr's desk at the time of his death July 5, 1962, consisting of "drafts of two chapters" which are "greatly expanded versions of portions of the substance" (RS 3) published in *The Responsible Self* (listed by Grant [168] as 1. "Metaphors and Morals," 41 pp. typewritten; 2. "The Meaning of Responsibility," 34 pp. + numerous addenda typewritten; Box 2, file 6); "numerous sketches and outlines of various projections of his ethics for publication"; "a series of addresses at The Riverside Church in New

York City, a series cut short by illness in the Winter of 1962" (RS 3); "On the Meaning of Responsibility" (lecture delivered at Cambridge University, May 25, 1960, 21 pp. handwritten; Box 2, file 1 [Grant 167]); "Der Sinn der Verantwortlichkeit" (lecture delivered in Bonn, June 28, 1960 [Grant 168]); and "Pt. II. Responsibility to Divine Action; I. Valuation" (fragment, 13 pp. handwritten; Box 2, file 4 [Grant 168]). Earl Lecture II. "The Idea of Responsibility" remains unpublished as well.

   In the subsequent discussion the major resource for our explorations is *The Responsible Self* supplemented with Yetter, Canestrari, and Elliott's 1952 student transcriptions of "Christian Ethics," mine and my wife's student notes of the 1961 "Christian Ethics," Niebuhr's own "Christian Ethics Lectures," "Christian Responsibility": Earl Lecture II. "The Idea of Responsibility," and "'The Responsible Self' Manuscript."

58. In *A Myth of Innocence: Mark and Christian Origins* Burton Mack says: "*metis* [is] . . . practical wisdom required of contingent circumstances that are threatening in some way. The contrast is *sophia*, that kind of knowledge that presupposes stable systems and generates general truths. . . . Assessing the situation, anticipating the way things might go, a sense of timing, waiting for the opportune moment, dodging, moving in quickly with a forthright initiative were all known about, storied, and practiced by the Greeks. The Cynics applied the logic of *metis* to the art of living" (68).

59. Other similar reflections on the body are sprinkled among his class lectures, such as this statement in relation to Schleiermacher: "Religion comes to actualization always in concrete situations--in them I'm aware of myself not as a bare self but as a self with a body" (*Prot* 25).

60. *Earl* II. 23 in Grant 74. While Grant calls Lecture II. "The Meaning of Responsibility," Niebuhr gave it originally at Pacific School of Religion under the name of "The Idea of Responsibility."

61. While Niebuhr's penchant is not for speaking of particular words but of larger patterns of our being as forms of life, such as symbols and metaphors, he nevertheless affirms that a language-act is a "form of his practical life" (RS 48), a "form" in which "our being" "comes to expression" (RS 149), and a "form religious life" takes in a specific history (MR 17).

62. Divine action for Niebuhr is not "the mighty acts of God" of *heilsgeschichte* as articulated by G. Ernest Wright and others of his theological generation. The One's action is not the paradigmatic external acts of the scripture that we should believe in but rather particularized acts contacting us in our immediate experience to which we invariably, one way or another, respond. Nor is the divine action Whitehead's God systematically upholding, and luring the self towards, the best possibility among lesser options. Although Niebuhr and Whitehead are similar in the constancy of the divine-human interaction and the shifting particularity of what God intends within what is possible in the changing situation, Niebuhr never delineates a metaphysical structure within which God acts. Avoiding the objectivism of either theological doctrines enacted in history or a metaphysical process for all entities, he always keeps it in the realm of personal experience. Yet paradigmatic images are always at work for him within experience. Unlike Whitehead, Niebuhr understands response to the moment's actions, including the One action, as interpreted through myth and metaphors. For

the Christian these are shaped by the symbolic form of Jesus Christ. While Christ functions in this way paradigmatically, Niebuhr focuses attention not on the general truth of doctrines in history but on the way the Christ symbol enables interpretation of and response to what is going on within the particularities of a given circumstance. Because Niebuhr does not give concrete examples of interpreting a situation by telling stories about others or himself, this distinction between his existential and Wright's objective approach is not as evident as it should be, but Niebuhr's thrust towards immediacy rather than generality is clear.

While he does speak of divine pattern in his conversion essay and subsequently from time to time (e.g. RS 77), the language of responsibility for the divine is more mysterious both as the indefinable One and ultimate action, and through various contextual metaphors--such as "the final circumambiency" (RS 153), "ultimate context" (RS 106; cf. 125), "this environment environing all our environments" (RS 175; cf. 155), and "a whole [or realm] in which we live and move and have our being" (RS 88 & 140). These wholistic metaphors, while contextual, do not imply structure, as pattern does, but suggest a greater sense of divine mystery that we indwell.

63. This phrase is used as a heading in *CEL* February 15, 1961 (on sheet dated October 14, 1959).

64. I am indebted for this insight to conversations about the erotic with Elizabeth B. Keiser. See her forthcoming *Homophobic Wrath and Paradisal Pleasure: Courtliness and the Sacred in* Cleanness *and Its Medieval Contexts* (Yale University Press).

65. Niebuhr's movement toward the concrete particular is evident in his change from accepting to criticizing G.H. Mead's view of the "generalized other" or "impartial spectator." In "The Ego-Alter Dialectic and the Conscience " Niebuhr quotes approvingly from Mead's *The Philosophy of the Present*: "We are in possession of selves just in so far as we can and do take the attitudes of others toward ourselves and respond to these attitudes" (353), and embraces this notion of seeing oneself from the other's perspective, making clear that the other is the impartial spectator: "It must and does regard itself with the eyes of another, of an impartial spectator or judge" (353). What he means by this "impartial spectator" or "'generalized other' is a sort of composite photograph which the self makes of the associates in his society" (354). With this generalized other the self carries on an inner conversation, as Mead says: "Our thinking is an inner conversation in which we may be taking the roles of specific acquaintances over against ourselves, but usually it is with what I have termed the 'generalized other' that we converse" (354). Niebuhr hastens to add: "The self does not deal with one 'generalized other' only but with many, and not all its 'others' are 'generalized'" (354). For Niebuhr early on, then, our encounter is with a multiplicity of generalized others each representing a specific sphere in life, such as family, professional, and religious communities, and our impartiality is not a disinterestedness but an attachment to a particular cause or value transcending my particular self. While Mead's view is already modified by Niebuhr in 1945, insisting on the particularity and plurality of the generalized other, he, nevertheless, is working out of a basic acceptance of Mead's generalized idea.

While there are many elements present in this article that will later become central to dialogical responsibility--Niebuhr quotes Mead speaking of "response" and "inner conversation," and himself uses such words as "dialogue" (352-53) and "responsible self" (356)--they have not yet emerged out of the essentially alien context within which they are embedded, for the generalized other is fundamentally deontological. This is evident most clearly when Niebuhr speaks of the responsible self in the language of law: "it is the self which judges or commands itself in the presence of the other. It gives a law to itself and unless it did this it would not be a responsible self" (356). The generalized other as used by Mead and accepted with minor modifications by Niebuhr in 1945 has been taken over in a more social context from Kant's notion of conscience as an inner court within which judgment occurs according to universal law.

By the 1960s responsibility has emerged for Niebuhr into sufficient clarity so as to be differentiated from all deontology. In this shift conscience is transformed from the deontological inner conversation with another as explicit "composite photograph" representing law, to responsible dialogue with particular selves as they exist in the ordinarily less than explicit constancies of interaction and response. He moves toward greater concreteness, from this abstract composite and juridical judgment to the particularity of interpersonal existence and patterns of response. And he moves toward the explicitly linguistic: the constancy of interaction or pattern of response is present in the "constant meanings of a common language" (RS 78).

66. An outstanding ethicist profoundly influenced by Niebuhr, James Gustafson affirms the importance of fittingness within a system of interdependence; yet he rejects what Niebuhr understands as the foundation of fittingness: divine immanence and its particularizing intentionality. "For Niebuhr, God is 'acting' in all actions upon us. He had more confidence in the agency model of God than I have. In distinction from that view, I believe we can appropriately say only that we have capacities to respond to persons and events in an interactive way, and that through those actions we respond to the divine governance, to the powers that bear down on us and sustain us. We have capacities to discern in particular events and relations something of what the divine governance requires, what our appropriate actions and relations are to nature, to other persons, and so forth. God is the ultimate source of the conditions for the possibilities of all our actions; we not only respond to these possibilities but, in some instances at least, they respond to us and interact with our action" (*Ethics* I: 273-74).

Gustafson has removed God in his ethics from an immediate presence acting upon me to a general "divine governance" and "source of the conditions of the possibilities of all our actions" and thereby alters significantly the meaning of fittingness, shifting it away from encounter with lived reality to thinking about objective structure. The result is to lose Niebuhr's radical affirmation of dynamic particularity, a relational lived universality, and the center of fittingness.

67. For a convivial rendering of a relational self from a Whiteheadian perspective see Catherine Keller's insightful and imaginative *From a Broken Web: Separation, Sexism, and Self*. Even though she explicitly criticizes his radical monotheism as patriarchal (180-82), as we have considered in Chapter Three, her talk about "person" and "integrity" is closer to Niebuhr than she realizes (see ch. 4, "The Selves of Psyche," especially 194-212).

68. See Chapter Seven and Eight for discussion of Niebuhr's view of justice and oppression; see *CE[RMK]* April 28, 1961 for Niebuhr's stress on need-meeting.

69. These excerpts from H. Richard Niebuhr's letter to Eleanor Swalgren Dorn, May 22, 1962, are published without permission since I have been unable to locate her, but

I hope, if she should see this, that she will agree that these words should be available to others.

70. On transformation, see KGA 101-03, *War* 515, MR 165-75 & 182-91, CC ch. 6, RMWC 21, 56, & 123-26. While he nowhere identifies transformation and liberation, he does on occasion advocate liberation. See *FaithWork* 429-30, CAW 599, *Attempt* 4, and *Illusions* 6.

71. Disagreeing with his brother's assertion that individuals possess a capacity for goodness that a society lacks, while insisting society can exert an ameliorating effect upon individuals, he once quipped about his brother's book: "My brother wrote a book called *Moral Man and Immoral Society*. It was a good theme even though later he disavowed it to some extent. I've been tempted to write a book called *Immoral Man and Moral Society*" (*Intro* September 28, 1960). For an incisive comparison of the two brothers on this issue and a description of H. Richard Niebuhr's epistolary criticism of residual liberalism in his brother see Richard Wightman Fox, "The Niebuhr Brothers and the Liberal Protestant Heritage."

72. Niebuhr's endorsement was practical. It was common knowledge at Yale Divinity School, for those who were interested, that he contributed significantly to opening Divinity School admission in the 1950s to women and it was evident in the 1960s that he treated them with equal seriousness as men once they arrived. When he had his first heart attack in the early spring of 1962, he asked a woman graduate student, Sallie McFague, to take over his seminar while he was recuperating (see Keiser, *Recovering* xx, n.6).

73. Linda Holler, in "Is There a Thou 'Within' Nature? A Dialogue with H. Richard Niebuhr," begins to mine the rich ecological lode in Niebuhr to affirm living and inanimate creatures' "moral integrity as existents within the community of being" (Holler 82). While I agree with her incisive criticism of dualism in Niebuhr, especially in his conception of historical reason, I see him as having more fully overcome that dualism in his culminating thought on responsibility than she does so that he is, I believe, closer to what she wants to affirm than she realizes. She has engaged Niebuhr with Buber's affirmation of a Thou in nature. While Buber is a very important dialogical companion for Niebuhr in overcoming the dualism of "any atomic I or atomic object" (RS 72), he never speaks, as Buber does, of a Thou in nature. This may be because, while wanting with Buber to affirm the sacred integrity of every entity, he no longer, as in his historicism, wants to conceive of one way of being that involves relatedness and another that does not--as both external history and the I-It do not--but rather affirms the underlying relatedness of all being regardless of our dualistic consciousness. While I would agree that G.H. Mead's reflexivity, which Niebuhr conjoins with his discussion of Buber, is objectivistic, I would not agree that reflexivity is Niebuhr's sole criterion for selfhood (Holler 98), as should be evident from the above discussion of the self's contextual, tacit, dialogical, and mythic relations to nature; nor is this objective sense of reflexivity the only one in Niebuhr (see my discussion of the self as an elusive irreducible "I," a self-transcending self in dialogue, speaking in the first person, in which the self is reflexive [bending back upon itself] in tacitly standing in yet behind all that it does or says, in *Recovering the Personal* 114-16 & 133-43). I think his sense of the inherent and invisible "power-over" dynamic in dualism is one of the main reasons why he struggled to free himself from modern dichotomous thinking--and thus from talk of "subjective worth rather

than objective utility" and from identifying the Thou within nature as "Subjective life" (Holler 82 & 83)--in order to affirm more fully the moral integrity of all existents.

74. I am grateful to Katharina von Kellenbach for introducing me to this term, "anti-Judaism," at the Coolidge Colloquium meeting in June 1986 at the Episcopal Divinity School in Cambridge, Massachusetts.

75. In his insightful exploration of Niebuhr's writings on war and pacifism, Richard B. Miller, in "H. Richard Niebuhr's War Articles: A Transvaluation of Value" (258-62), shows how Niebuhr avoids conventional discourse about either as he is guided by action theory, metaphor and symbol, and social faith in developing an alternative grounded in God's sovereign immanent activity. Yet he concludes by identifying Niebuhr with the conventional just war theory of Paul Ramsey and so slides away from the radicality of Niebuhr's third alternative. While critical of all war-making, Niebuhr, it is true, does not reject it as a principle. If acceptance of the moral possibility of war is what is meant by just war, then this attribution is understandable. But as is evident in Miller's own article, Niebuhr is seeking to transcend the conventional discourse and as is evident in "War as Crucifixion," he rejects traditional just war theory. He would not say that any war is just; as Miller makes clear Niebuhr confesses both sides are invariably sinful and self-interested. Just war theory discriminates the more just cause between combatants; this is something Niebuhr refuses to do. If war is crucifixion it cannot be just, though redemptive good may, by the grace of God, come from it.

76. With regard to the happy warrior of the Cold War Niebuhr once remarked: "we can't live on the basis of competition with Russia. We don't consider what our responsibilities are given our abilities, but only how to keep up with the Russians. The good that comes out of competition cannot justify this kind of competition." He therefore advocated disarmament with inspections but said that "we need moral disarmament before physical disarmament" (*WhatSay* December 6, 1961).

77. See "Man the Sinner" in which Niebuhr makes this same point in his conclusion and adds that restraint should be medicinal rather than vindictive and should be subordinate to a strategy of reconciliation (*Man* 280).

78. While Richard Miller, in his essay on Niebuhr's war articles, names the immanence of divine sovereignty as the foundation of Niebuhr's ethics, he veers away from its radical significance in identifying it at the end of his article as deontological: "Niebuhr extends, or universalizes the moral law" (259). The law he claims Niebuhr arrives at, as Paul Ramsey does, is "other-regard" (260) and the principle by which he legitimates war or pacifism is "the extent to which the self has been displaced from the center" (262). Miller connects this principle of other-regard and self-displacement with repentance: "repentance focuses our gaze in the direction of the divine--the eternal--rather than on the moral demands of the passing moment" (244).

While Miller is certainly right that Niebuhr does stress repentance and other-regard, he does not do this within the dualistic framework of deontological ethics. Miller has set up an either/or: either I focus on God or on the particular moral situation. But this is to miss the heart of Niebuhr's ethics: response to the immanent action of God within the context of the community of being. Repentance is a turning to recognize the divine presence acting on us in every moment and is an expansion of our context to total being. To respond to God is not to shift regard from self to other but is to discover a regard for all of being that includes the other and one's own self.

To respond to God is to respond to the world--both/and. But it is also to respond to God in the particular moral situation because that is where God is acting on us.

Niebuhr's is not Tillich's method of correlation, correlating the religious answers with the world's questions, or applying the absolute to the particular (258). Rather it is to discover the absolute in the particular (an absolute which is not a value [258] but an action), to discover the answer comes in interaction with God in our concrete religious and worldly being. While there are several reasons why Niebuhr refuses to provide general ethical judgments--such as his commitments to existentialism that persons must interpret and decide for themselves, to relativism that persons look and must look from their own perspective, and to inwardness that each self must articulate principles emergent out of its own life situation rather than receive external laws or goals imposed from without--but the heart is that ethical decisions arise in each person's response to the specific action of God on him or her in the particular moral circumstance within the entire community of being. What each should do depends on how God is acting on you and how you are situated within the community of being--that is, whether through repentance you have opened to this Action and to its and your entire context. Neither God's particular action nor my specific situation, Niebuhr believes, can be generalized as a moral law such as other-regard and self-displacement.

79. For sharp criticism after *The Church Against the World* see *Utilit* (1946), *RespCS* (1946), *Disorder* (1949), *EthCrisis* (1961); for illustrative criticism see *CCh* (1941), *Towards* (1944), *Hidden* (1945-46), *Gospel* (1950), *Attempt* (1951), *Who* (1954), *ProtDem* (1961).

80. For a similar method of analysis, although not connected with Niebuhr, from which I have benefitted, see Joe Holland and Peter Henriot, *Social Analysis: Linking Faith and Justice*.

Bibliography

I. Niebuhr's Works
    A. Published Cited
    B. Unpublished Cited (Other than on Responsibility)
    C. Resources on Responsibility
        i. Published
        ii. Unpublished
II. Works about Niebuhr Cited
III. Other Works Cited

I. NIEBUHR'S WORKS

A. PUBLISHED CITED

(Chronologically arranged according to publication or composition, if much earlier.)

"Winter Peace." By H.R.N. *The Keryx* 2.5 (December 1912): 1.

"An Aspect of the Idea of God in Recent Thought." *Theological Magazine of the Evangelical Synod of North America* 48 (1920): 39-44.

"The Alliance Between Labor and Religion." *Theological Magazine of the Evangelical Synod of North America* 49 (1921): 197-203.

"Christianity and the Social Problem." *Theological Magazine of the Evangelical Synod of North America* 50 (1922): 278-91.

"Back to Benedict?" *Christian Century* 42 (July 2, 1925): 860-61.

"Theology & Psychology: A Sterile Union." *Christian Century* 44 (January 13, 1927): 47-48.

"Jesus Christ Intercessor." *International Journal of Religious Education* 3 (1927): 6-8.

"Christianity and the Industrial Classes." *Theological Magazine of the Evangelical Synod of North America* 57 (January 1929): 12-18.

"Churches That Might Unite." *Christian Century* 46 (February 21, 1929): 259-61.

The Social Sources of Denominationalism. New York: Henry Holt and Company, [October] 1929. Living Age Books. New York: Meridian Books, 1957.

"From the Religion of Humanity to the Religion of God." *Theological Magazine of the Evangelical Synod of North America* 57.6 (November 1929): 401-09.

"Moral Relativism and the Christian Ethic." *Theological Education and the World Mission of Christianity: Preliminary Papers for the Conference on Theological Education.* New York: International Missionary Council, 1929. 1-11. Paper given at a Conference of Theological Seminaries, meeting at Drew Theological Seminary, Madison, New Jersey, November 29-December 1, 1929.

"Can German and American Christians Understand Each Other?" *Christian Century* 47 (July 23, 1930): 914-16.

"The Irreligion of Communist and Capitalist." *Christian Century* 47 (October 29, 1930): 1306-07.

"Religion and Ethics." *World Tomorrow* 13 (November 1930): 443-46.

"Religious Realism in the Twentieth Century." *Religious Realism.* Ed. D. C. Macintosh. New York: The Macmillan Company, 1931. 413-28.

"Translator's Preface." *The Religious Situation.* By Paul Tillich. New York: Henry Holt & Co, 1932. vii-xxii. Living Age Books. New York: Meridian Books, 1956. 9-24.

"The Grace of Doing Nothing." *Christian Century* 49 (March 23, 1932): 378-80. *The Christian Century Reader.* Ed. Harold E. Fey and Margaret Frakes. New York: Association Press, 1962. 216-21.

"A Communication: The Only Way into the Kingdom of God." *Christian Century* 49 (April 6, 1932): 447. *The Christian Century Reader*. Ed. Harold E. Fey and Margaret Frakes. New York: Associated Press, 1962. 228-31.

"Faith, Works, and Social Salvation." *Religion in Life* 1.3 (Summer 1932): 426-30.

"The Social Gospel and the Mind of Jesus." Originally delivered to the American Theological Society, April 21, 1933. *The Journal of Religious Ethics* 16.1 (Spring 1988): 115-27.

"Inconsistency of the Majority." *The World Tomorrow* 17 (January 18, 1934): 43-44.

"What then Must We Do?" *Christian Century Pulpit* 5 (1934): 145-47.

"Man the Sinner." *Journal of Religion* 15 (1935): 272-80.

The Church Against the World. H. Richard Niebuhr, Wilhelm Pauck, and F. P. Miller. Chicago, New York: Willet, Clark & Co., 1935. H. Richard Niebuhr, "The Question of the Church" and "Toward the Independence of the Church." 1-13 & 123-56. *Theology in America: The Major Protestant Voices from Puritanism to Neo-Orthodoxy*. Ed. Sydney E. Ahlstrom. Indianapolis and New York: Bobbs-Merrill Company, 1967. 590-618.

"The Attack Upon the Social Gospel." *Religion in Life* 5 (1936):176-81.

The Kingdom of God in America. Chicago and New York: Willett, Clark and Company, 1937. Harper Torchbooks. New York: Harper & Brothers, 1959.

"Value-Theory and Theology." *The Nature of Religious Experience: Essays in Honor of Douglas Clyde Macintosh*. Ed. J. S. Bixler, R. L. Calhoun, H. R. Niebuhr. New York: Harper & Brothers, 1937. 93-116.

"Life Is Worth Living." *Intercollegian and Far Horizons*. 57 (October 1939): 3-4, 22.

"The Christian Evangel and Social Culture." *Religion in Life* 8.1 (Winter 1939): 44-48.

The Meaning of Revelation. New York: The Macmillan Company, 1941.

"The Christian Church in the World's Crisis." *Christianity and Society* 6 (1941): 11-17.

"War as the Judgment of God." *Christian Century* 49 (May 1942): 630-33.

"Is God in the War?" *Christian Century* 49 (August 1942): 953-55.

"War as Crucifixion." *Christian Century* 60 (April 1943): 513-15.

"Faith in Gods and in God." Originally published as "The Nature and Existence of God: A Protestant's View." *Motive* 4 (December 1943): 13-15 & 43-46. Revised in *Radical Monotheism and Western Culture, with Supplementary Essays*. New York: Harper & Brothers, 1960. 114-26.

"Towards a New Other-Worldliness." *Theology Today* 1 (1944): 78-87.

"The Ego-Alter Dialectic and the Conscience." *Journal of Philosophy* 42 (1945): 352-59.

"Ethics, Christian." *Encyclopedia of Religion*. Ed. Vergilius Ferm. New York: The Philosophical Library, 1945. 259.

"The Hidden Church and the Churches in Sight." *Religion in Life* 15 (1945-46): 106-16.

"The Responsibility of the Church for Society." *The Gospel, the Church, & the World*. Ed. Kenneth Scott Latourette. New York: Harper & Brothers, 1946. 111-33.

"Utilitarian Christianity." *Christianity and Crisis* 6 (1946): 3-5.

"The Disorder of Man in the Church of God." *Man's Disorder and God's Design*. Vol. 1: *The Universal Church in God's Design*. New York: Harper & Brothers, 1949. 78-88.

"The Gospel for a Time of Fears." *The Washington Federation of Churches and the School of Religion, Howard University.* Washington, D.C.: Henderson Services, 1950. 1-22. Three Lectures: I. Our Eschatological Time, II. The Eternal Now, III. The Gospel of the Last Time. Delivered Howard University, Washington, D.C., April 18, 1950.

Christ and Culture. New York: Harper & Brothers, 1951. Harper Torchbooks. New York: Harper & Brothers, 1956.

"An Attempt at a Theological Analysis of Missionary Motivation." Paper presented April 1951. *Occasional Bulletin from the Missionary Research Library* 14.1 (January 1963): 1-6.

"The Center of Value." *Moral Principles of Action: Man's Ethical Imperative.* Ed. Ruth Nanda Anshen. New York: Harper & Brothers, 1952. 162-75. *Radical Monotheism and Western Culture, with Supplementary Essays.* New York: Harper & Brothers, 1960. 100-13.

"Reflections on Faith, Hope and Love." [1953.] *Journal of Religious Ethics* 2 (Spring 1974): 151-56.

"Who are the Unbelievers and What Do They Believe?" Report submitted to Secretariat for Evangelism, World Council of Churches, Second Assembly. *The Christian Hope and the Task of the Church.* New York: Harper, 1954. 35-37.

Christian Ethics: Sources of the Living Tradition. Ed. with Introductions by Waldo Beach and H. Richard Niebuhr. New York: The Ronald Press Company, 1955.

The Purpose of the Church and Its Ministry: Reflections on the Aims of Theological Education. H. Richard Niebuhr, in collaboration with Daniel Day Williams and James M. Gustafson. New York: Harper & Brothers, 1956.

Faith on Earth: An Inquiry into the Structure of Human Faith.[1958.] Ed. Richard R. Niebuhr. New Haven & London: Yale University Press, 1989.

Radical Monotheism and Western Culture, with Supplementary Essays. New York: Harper & Brothers, 1960.

"Reformation: Continuing Imperative." *Christian Century* 77 (1960): 248-51. *How My Mind Has Changed.* Ed. with an Introduction by Harold E. Fey. Meridian Books. New York: World Publishing Company, 1961. 69-80.

"On the Nature of Faith." *Religious Experience and Truth: A Symposium.* Ed. Sidney Hook. New York: New York University Press, 1961. 93-102.

"The Protestant Movement and Democracy in the United States." *Religion in American Life.* Vol 1: *The Shaping of American Religion.* Eds. James Ward Smith & A. Leland Jamison. Princeton: Princeton University Press, 1961. 20-71.

"The Ethical Crisis." Delivered at Wayne State University, November 1961. *Universitas: A Journal of Religion and the University* 2.2 (Spring 1964): 41-50.

"The Illusions of Power." *The Pulpit* 33 (April 1962): 4(100)-7(103).

The Responsible Self: An Essay in Christian Moral Philosophy. [1960, 1962.] Preface by Richard R. Niebuhr. Introduction by James M. Gustafson. New York, Evanston, and London: Harper & Row, 1963.

B. UNPUBLISHED CITED (Other than on Responsibility)

"The Problem of the Individual in Richard Dehmel." Unpublished M.A. thesis. Department of Germanics, Washington University, St. Louis (June 1917). 1-50.

"Ernst Troeltsch's Philosophy of Religion." Unpublished Ph.D. dissertation. Yale University, 1924. 1-270.

"Theology in a Time of Disillusionment." Unpublished lecture, handwritten, delivered as Alumni Lecture, Yale Divinity School, 1931. 1-22. Niebuhr Box 1, file 7.

"Protestant Theology Since Schleiermacher." Student lecture notes, handwritten by Joe E. Elmore, Yale Divinity School, Fall 1951.

"Address on Dr. Martin Buber's 80th Birthday." Unpublished lecture, typed transcript, delivered at New York City (April 17, 1958): 1-10. Niebuhr Box 1, file 7.

"Introduction to Theological Study." Student lecture notes, and written by R. Melvin Keiser, delivered at Yale Divinity School, fall semester, 1960. 1-16.

"Next Steps in Theology." Four Lectures: I. Toward the Future, II. Toward New Symbols, III. Toward the Recovery of Feeling, IV. Toward the Service of Christendom. Unpublished Cole Lectures, transcribed from tape recording, delivered at Vanderbilt University, April 10-12, 1961. 1-114. Niebuhr Box 2, file 5.

"Toward the Future." "Next Steps in Theology." Lecture I. Unpublished Cole Lectures, transcribed from tape recordings, delivered at Vanderbilt University, April 10-12, 1961. 1-21. Niebuhr Box 2, file 5.

"Toward the Recovery of Feeling." "Next Steps in Theology. "Lecture III. Unpublished Cole Lectures, transcribed from tape recordings, delivered at Vanderbilt University, April 10-12, 1961. 1-30. Niebuhr Box 2, file 5.

"The Christian Theory of Sin." Student Seminar notes, handwritten by R. Melvin Keiser, taught at Yale Divinity School, fall semester, 1961. 1-34.

"What Has a Christian To Say in the Cold War?" Student notes, handwritten by R. Melvin Keiser, Common Room Conversation, Yale Divinity School (December 6, 1961).

"The Hope of Glory." Student notes, handwritten by R. Melvin Keiser, delivered at Yale Divinity School Chapel, December 12, 1961. Niebuhr Box 1, file 11.

"The Religious Emotions." Student seminar notes, handwritten by R. Melvin Keiser, taught at Yale Divinity School, spring semester, 1962. 1-26.

C. Resources on Responsibility

(Chronologically arranged.)

i. Published

"The Social Gospel and the Mind of Jesus." Originally delivered to the American Theological Society, April 21, 1933. *The Journal of Religious Ethics* 16.1 (Spring 1988): 115-27.

The Church Against the World. H. Richard Niebuhr, Wilhelm Pauck, and F. P. Miller. Chicago, New York: Willet, Clark & Co., 1935. H. Richard Niebuhr, "The Question of the Church" and "Toward the Independence of the Church." 1-13 & 123-56. *Theology in America: The Major Protestant Voices from Puritanism to Neo-Orthodoxy*. Ed. Sydney E. Ahlstrom. Indianapolis and New York: Bobbs-Merrill Company, 1967. 590-618.

"The Attack Upon the Social Gospel." *Religion in Life* 5 (1936): 176-81.

"The Christian Church in the World's Crisis." *Christianity and Society* 6 (1941): 11-17.

"War as the Judgment of God." *Christian Century* 49 (May 1942): 630-33.

"Is God in the War?" *Christian Century* 49 (August 1942): 953-55.

"War as Crucifixion." *Christian Century* 60 (April 1943): 513-15.

"Towards a New Other-Worldliness." *Theology Today* 1 (1944): 78-87.

"The Ego-Alter Dialectic and the Conscience." *Journal of Philosophy* 42 (1945): 352-59.

"Ethics, Christian." *Encyclopedia of Religion*. Ed. Vergilius Ferm. New York: The Philosophical Library, 1945. 259.

"The Responsibility of the Church for Society." *The Gospel, the Church, & the World.* Ed. Kenneth Scott Latourette. New York: Harper & Brothers, 1946. 111-33.

"Outline and Bibliography for Niebuhr's Lecture Course in Christian Ethics, Winter and Spring Terms, 1952-53." Appendix. *To See the Kingdom: The Theological Vision of H. Richard Niebuhr.* By James W. Fowler. Nashville & New York: Abingdon Press, 1974. 271-75.

The Responsible Self: An Essay in Christian Moral Philosophy. Preface by Richard R. Niebuhr. Introduction by James M. Gustafson. New York, Evanston, and London: Harper & Row, 1963. (Containing the Robertson Lectures, delivered at the University of Glasgow, Spring 1960; and as Appendix the Earl Lectures, much of I. "The Root Metaphors of Morality," February 27, 1962 [as A. Metaphors and Morals], and all of III. "Responsibility to God," March 1, 1962 [as B. Responsibility and Christ].)

ii. Unpublished

"Christian Ethics." Student lecture notes, transcribed by Robert Yetter, Gene Canestrari, and Ed Elliott, delivered at Yale Divinity School, spring semester, 1952. 1-182.

"Pt. II. Responsibility to Divine Action; I. Valuation." Handwritten. n.d. Box 2, file 4. (Grant 168.) 1-13.

"On the Meaning of Responsibility." Handwritten. Lecture delivered at Cambridge University, May 25, 1960. Niebuhr Box 2, file 1. (Grant 167.) 1-21.

"Der Sinn der Verantwortlichkeit." Typewritten. Lecture delivered in Bonn, June 28, 1960. (Grant 168.) 1-20.

"Christian Ethics." Student lecture notes, handwritten by Elizabeth Bassett Keiser, delivered at Yale Divinity School, spring semester, 1961. 1-113.

"Christian Ethics."　Student lecture notes, handwritten by R. Melvin Keiser, delivered at Yale Divinity School, spring semester, 1961. 1-58.

"Christian Ethics Lectures."　Niebuhr's lecture notes, handwritten for class in "Christian Ethics" at Yale Divinity School, [contains layers from previous years mixed with most recent] spring semester, 1961. Niebuhr Box 1, file 10. 1-239.

"Christian Responsibility."　The Earl Lectures delivered at Pacific School of Religion, 1962.　Consists of three lectures (written and on cassette tapes): I. "The Root Metaphors of Morality" (delivered February 27, 1962), II. "The Idea of Responsibility" (February 28, 1962), and III. "Responsibility to God" (March 1, 1962).　Niebuhr Box 2, file 1.

"Addresses at The Riverside Church in New York City, a series cut short by illness in the Winter of 1962."　(Preface, RS 3.)

"'The Responsible Self' Manuscript."　Drafts of two chapters for projected book. I. "Metaphors and Morals," 41 pp. (typewritten); II. "The Meaning of Responsibility," 34 pp. + numerous addenda (typewritten).　(Found on Niebuhr's desk at time of his death [Preface, RS 3; Grant 168].)　Niebuhr Box 2, file 6.

"Numerous sketches and outlines of various projections of his ethics for publication."　[Found on Niebuhr's desk at time of his death.] (Preface, RS 3.)

II. WORKS ABOUT NIEBUHR CITED

Ahlstrom, Sydney E.　"H. Richard Niebuhr's Place in American Thought." *Christianity and Crisis*, 23.20 (November 25, 1963): 213-17.

Barbour, John D.　"Niebuhr Versus Niebuhr: On Tragedy in History." *The Christian Century* 101.36 (November 21, 1984): 1096-99.

Chrystal, William G.　"The Young H. Richard Niebuhr." *Theology Today* 38.2 (July 1981): 231-35.

Fowler, James W. *To See the Kingdom: The Theological Vision of H. Richard Niebuhr.* Nashville & New York: Abingdon Press, 1974.

Fox, Richard Wightman. "The Niebuhr Brothers and the Liberal Protestant Heritage." *Religion and Twentieth-Century American Intellectual Life.* Ed. Michael J. Lacey. Woodrow Wilson International Center for Scholars, Cambridge and New York: Cambridge University Press, 1989.

Grant, C. David. *God the Center of Value: Value Theory in the Theology of H. Richard Niebuhr.* Forth Worth: Texas Christian University Press, 1984.

Gustafson, James M. *Ethics from a Theocentric Perspective.* Vol. I. *Theology and Ethics.* Chicago: The University of Chicago Press, 1981.

Harrison, Beverly Wildung. "H. Richard Niebuhr: Towards a Christian Moral Philosophy." Unpublished Ph.D. dissertation. Union Theological Seminary, 1974.

Hauerwas, Stanley. *The Peaceable Kingdom: A Primer in Christian Ethics.* Notre Dame, London: University of Notre Dame Press, 1983.

Hoedemaker, Libertus A. *The Theology of H. Richard Niebuhr.* Philadelphia and Boston: Pilgrim Press, 1970.

Holler, Linda. "Is There a Thou 'Within' Nature? A Dialogue with H. Richard Niebuhr." *The Journal of Religious Ethics* 17.1 (Spring 1989): 81-102.

Keiser, R. Melvin. *Recovering the Personal: Religious Language and the Post-Critical Quest of H. Richard Niebuhr.* Atlanta: Scholars Press, 1988.

Miller, David L. *The New Polytheism: Rebirth of the Gods and Goddesses.* Dallas: Spring Publications Inc., 1974, 1981.

Miller, Richard B. "H. Richard Niebuhr's War Articles: A Transvaluation of Value." *The Journal of Religion* 68.2 (April 1988): 242-62.

Niebuhr, Reinhold. "Must We Do Nothing?" *Christian Century* 49 (March 30, 1932): 415-17. *The Christian Century Reader*. Ed. Harold E. Fey and Margaret Frakes. New York: Association Press, 1962. 222-28.

Welch, Sharon D. *A Feminist Ethic of Risk*. Minneapolis: Fortress Press, 1990.

Yeager, D. M. "On Making the Tree Good: An Apology for a Dispositional Ethics." *The Journal of Religious Ethics* 10.1 (Spring 1982): 103-20.

III. OTHER WORKS CITED

Cauthen, Kenneth. *The Impact of American Religious Liberalism*. New York and Evanston: Harper & Row, 1962.

Edwards, Jonathan. *Dissertation Concerning the End for which God Created the World*. *Jonathan Edwards: Representative Selections, with Introduction, Bibliography, and Notes*. Ed. Clarence H. Faust and Thomas H. Johnson. New York: Hill and Wang, 1962.

---. *The Nature of True Virtue*. Ann Arbor Paperbacks. Ann Arbor: The University of Michigan Press, 1960.

---. "Personal Narrative." *Jonathan Edwards: Representative Selections, with Introduction, Bibliography, and Notes*. Ed. Clarence H. Faust and Thomas H. Johnson. New York: Hill and Wang, 1962.

Faust, Clarence H. and Thomas H. Johnson, eds. *Jonathan Edwards: Representative Selections, with Introduction, Bibliography, and Notes*. New York: Hill and Wang, 1962.

Eliot, T. S. "East Coker." *Four Quartets*. A Harvest Book. New York: Harcourt, Brace & World, 1943, 1971.

Fey, Harold E. *How My Mind Has Changed*. Meridian Books. Cleveland and New York: The World Publishing Company, 1961.

Hauerwas, Stanley. *Character and the Christian Life: A Study in Theological Ethics*. San Antonio: Trinity University Press, 1975, 1985.

Holland, Joe and Peter Henriot. *Social Analysis: Linking Faith and Justice*. Washington, D.C.: The Center of Concern; Maryknoll: Orbis Books, 1983, rev.

Hutchison, William R. *The Modernist Impulse in American Protestantism*. Oxford, New York, Toronto, Melbourne: Oxford University Press, 1982.

Keiser, Elizabeth B. *Homophobic Wrath and Paradisal Pleasure: Courtliness and the Sacred in* Cleanness *and Its Medieval Contexts* (forthcoming Yale University Press).

Keiser, R. Melvin. "Phenomenology and Spiritual Maturity in the Tillichian *Magisterium*." *Religion & Intellectual Life* 3.4 (Summer 1986): 108-17.

Keller, Catherine. *From a Broken Web: Separation, Sexism, and Self*. Boston: Beacon Press, 1986.

Long, Charles H. *Significations: Signs, Symbols, and Images in the Interpretation of Religion*. Philadelphia: Fortress Press, 1986.

Mack, Burton. *A Myth of Innocence: Mark and Christian Origins* Philadelphia: Fortress Press, 1988.

Miller, Perry. "From Edwards to Emerson." *Errand into the Wilderness*. Cambridge: The Belknap Press of Harvard University Press, 1956. 184-203.

Niebuhr, Reinhold. *How My Mind Has Changed*. Ed. Harold E. Fey, Meridian Books. Cleveland and New York: The World Publishing Company, 1961. 116-32.

Polanyi, Michael. *Personal Knowledge: Towards a Post-Critical Philosophy*. London: Routledge & Kegan Paul, 1958.

---. *The Tacit Dimension*. Anchor Books. New York: Doubleday & Company, 1967.

Tillich, Paul. *Systematic Theology*. 3 vols. Chicago: The University of Chicago Press, 1951, 1957, 1963.

Whitehead, Alfred North. *Religion in the Making*. Meridian Books. Cleveland and New York: The World Publishing Company, 1960; 1965.

in liberalism, 6-7
See also Church; Responsibility ethics, need-meeting; Virtues
Luther, Martin, 44, 45

McFague, Sallie, 72
Macintosh, Douglas Clyde, 8, 42, 212 n. 18, 214 n. 33
Mack, Burton, 71, 218 n. 58
Malebranche, 16
Marcion, 192
Marriage: 133-134
See also Oppression, sexism
Marx, Karl, 42, 127, 164, 201
Mead, George Herbert, 38, 42, 88, 170-171, 219 n. 65, 221 n. 73
Merleau-Ponty, Maurice, x, 68
Metaphysics: 28, 60, 105
See also Troeltsch
Metis: 71, 83, 218 n. 58
Miller, David L., 215 n. 51, 216 n. 54
Miller, Perry, 137
Miller, Richard B. 97, 222-223 n. 75 & 78
Modernity and its deconstruction: x-xi
See also "Critical"; Dualism; God; History; Inclusiveness; Integrity; Interactional; Language; Oppression; Part-Whole thinking; Phenomenology; Postcritical; Responsibility ethics; Self; Tacit; Triadic; Universality; Value; World
Mutuality: xi, 121, 133
Mystery: xii, 26, 189, 197, 199-200, 201-202
See also God
Mysticism: 16-21, 23, 27, 29, 33
See also God, immanence

Nature:
as context/object (thing-like), 135-137
as myth, 136
sun and rain, 52, 106, 136
See also World
Neo-orthodoxy: ix-xi, 53-54
Newness: 92-93, 200
Niebuhr, H. Richard:
biography, v, vi, xii, xiv, 3, 65, 168-169
conversion, ix, xi-xv, 23-40, 41, 44-45, 56
influences on, 14-22, 29-36, 42-45
liberalism, 3-22
limitations, xv-xvii
See also Responsibility ethics, social praxis
style of thinking/writing, 42, 44, 48-49
See also Language; Reason

Universality:
      abstract, 60, 71, 84-85
      relational, 60, 71, 84-85, 88-90, 200

Value: 7-8, 15, 20-21, 23, 26-31, 43, 53-54, 95-96, 223 n. 78
      holy, 53-54, 85
      sacred, 61, 200
      See also Being and value; Commitment; Ethics; Responsibility ethics;
          Troeltsch
Virtues: 87, 106-125, 180-181, 183
      theological/natural, 123-125
      See also Church

War: *See* Oppression
Weber, Max, 42
Welch, Sharon, 52-57, 62
Wells, H. G., 4, 6, 8, 42, 45, 49
Whitehead, Alfred North, 42, 47, 49-50, 60-61, 192, 218 n. 62
Wittgenstein, Ludwig, x, 104
World:
      contextual metaphors for, 53, 60, 66, 67, 69, 112, 113-114, 116, 155, 181,
          187, 189-191
      dualistic view of, x
      See also Church, and world; Ethos; Nature
Wright, G. Ernest, 218-219 n. 62

Yeager, D. M., 97

Zarathustra, 13

DATE DUE